Identity Dι

# Identity
# Destabilised

## Living in an Overheated World

Edited by
Thomas Hylland Eriksen and Elisabeth Schober

**Pluto**Press
www.plutobooks.com

First published 2016 by Pluto Press
345 Archway Road, London N6 5AA

www.plutobooks.com

British Library Cataloguing in Publication Data
A catalogue record for this book is available from the British Library

ISBN   978 0 7453 9913 3   Hardback
ISBN   978 0 7453 9912 6   Paperback
ISBN   978 1 7868 0004 6   PDF eBook
ISBN   978 1 7868 0006 0   Kindle eBook
ISBN   978 1 7868 0005 3   EPUB eBook

This book is printed on paper suitable for recycling and made from fully managed and sustained forest sources. Logging, pulping and manufacturing processes are expected to conform to the environmental standards of the country of origin.

Typeset by Stanford DTP Services, Northampton, England

Simultaneously printed in the European Union and United States of America

# Contents

# Figures and Tables

## FIGURES

## TABLES

# Preface

For more than a hundred years, anthropology was mainly about the study of the Other. Anthropologists, based in metropolitan universities, travelled to remote places in order to identify other peoples' culture and social life, often – but not always – relating their findings to a general theory accounting for human diversity, but also human universals. In the last decades of the twentieth century, a growing number of anthropologists did fieldwork in their own countries. Many studied 'the Other within', such as ethnic minorities, indigenous groups or sub-cultures, using the same tools as their peers had applied to studies overseas. However, quite a few ventured into mainstream society, doing research on the ethnic majority, convinced that the methods of anthropology – long-term participant observation, comparison, the study of actions as well as statements – were well suited for this purpose.

Over the last few decades, global communication networks have grown denser, mobility has increased and social change has unravelled the world as it was previously imagined by anthropologists. Although the view that the world consisted of separate, bounded 'cultures' was always debatable, it now became indefensible. The human world could no longer be imagined as an archipelago of cultures; it was rather an intricate meshwork of partial connections, creolisation processes, cultural hybridity, social differentiation and their counter-reactions in the shape of identity politics attempting to reinstate boundaries and purity.

The contemporary, overheated world of accelerated change has three main implications for the anthropological study of social identities, all of which are dealt with in this book.

First, anthropology can no longer be envisioned as the study of the Other. The boundary separating Self and Other is no longer self-evident; in a world of overlapping interconnections, the very existence of boundaries is being negotiated and interrogated, and it is by no means clear where the anthropological Self ends and the exotic Other begins, nor where the boundaries of a group can or should be drawn.

Second, non-anthropologists around the world have for many years been active in defining who they are and discussing intricate questions pertaining to identity, and they do not necessarily require the service of anthropologists to do so on their behalf. This is a second boundary that has been destabilised – that between the academic discourse on identity and local discourses on identity.

Third, the volatility of processes of identification in an overheated world leads to new kinds of paradoxes and complexities that it is necessary to come to grips with. There is nowhere a single narrative about social identity, but rather competing perspectives, ideologies and persuasions concerning the relationship of the individual to the group, the past to the present, tradition to change, purity to mixing.

This book attempts to capture the essentials of these dynamics, by updating social science perspectives on identity with fresh materials from around the world and a theoretical approach which emphasises the speed of change, the implications of reflexive modernity and of global neoliberalism in accounting for destabilised identities in the twenty-first century and, in some cases, their restabilisation.

The contributions by the editors, Hann, Thorleifsson, Stensrud and Pijpers as well as the process leading up to this publication have been funded by the European Research Council Advanced Grant project 'Overheating', ERC grant number 295843.

Thomas Hylland Eriksen
Elisabeth Schober

# 1. Introduction
## The Art of Belonging in an Overheated World

*Thomas Hylland Eriksen and Elisabeth Schober*

Identity and modernity; globalisation, culture and identity; changing identities in the (post-)modern world; cultural creolisation and the politics of identity; ambivalence and fundamentalism; identity, gender and power; intersectionality; social identity, cultural identity, gender identity, ethnic identity, sexual identity, national identity, class identity, regional identity, linguistic identity, the hybridisation of identities and the essentialisation of hybridity. For a while in the 1990s, the concept of identity seemed to be everywhere. It has subsequently faded away somewhat as a keyword in the social sciences, which is to be regretted, since we live in a time when good and focused research on social identification is acutely needed. The need for the term identity is possibly even more pressing today than in the last century, if the high-speed transformations we have witnessed in a number of locations across the globe over the last few years are any indication at all. In a fast changing world with rapidly increasing connectivity and mobility, with mounting environmental challenges, rapid economic transformations and the rise of often virulent nationalisms, forms of belonging to places, groups or communities are being challenged in new ways that social scientists arguably still need to have a language for.

Although it might seem that though the intellectual energy of the concept of identity was spent after the turn of the millennium, it cannot be denied that people in otherwise very different societies continue to raise strikingly similar questions about who they are and what this entails. In rapidly changing surroundings, the answers are fraught with controversy, often pitting ambivalence and doubt against withdrawal and the reassertion of boundaries.

This book represents an approach to identity which aims to take previous research a step further. Shifting, multiple, contested and unstable social identities that hold out a promise as the basis of a meaningful sense of belonging will be at the centre – identities which we view through a particular lens, namely that of accelerated change. It is as if modernity shifted into a higher gear towards the end of the twentieth century (Eriksen 2014, 2016). Phenomena that led to rapid changes in the postwar decades – migration, urbanisation, tourism, communication technology – are changing even faster in the 2010s. Adjusting to new circumstances is therefore necessary, and several options are available. To use Alfred Hirschman's famous tripartite classification of strategies in organisations (Hirschman 1971): should they opt for exit (withdrawal into the secure and safe), voice (resistance and protest) or loyalty (adapting to the powers that be)? Or perhaps a pragmatic blend of the three? And how can a world that has been ripped apart, whether because of industrial development, migration or the expansion of finance capital, be patched together again so that it appears meaningful and secure? How can continuity with the past be created in a convincing way when change is taking place at enormous speed? And in what ways do global crises influence forms of belonging and the sense of self? That is what this book is about, and we now proceed to presenting some of the main themes that, in our view, should be explored in an updated anthropology of identity.

## OVERHEATING AND SOCIAL IDENTITY

Seen from a bird's-eye perspective, it is difficult to deny that the early twenty-first century appears to be an unusually hectic and restless period in the history of humanity. There seems to be rapid change everywhere. Ranging from foreign direct investment and the number of internet connections to global energy use, urbanisation in the global south and increased migration rates, rapid transformations are having impacts on social life in many ways, and have in some respects visibly stepped up their pace only since the 1990s. Dramatic alterations to the environment, economic transformations and social rearrangements are the order of the day in so many parts of the world, and in so many areas, that it may not be an exaggeration to speak of the global situation as being overheated (Eriksen 2016; see also Spooner 2015).

*Overheating* may serve as a central metaphor for the current phase of globalisation. The term calls attention to both accelerated change and the tensions, conflicts and frictions it engenders, as well as – implicitly – signalling the need to examine, through dialectical negation, deceleration or cooling down. Generally speaking, when things are suddenly brought into motion, they create friction; when things rub against each other, heat is generated at the interstices. Heat, for those who have been caught unawares by it, may result in torridness and apathy, but it may also trigger a number of other transformations, the trajectories of which may not be clear at the outset. When water is brought to boiling point, for instance, it actually changes into a different substance. In a similar fashion, we arguably find ourselves at a 'systemic edge' (Sassen 2014: 221) these days, with economic, social and cultural forms of globalisation expanding into ever new territories, often changing the very fundamentals of customary life for those who find themselves subject to the whirlwinds of change. These processes are not unilaterally negative or positive for those affected by them, since what may be perceived as a crisis by some could very well represent positive opportunities to others, and the potential for spontaneous transformative moments is always present. Even climate change is sometimes welcomed, for example in cold regions where agriculture becomes feasible, or in the far north, where the melting of the Arctic ice creates exciting opportunities for oil companies and may lead to the opening of new shipping routes. Overheating consists of a series of unintended, and interrelated, consequences triggered by global neoliberal deregulation, technological developments rendering communication instantaneous and transportation inexpensive, increased energy consumption and a consumerist ethos animating the desires of a growing world population.

Changes in economic, social and environmental circumstances are often perceived locally as being exogenous, in the sense that large segments of those societies affected did not initiate the changes themselves; indeed, while some local key actors usually collaborate in bringing about, and benefit from, these changes, a good number of people are generally left with the feeling that they were not even asked by anybody in power for their opinion. Such rapid changes in the social fabric may affect, challenge or – sometimes – strengthen people's existing perceptions of themselves, their social belonging, who they are and where they are going. Making social and cultural identities sustainable in a world where change is unpredictable, frequently exogenous and often resulting in unintended consequences can be compared to rebuilding a ship at sea. It requires flexibility and improvisation, or novel forms of boundary-making. Others may discover that they are committed to change in such a way that it is stagnation, rather than change, that challenges their self-understanding, or they may approach the transformations around them with a lack of care and a fundamental sense of indifference.

Some questions people may typically ask in a situation of rapid change are: How can I be the person that I want to be when there is so much change? What is the essence of being me/us? What are the forces threatening our ability to remain who we think we should be? What kind of changes do we embrace, and what kind of changes do we see as a threat? The work of tracing a line connecting the past to the future, via the present, in a compelling and meaningful way, is easy when there is just repetition, but difficult when there is no clear script relating the past to the future, no story of either continuity or development which is persuasive. All the chapters in this collection engage with this problematic, from Drotbohm's study of migrant lives which are cooled down upon enforced return to a slow place, via Kearney's exploration of collective healing as a response to fast and catastrophic changes affecting cultural identity, Thorleifsson's study of the ongoing negotiation of identity in a contested frontier area and Martin's analysis of alienation among football supporters unsure of their identity amidst the transformation of their club into a global brand, to Banović's story about destabilised gender identity in Montenegro and Schober's 'navy nostalgia' in the Philippines, where the changes brought about by recent foreign direct investment makes indigenous people long for the 'good old times' when the US military was still around. Whereas MacClancy forcefully argues against frozen identities, showing how they are being resisted, Neumann takes a long historical view and points to how the flow of irreversible time is being punctuated by the construction of monuments creating a sense of stability, continuity – and collective identity.

The issues raised can be related analytically to the broader question of how social reproduction and social identity are related during times of dramatic change. If it is true, as we claim, that accelerated change is now being experienced across the world (although, naturally, in an uneven fashion in particular places, with some communities being entirely unaffected), then the actual reproduction of the social fabric of life – and its connection to the way people make sense of their day-to-day affairs – is a 'burning' issue for many. Social reproduction and its inter-linkages with identity may, moreover, be studied through the lens of more specific fields, from cultural reproduction to the reproduction of families, gender relations, class dynamics, ethnic divisions and so on, which are all affected by overheating. As Wimpelmann (this volume) points out, the emergence of new elites in Afghanistan has not eclipsed the old ones but led to a continuing tension, while Pijpers shows how the uneven speed of change in competing Sierra Leonean power structures exacerbates chronic tensions, leading to frequent contestations that boil down to the question of how livelihoods can be secured through identity claims made amidst accelerated transformations.

The term reproduction has played a central role in (neo-)Marxist debates about the meaning of work and labour. Marx understood labour as a key factor in the productive process, with his collaborator Engels (2010 [1884]) introducing an understanding of economic production that tightly linked it to the social reproduction of families. Engels's understanding of the gendered division of labour, which shapes how men and women partake in economic activities, was later found to conceal more than it actually reveals by Marxist feminists. The reproduction of labour, Harris and Young (1981) argued, as important as it may be, cannot simply be conflated with the wider processes of social and biological reproduction that are undertaken within households, where a number of other non-economic societal values are being (re-)created as well. The old Marxist tension between production and reproduction was later developed in another direction in the work of Pierre Bourdieu (1977; cf. Robbins 2000: 42–65; see also Goody 1976). Bourdieu stresses the social and cultural dimensions of reproduction, with reproduction being turned into a concept that deals with the transmission of social formations from one generation to another. In Bourdieu's understanding of the term, there is some space left for transformations to take place *within* routine processes of cultural reproduction. Change, in his view, has usually been a gradual, subtle process confined by pre-existing structural confines.

Through his sweeping study of the cultural reproduction of classes in French society (Bourdieu 1984), however, Bourdieu was essentially investigating the postwar period, which fizzled out in the 1980s. During the last decade of his life, Bourdieu was in fact deeply troubled by the onset of neoliberal regimes in the European Union. He understood globalisation and the shockwaves that it produced in Europe from the early 1990s onwards as destabilising the at times deeply oppressive, but at least *predictable* regimes of reproduction that he had studied for most of his academic career. With Bourdieu lamenting the end of the modernist era in his last important book (Bourdieu et al. 2000), one cannot but wonder what the French sociologist would have made of the changes unfolding since his death, an era during which the social, cultural and economic reproduction of people's life-worlds in many places has become ever more destabilised, with concepts such as neoliberalism, Anthropocene and the precariat having rapidly become buzzwords in academic and intellectual discourse.

Since the early 2000s, the concept of identity, which we seek to bring into conversation with local social reproduction and large-scale change, has become increasingly contested in the social sciences, with Rogers Brubaker and Frederick Cooper arguing, at the turn of the millennium, that the social sciences might actually be better off without identity as part of its analytical toolbox (Brubaker & Cooper 2000; cf. MacClancy, this volume). At the same time, the everyday, emic usage of identity as a category of practice, an existential discourse, a feature of commercial life and an important, sometimes virulent form of politics, has spread to such an extent that 'identity' has reached near universal currency in the way social relations are made sense of in the world: from Peru to the Philippines, from Norway to Montenegro, the tendency is for people to decipher their collective plights, fortunes and futures through the lens of social identity (see e.g. Brandstädter et al. 2013; Jenkins 2014). Since it is obvious that we need to retain a concept for the analysis of these significant phenomena related to people's collective views about themselves and others, we shall argue for an understanding of the term inspired by Reinhard Koselleck's conceptual history approach. If identity is one of the key *Grundbegriffe* (basic concepts) of our times, then its very contestedness, ambiguity and historically shifting meaning attest to the fundamental role it continues to play in people's understandings of themselves. Through his meticulous tracing of concepts through their historical transformations, Koselleck (2002) showed that basic concepts are inherently contradictory and multi-layered, and that they acquire new meanings, particularly during tumultuous times. This understanding of *Grundbegriffe* is supremely compatible with the way in which conceptualisations of identity twist and turn in the present era. To some of these changes we now turn.

## BOUNDARIES AND FUZZY ZONES

Although the social science usage of the initially philosophical term identity began in developmental psychology (Erikson 1963), the bulk of the literature over the last decades of the twentieth century dealt with collective identities, often national, ethnic or religious. Whereas Gellner quipped that '[n]ationalism is not the awakening of nations to self-consciousness: it invents nations where they do not exist' (Gellner 1964: 169), his student A.D. Smith (1986) took a different position, arguing that the transformation of ethnic groups into nations was a continuous historical process, not a conjuring trick.

Gellner and Smith nevertheless share a premise made famous in Barth's essay on ethnicity (Barth 1969a), as well as in Anderson's definition of the nation as being imagined as 'inherently limited' (Anderson 1983: 6). In all of these theorisations, identity categories were delineated as being *bounded*. While cultural meaning is often described through the concept of flow, thereby depicted as continuous, identity categories were seen as discontinuous and bounded (Eriksen 2015: 9). With the boundary understood by Barth as an 'osmotic' entity across which transactions, communication and even the flow of people could take place (Barth 1969a: 21), the existence of a clear dividing line was nevertheless a premise for the study of inter-ethnic processes. However, the very concept of the boundary has subsequently been problematised in a number of ways.

First, as argued by A.P. Cohen (1994), the concept of the *frontier*, seen as an ambiguous zone of negotiation, may in many cases be a more apt metaphor than the more rigid notion of the boundary. Indeed, the idea that ethnic groups are actually firmly bounded may be seen as an involuntary expression of methodological nationalism (Wimmer and Glick Schiller 2002), using the nation-state and its fixed borders as a template for sub-, non-, trans- and pre-national groups. Although few of the chapters in this volume explicitly deal with frontier areas (Thorleifsson's is the most obvious example), they all interrogate the boundary as such, since it is being destabilised on the ground by uneven processes of change.

Second, as pointed out by Fardon (1987) and others, in many parts of the world the bounded ethnic group was often a colonial invention. Precolonial groups were often more fluid and overlapping than the groups emerging from population censuses and modern state-building.

Third, research on transnationalism (Glick Schiller et al. 1992; Olwig 2007) has shown that migrants often have an ambiguous national and local identity, with consequences for their ethnic identity. Many have economic and social obligations in two or more locations, bringing with them novel emotional attachments and identifications as well. In the second and third generation, this kind of complexity is further accentuated, as many have scarcely even visited their ancestral homeland. Some have intermarried. Some have changed their language or religion, food habits, body language and dress. Many actively resist being 'boxed' into a fixed category.

Fourth, there has been an increased empirical interest in the frontier zones of collectivities, where identity is precarious and contestable. Echoing the effects of the poststructuralist turn in gender studies, students of ethnicity are now likely to discover relatively permanent frontier areas where persons can be identified as neither/nor or both/and. In the Caribbean, people of mixed African and European origins hold such an ambiguous position, as do people of mixed Indian and African origins. Sometimes spoken of as 'ethnic anomalies', people with a complex and contestable ethnic identity may form a substantial part of a population, although few are as extreme as the golfer Tiger Woods, who once described himself as Cablinasian, 'a mixture of Caucasian, Black, north American Indian and Asian' (Jenkins 2002: 115).

By concentrating on the core actors of collectivities, those who engage in the politics of culture and identity, classic ethnicity studies tended to overlook the often substantial numbers of persons at the margins. The increased interest in the fuzzy edges of collectivities has developed in tandem with similar developments in other areas, notably studies of cultural mixing or hybridity (Werbner & Modood 1997). The concept of cultural creolisation (Drummond 1980; Hannerz 1996; Stewart 2007), moreover, denotes a particular form of cultural mixing resulting from sustained interaction between formerly discrete groups.

There is no intrinsic reason why cultural mixing should necessarily lead to the merging of collective identities. As research on ethnicity and nationalism has made abundantly clear, it is *presumptions* of difference, not objective differences, that keep boundaries intact. Indeed, as Harrison (2002) has argued, perceived similarities may sometimes be pivotal in spurring boundary work and inter-group competition. Groups are constituted as social entities, not as cultural ones. There is nevertheless an intrinsic relationship between social cohesion and cultural meaning, and when the social integrity of a group is threatened, the threat is often interpreted as an assault on the 'cultural stuff' believed to hold them together as a group. At the same time, perceived loss of cultural boundaries can entail a sense of impurity or lamentations over corruption (e.g. Schober, this volume) that may affect identification in two main ways: purification or affirmations of impurity. Cultural variation within any group is considerable, and cultural flows across boundaries ensure that mixing, in the contemporary world, is virtually everywhere. However, the impression sometimes given that 'everything' seems to be in continuous flux, that an infinity of opportunities seem to be open and that no groups, cultural identities or ethnic categories are fixed is caused by a conflation of discrete phenomena. Strong identities and fixed boundaries do not preclude cultural mixing. Ethnic variation may well exist without significant cultural variation. Processes of cultural mixing do not in themselves affect group identities and forms of boundedness.

This means that the ambiguous grey zones, which can be located in the space between categories and boundaries under pressure, are privileged sites for studying the interplay between culture and identity. This is not because all boundaries will eventually disappear, but because they are made visible through their negotiation and renegotiation, transcend-ence, transformations and reframing under conditions of accelerated change.

In a situation of overheating, there is often a tension between boundedness and openness. Many intellectuals have recently tried to think essentialism away, emphasising the flexible and fluid character of human identification – yet, it may seem that few are listening outside the seminar room. An eloquent expression of this position is that of Zygmunt Bauman: 'If the *modern* "problem of identity" is how to construct an identity and keep it solid and stable, the *postmodern* "problem of identity" is primarily how to avoid fixation and keep the options open' (Bauman 1996: 18). Perhaps many in societies with a strong individualist ethos and a positive attitude to change, such as the city of Gladstone described by Eriksen (this volume), evade strong group commitments, preferring to keep their options open for change and mobility, should an attractive opportunity present itself.

There may be sound normative reasons to endorse Bauman's position, but it is ultimately insufficient as a guideline for empirical research. Notwithstanding globalisation and the universalisation of some of the categories of modernity, differences and boundaries continue to exist. However, in a context of overheating, keeping the boundaries intact requires hard work and, as we have suggested, it is an empirical question to what extent maintaining strict divisions is even desirable.

## GLOBALISATION AND IDENTITY THEORY

Many social scientists have questioned a widespread epistemic orientation called 'methodological nationalism' in recent years (e.g. Wimmer & Glick Schiller 2002), which has entailed taking nation-states as 'natural' units of analysis in social scientific research. In light of this critique, it is now common to argue that the world has changed in such a way that the nation-state is no longer an appropriate synonym for 'society'. To a certain degree, Appadurai (1990), Hannerz (1996) and other scholars of globalisation are correct in arguing that identification and social alignments increasingly follow different lines than was formerly the case, since capitalism and modern communication technology have reworked the spatial dimension of human life. Robertson speaks of 'the present sense of the world as a single place' (Robertson 1992: 184), and Urry (2000) has suggested replacing the term 'society' with 'mobility' as a foundational concept for explorations of contemporary social life. Yet this view, despite its merits, overlooks how traditional forms of identification are in fact not being completely eradicated, but often only reshaped, albeit at times in often dramatic ways. What is needed is research on the dynamic relationship between openness and boundedness, quests for purity and celebrations of mixing, identities looking to the past and identities based on visions of the future. This is one major perspective that is being highlighted in the approach to identity based on the idea of overheating. Boundaries have been destabilised, but they are at the same time being restabilised. Urry's radical bid of replacing the term 'society' with 'mobility' would doubtless lead to an analytical focus quite different from a conceptualisation (still common in social science) that assumes, almost in an axiomatic way, that stable societies are the stuff that social life is made of. At the same time, much would be lost if the concept of society and similar conceptualisations of stability and continuity were relegated to the dustbin of history, since it is an empirical fact that people all over the world seek stability, continuity, security and predictability (Eriksen et al. 2010), often by defending, creating or reconfiguring spatial belonging, border demarcations and collective memories anchored in particular places (Connerton 2009). What has been 'dis-embedded' is, in a multitude of ways, being 're-embedded'.

Less revolutionary, but still fairly radical, attempts to renew the conceptual apparatus of the social sciences can be found in works by, *inter alia*, Bourdieu (1977), Giddens (1991), Castells (1996–1998), Bauman (2000) and Beck (2009), who have suggested terms such as multidimensional social spaces (Bourdieu), the era of reflexive modernity (Giddens), the global network society (Castells) and globalised risk society (Beck) in a series of attempts to conceptualise the social in a time characterised by accelerated change and fuzzy boundaries. Notwithstanding their differences, their shared premise is the assumption that boundaries have been destabilised, are being questioned and challenged, and may be deconstructed, reconstructed or made to appear in new places.

Any complex society offers an almost infinite number of possible criteria for delineating subjective communities for whom the term 'we' can be used meaningfully: We, the supporters of the Labour Party. We commuters. We lesbians. We jazz musicians. We Christians. We copywriters. We Israelis. We women. Regardless of the many possible forms of 'we-hood', an underlying question remains, and is made acutely relevant in highly differentiated societies, namely which symbolic basis exists for a shared subjective identity encompassing a number of persons who can identify as a collectivity. In spite of decades of criticism of the methodological nationalism that social scientific works have suffered from, the nation still has, in many parts of the world, an indisputable and enduring ability to create strong abstract communities, quite contrary to what many theorists of globalisation predicted towards the end of the last century. It has its detractors, and it has its 'entropy-resistant' persons or groups who will not be part of it even if sharing the same territory, but national identities remain surprisingly strong in most parts of the world. The political struggles and controversies dividing many European populations these days do not mainly concern the nation as such, but how it should be delineated symbolically and demographically; who should be included, and on what conditions. The nation (or ethnic group) must now share the field of belonging with various other symbolic communities, many of them shifting, unstable and transnational, some complementary, some competing. Yet, as Chris Hann (this volume) argues, social identities cannot be manipulated at will, nor can they be fully understood in terms of rational-choice theory. They are 'imagined, but not imaginary', as Jenkins (2002: 114) puts it, no less real for being socially constructed.

## MEMORY AND FORGETTING

Most of the chapters in this book do not primarily take on national or ethnic identities, but all collectivities described here face some of the same challenges, whether they are pioneers in a new city (Stensrud) or football supporters seeing their club going through a dramatic transformation (Martin). One concerns boundaries and the grammar of inclusion and exclusion; another concerns the destabilising and often alienating forces of economic and cultural globalisation; a third is about the relationship between the past, the present and the future. If, as John Peel once said, the present is 'really nothing more than the hinge between the past and the future' (Peel 1989: 200), the delineation of the past, and its substance, remains supremely important, even in a state of accelerated structural amnesia.

Paul Connerton, whose work on social memory (Connerton 1989) has been very influential in anthropology, has later described a world divesting itself of its collective memory at an enormous speed (Connerton 2009). Connerton describes a number of ways in which modern societies obliterate their pasts, including so-called urban renewal. Distinguishing between monuments and loci of memory, he fears not for the future of monuments, or their pasts (cf. Neumann, this volume), but for the continuity in everyday sites of encounters to which people have attached their tangible, corporeal experiences, and which are under threat, at least in cities that can afford to get rid of their past in efficient and unceremonious ways.

There is merit in Connerton's argument. Uprootedness through migration may effect similar feelings of not belonging, and besides, this is not a phenomenon confined to city life. Rapid transformations of rural terrains may also well create problems for the reproduction of identity: if your personal and collective attachment is to a landscape, it will suffer when your surroundings are no longer recognisable. These changes, which influence collectivities, may be spurred on by economic investments – Connerton may have had the urban renewal of east London in mind – but they can also take the shape of ecological devastation motivated by economic interests, as in the coal-rich regions of New South Wales. Connerton's largely Durkheimian perspective is nevertheless incomplete; it posits rapid change as unequivocally negative, and is insensitive to internal variation. Overheating is never the only game in town. It is always accompanied by eddies and billabongs, stagnation and reversals, some of them voluntary, others enforced. Through migration, the shift from a fast life to a slow one can be excruciating (see Drotbohm, this volume), and in any given society, change follows different rhythms.

Moreover, recent works in social anthropology have shown how a 'sense of temporal acceleration prompted by unprecedented social and economic transformations' may in fact lead to quite the opposite of what Connerton has feared, namely a conscious appraisal of the past in the shape of nostalgia, as Olivia Angé and David Berliner (2015: 2) have pointed out. Nostalgia, in fact, is often 'an act anchored in the present context that says a lot more about contemporary social configurations than about the past itself' (Angé & Berliner 2015: 3), a process that is also sharply expressed by Thorleifsson and Schober (this volume), who both explore how nostalgia for a lost time may arise under conditions of rampant neoliberalism.

To be sure, how temporality is made sense of greatly varies in individual lives. Through his conceptualisation of disjunctures, Appadurai (1990) shows how people lead multi-scalar and multi-temporal lives by engaging in 'scapes' of different scope. Temporality, however, can also vary within cultural and social worlds. Some phenomena change quickly while others seem sluggish or even stable. Just after the First World War, the sociologist William Ogburn proposed the term 'cultural lag' (Ogburn 1922) to describe a situation where ideas and concepts about the world lag behind changes in the physical world. In this kind of situation, the disjunctures are systemic, and the maps cannot be made to fit the territory. An ideology of economic growth may be dysfunctional in a world of severe ecological problems, and an ideology of cultural cohesion at the level of the nation may not be appropriate in an increasingly diverse population. The use of smartphones has exploded worldwide since their introduction in 2007, but people still go to church, the mosque or the temple. As a response to the problems raised by Connerton, many find oases of continuity; but in an overheated situation, they actively have to seek them out.

Finally, there are variations within any society concerning the speed of change. In Mauritius, which has, since the mid 1980s, shifted from complete reliance on sugar to a diverse economy with a large manufacturing sector, there is rapid change in some places. The capital, Port-Louis, quite dilapidated thirty years ago, now has a large, posh shopping mall and a tourist-friendly seafront; there are new highways and hotels, and an ambitious 'cyber-city' has been built near the university. Yet at the same time, several Mauritian towns and coastal villages have changed little since Eriksen's first fieldwork in 1986. It cannot, moreover, be taken for granted that their residents appreciate the continuity they experience in their daily lives. In modern societies, social identities are often based just as much on visions of progress and improvement as on incorporated memories and inherited routines.

## SPEED AND DIVERSIFICATION

A great deal of anthropological research on identity or identification has taken change as a premise – though Barth (1969b) is an interesting exception – but the variable speed and distinct forms of change we have alluded to have rarely been addressed explicitly. The 'urban ecology' approach of the Chicago School, developed largely by Robert Park in the 1920s (see Hannerz 1980), studied ethnic relationships and processes of exclusion and inclusion in a setting – early twentieth-century Chicago – characterised by migration and rapid economic change. Somewhat later, the situational approaches and network analyses of the Manchester School were developed in a context of rapid urbanisation in Northern Rhodesia (now Zambia), and their focus gradually shifted from 'detribalisation' (Wilson 1942) to 'retribalisation' (Mitchell 1956; Epstein 1958) as it soon became clear that 'trade unions transcended tribes' (Mayer 1962: 63) only to a limited extent, and that tribal (or ethnic) identities continued to be highly socially relevant, albeit in new ways and novel settings. Building on this work, anthropologists such as Parkin (1969), writing about Luo in Nairobi, and Abner Cohen (1969), on Hausa in Ibadan, similarly showed how changed circumstances led to a reorganisation and reconceptualisation of ethnic identities in urban Africa.

A more recent, and still very productive, area of anthropological and sociological research concerns the identity implications of transnational migration into Western Europe and North America, and this concerns both majorities, minorities and – not least – their mutual relationships. It was in this context that Steven Vertovec (2007) proposed the term 'super-diversity' to designate a new social pattern, where migrant mobility and cultural streams have accelerated and changed in character. Whereas people formerly came from a few places and went to a few places, Vertovec argues, they now come from many places and go to many places. The legal status of new migrants is also often ambiguous, and it is not always easy to classify a person as either a student, a tourist, a labour migrant or a refugee. Some seasonal workers stay on, while some permanent migrants move away. The number of languages spoken in London is now well above 300, but even in Oslo, with just 700,000 inhabitants, nearly

200 languages are spoken. However, Vertovec's concept of super-diversity does not merely concern increased ethnic and linguistic variation. The 'diversification of diversity' he describes also indicates a situation where it cannot be taken for granted how people identify and on what grounds they define their social identity. As Susanne Wessendorf (2015) shows, in a study of Hackney, London, the super-diversity of this area often (but not always) entails the creation of shifting public arenas and foci of group identification that are not based on ethnic or religious origins but on shared interests or activities. Whether this kind of fluid identification is sufficient to create a sense of belonging is an empirical question, and it deserves to be raised in earnest.

## THE FIXED AND THE FLUID

As the foregoing shows, we take a broad view of identity in this book, delineating it as social belonging and reflexive 'we-hood'; it is personal, but invariably has a collective dimension, it allows people to connect the past with the present, to make sense of continuities and changes, to negotiate their connections to place, and there are no *a priori* assumptions about the primacy of such things as ethnic, national, gendered or religious identities over other criteria of belonging. It shifts between being an emic and an analytical concept. To many people, pressing existential questions are likely to be the crucial ones, but analysis reveals underlying structural, collective and systemic aspects which trigger responses at the personal level. Like Handelman (1977), Brubaker (2002) and Jenkins (2014), the authors of this book do not take groupness for granted, but explore, through their case studies, how groups are being shaped and contested, how boundaries are established or destabilised in the interplay between exogenous and endogenous forces. During times of accelerated change, boundaries around groups may not merely be fluid; they may actually become moving targets that people seek to catch up with. Cohesion, built around a shared identity, may come in various forms and degrees, and it shifts and has to be readjusted.

There is no reason to assume that responses to change are homogeneous, consistent or unequivocal: there is always diversity, ambivalence and social inequality in the communities we study. At the same time, there may well exist a hegemonic narrative about the nature and implications of change, but it may be contested from within. One woman's crisis may be another's golden opportunity. Identifying the winners and losers in a situation of change is often useful (but not always unequivocally and unambiguously feasible); the challenge for many, whether they welcome or resist a particular form of exogenous change, nonetheless consists in 'rebuilding the ship at sea', a task undertaken in numerous ways.

In this kind of setting, many overheating effects can be observed. There are tendencies of boundary making and withdrawal into primordial identities both among minorities and majorities (the parallel in Europe between the extreme Right and militant Islamism is striking); there are vibrant debates about what it takes to be a good member of a category (a good Montenegrin, settler, return migrant and so on), and processes of hybridisation or creolisation at the level of symbolic culture may or may not match parallel processes of mixing in social life: you can stay endogamous, homosocial and heterosexual (cf. Banović, this volume), even if the cultural stuff that makes up your world is taken from diverse sources. Social identification has to be reconceptualised when circumstances change, and although there is no linear or predictable direction to changes in identification, there are a few likely scenarios or, perhaps, a range of options available in any given situation. It is likely that there will, in any discourse and practice surrounding perceived change, be elements of traditionalism, willingness to adjust, resistance and loyalty, quests for purity and celebrations of mixing.

The belief that modernity would lead to the obsolescence of 'primordial identities' has long been abandoned, but it can be important to distinguish between tradition (which recommends itself) and traditionalism (a reflexive choice). In the literature on indigenous peoples and their attempts to (re)define their place in a world where nearly everybody is forced to be a citizen, discourses about tradition and its entanglements with the state and its institutions have a central place, whether the study concerns Australian Aborigines' attempts to produce narratives creating the necessary hinges between past and future (Kearney, this volume) or the Filipino Aeta's quest for land and livelihood (Schober, this volume; see also Forte 2009). The authors tackling these issues in this volume, incidentally, all point to a certain quality of endurance that is displayed by the communities they study. Indigenous people complicate the picture of how social reproduction and identity matters are currently undergoing change because they tend to have been under great duress from various outside actors for much longer periods, which makes their strategies to create continuity during the recent era of accelerated change all the more worth noting.

Most of the processes of identification and re-identification discussed in the following chapters do not concern ethnic, national or regional identities as such. For example, rapid economic change, such as in contemporary Kabul (Wimpelmann), leads to a reconfiguration of class and new social distinctions. We are, moreover, looking at issues concerning identification with places in situations of rapid demographic, ecological and economic transitions in 'boomtowns' (Stensrud, Eriksen); the impact of disembedded, globalised commercialisation on identification (Martin); the clash between a transnational gay/lesbian discourse and traditional Balkan views of masculinity (Banović); the emergence of a 'frozen cosmopolitanism' among return migrants in the Cape Verde islands (Drotbohm); the desire to relinquish group identity for the sake of our common humanity (MacClancy). A key assumption is that rapid change – be it in the realm of the economy, politics or the environment – potentially limits people's options for economic, social and cultural reproduction. This, in turn, challenges collective identities which are often based on notions of continuity – temporal, spatial, social – leading to a broad but finite range of options for the people affected by and/or contributing to those changes.

Several zones of tension are at play in situations where the social world is being destabilised owing to rapid change in certain domains. As pointed out, not everything accelerates in the generally overheated early twenty-first century. Local or regional *deceleration* is also a possible consequence of globalised acceleration, and change is never uniform. It affects different aspects of individual life-worlds, but also different parts of a society, in different ways. The gap between acceleration and stability, or between rapid and slow change, is a main source of destabilisation in the realm of the social, as the chapters on 'boomtowns' indicate. Some sectors, areas or activities are 'left behind' or 'opt out', while others change very fast, creating – perhaps – disequilibrium or destabilisation in the system as a whole. Sometimes, there may also be an interesting rural/urban contrast or highland/lowland distinction (e.g. Schober) to be explored.

Second, *displacement* is a central theme in several of the papers, explicitly or implicitly, literally (e.g. Drotbohm) or metaphorically (e.g. Banović, Pijpers). Physical mobility is a main focus in research on transnationalism and diasporas, yet 'displacement' may also be an appropriate term for describing a situation where the physical surroundings have changed dramatically. The Australian environmental philosopher Glenn Albrechts accordingly coined the term 'solastalgia' to describe the feeling of loss and disorientation experienced as a result of environmental destruction (Albrechts 2005).

Another important distinction, which lies at the core of processes of rapid change, concerns the relationship between past and future as a source of identification and motivation. Alfred Schütz's distinction between 'in-order-to' and 'because-of' motivations (Schütz 1976), developed in Kearney's chapter, addresses this contrast at a micro-level.

Thorleifsson's chapter speaks to the same issues, but from the perspective of a marginal part of Israel, where the hinge between past, present and future is precarious. Nostalgia for a golden era and/or ideas about progress or development may articulate these notions in local political contexts, but the cultural production of continuity amidst changing circumstances is perhaps nowhere more evident than in the frozen moments described in Neumann's chapter about monuments, which counteract change, decay, alienation and displacement by creating continuities across a bumpy terrain.

To the dialectics of past and future, change and stagnation, overheating and cooling down, the frozen moment and the changing reality may be added to some classic and enduring themes in theories of identification: the production of comparability through intensified contact across borders creates a transnational (or even global) discourse about similarities and differences, whereby a global grammar for talking about identity may emerge, based on 'contrasting' and 'matching'. While collective identification has often been studied from a political perspective, the commercialisation of identity is increasingly the subject of scholarly attention, as witnessed in several of the chapters. With the current intensification of market mechanisms, and the growing transnationalisation of production and exchange, reconfigurations of collective identities may often take commercial forms instead of, or in addition to, political forms. However, the boundary-making entailed in identity talk is often challenged by ideologies and practices of hybridity and mixing. Finally, the tension between universalising and particularising processes, a fundamental dimension in current and recent theorising about modernity and globalisation, takes on its own dynamics in the volatile, unstable and unpredictable settings explored in the chapters that follow.

## REFERENCES

Albrechts, G. 2005. Solastalgia, A New Concept in Human Health and Identity. *PAN/ Philosophy Activism Nature* 3: 41–44.

Anderson, B. 1983. *Imagined Communities: An Inquiry into the Origins and Spread of Nationalism*. London: Verso.

Angé, O., and D. Berliner. 2015. Introduction: Anthropology of Nostalgia – Anthropology as Nostalgia. In O. Angé and D. Berliner (eds), *Anthropology and Nostalgia*. Oxford: Berghahn, pp.1–16.

Appadurai, A. 1990. Disjuncture and Difference in the Global Cultural Economy. In M. Featherstone (ed.), *Global Culture: Nationalism, Globalization, and Modernity*. London: Sage, pp.295–310.

Barth, F. 1969a. Introduction. In F. Barth (ed.), *Ethnic Groups and Boundaries: The Social Organization of Cultural Difference*. Oslo: Universitetsforlaget, pp.9–38.

—— (ed.) 1969b. *Ethnic Groups and Boundaries: The Social Organization of Cultural Difference*. Oslo: Universitetsforlaget.

Bauman, Z. 1996. From Pilgrim to Tourist; Or A Short History of Identity. In S. Hall and P. Du Gay (eds), *Questions of Cultural Identity*. London: Sage, pp.18–36.

—— 2000. *Liquid Modernity*. Cambridge: Polity.

Beck, U. 2009. *World at Risk*. Cambridge: Polity.

Bourdieu, P. 1977. *Outline of a Theory of Practice*. Cambridge: Cambridge University Press.

—— 1984. *Distinction: A Social Critique of the Judgement of Taste*. London: Routledge.

Bourdieu, P., et al. 2000. *The Weight of the World: Social Suffering in Contemporary Society*. Stanford: Stanford University Press.

Brandstädter, S., P. Wade and K. Woodward (eds). 2013. *Rights, Cultures, Subjects and Citizens*. London: Routledge.

Brubaker, R. 2002. Ethnicity without Groups. *European Journal of Sociology* 43(2): 163–89.

Brubaker, R., and F. Cooper. 2000. Beyond 'Identity'. *Theory, Culture and Society* 29(1): 1–47.

Castells, M. 1996–1998. *The Information Age*, 3 vols. Oxford: Blackwell.

Cohen, A. 1969. *Custom and Politics in Urban Africa*. London: Routledge and Kegan Paul.

Cohen, A.P. 1994. *Self Consciousness: An Alternative Anthropology of Identity*. London: Routledge.

Connerton, P. 1989. *How Societies Remember*. Cambridge: Cambridge University Press.

—— 2009. *How Modernity Forgets*. Cambridge: Cambridge University Press.

Drummond, L. 1980. The Cultural Continuum: A Theory of Intersystems. *Man* 15(2): 352–74.

Engels, F. 2010 [1884]. *The Origin of the Family, Private Property and the State*. London: Penguin.

Epstein, A.L. 1958. *Politics in an Urban African Community*. Manchester: Manchester University Press.

Eriksen, T.H. 2014. *Globalization: The Key Concepts*, 2nd edn. London: Bloomsbury.

—— 2015. The Meaning of 'We'. In P.A. Kraus and P. Kivisto (eds), *The Challenge of Minority Integration*. Berlin: De Gruyter Open, pp. 1–21.

—— 2016. *Overheating: An Anthropology of Accelerated Change*. London: Pluto.

Eriksen, T.H., E. Bal and O. Salemink (eds). 2010. *A World of Insecurity*. London: Pluto.

Erikson, E.H. 1963 [1950]. *Childhood and Society*. New York: Norton.

Fardon, R. 1987. 'African Ethnogenesis': Limits to the Comparability of Ethnic Phenomena. In L. Holy (ed.), *Comparative Anthropology*. Oxford: Blackwell, pp.168–88.

Forte, M. (ed.). 2009. *Indigenous Cosmopolitans: Transnational and Transcultural Indigeneity in the Twenty-First Century*. New York: Peter Lang.

Gellner, E. 1964. *Thought and Change*. London: Weidenfeld and Nicolson.

Giddens, A. 1991. *Modernity and Self-Identity*. Cambridge: Polity.

Glick Schiller, N., L. Basch and C. Blanc-Szanton (eds). 1992. *Towards a Transnational Perspective on Migration: Race, Class, Ethnicity, and Nationalism Reconsidered*. New York: New York Academy of Sciences.

Goody, J. 1976. *From Production to Reproduction: A Comparative Study of the Domestic Domain*. Cambridge: Cambridge University Press.

Handelman, D. 1977. The Organization of Ethnicity. *Ethnic Groups* 1: 187–200.

Hannerz, U. 1980. *Exploring the City: Inquiries toward an Urban Anthropology*. New York: Columbia University Press.

—— 1996. *Transnational Connections*. London: Routledge.

Harris, O., and K. Young. 1981. Engendered Structures: Some Problems in the Analysis of Reproduction. In J.S. Kahn and J.R. Llobera (eds), *The Anthropology of Pre-Capitalist Societies*. London: Macmillan, pp.109–47.

Harrison, S. 2002. The Politics of Resemblance: Ethnicity, Trademarks, Head-Hunting. *Journal of the Royal Anthropological Institute* 8: 211–32.

Hirschman, A. 1971. *Exit, Voice, Loyalty: Responses to Decline in Firms, Organizations and States*. Cambridge, MA: Harvard University Press.

Jenkins, R. 2002. Ethnicity and Nationalism in the Modern World. In J. MacClancy (ed.), *Exotic No More: Anthropology on the Front Lines*. Chicago: University of Chicago Press, pp.114–28.

—— 2014. *Social Identity*, 4th edn. London: Routledge.

Koselleck, R. 2002. *The Practice of Conceptual History: Timing History, Spacing Concepts*. Stanford: Stanford University Press.

Mayer, P. 1962. Migrancy and the Study of Africans in Towns. *American Anthropologist* 64: 576–92.

Mitchell, J.C. 1956. *The Kalela Dance: Aspects of Social Relationships among Urban Africans in Northern Rhodesia*. Rhodes-Livingstone Institute Paper. Manchester: Manchester University Press.

Ogburn, W.F. 1922. *Social Change with Respect to Culture and Original Nature*. New York: Huebsch.

Olwig, K.F. 2007. *Caribbean Journeys: An Ethnography of Migration and Home in Three Family Networks*. Durham, NC: Duke University Press.

Parkin, D. 1969. *Neighbours and Nationals in an African City Ward*. London: Routledge and Kegan Paul.

Peel, J.D.Y. 1989. The Cultural Work of Yoruba Ethnogenesis. In E. Tonkin, M. McDonald and M. Chapman (eds), *History and Ethnicity*. London: Routledge, pp.198–215.

Robbins, D. 2000. *Bourdieu and Culture*. London: Sage.

Robertson, R. 1992. *Globalization*. London: Sage.

Sassen, S. 2014. *Expulsions: Brutality and Complexity in the Global Economy*. Cambridge, MA: Belknap Press.

Schütz, A. 1976 [1964]. *Collected Papers*, Vol. 2: *Studies in Social Theory*. The Hague: Martinus Nijhoff.

Smith, A.D. 1986. *The Ethnic Origins of Nations*. Oxford: Blackwell.

Spooner, B. 2015. Globalization via World Urbanization. In B. Spooner (ed.), *Globalization: The Crucial Phase*. Philadelphia: University of Pennsylvania Press, pp.1–21.

Stewart, C. (ed.). 2007. *Creolization: History, Ethnography, Theory*. Walnut Creek, CA: Left Coast Press.

Urry, J. 2000. *Sociology Beyond Societies: Mobilities for the Twenty-First Century*. London: Routledge.

Vertovec, S. 2007. Super-Diversity and its Implications. *Ethnic and Racial Studies* 30(6): 1024–54.

Werbner, P., and T. Modood (eds). 1997. *Debating Cultural Hybridity*. London: Zed.

Wessendorf, S. 2014. *Commonplace Diversity: Social Relations in a Super-Diverse Context*. London: Palgrave.

Wilson, G. 1942. *An Essay on the Economics of Detribalization in Northern Rhodesia*, Parts 1 and 2. Rhodes-Livingstone Institute Papers. Livingstone: Rhodes-Livingstone Institute.

Wimmer, A., and N. Glick Schiller. 2002. Methodological Nationalism and Beyond: Nation-State Building, Migration and the Social Sciences. *Global Networks* 2(4): 301–34.

# 2. Down With Identity!
# Long Live Humanity!

*Jeremy MacClancy*

Only connect!
—E.M. Forster, *Howard's End*

Where are we anthropologists with the study of identity today? In the postwar beginnings of European anthropology, anglophone ethnographers stressed in their village-based studies social harmony and consensus. They isolated honour and shame as promising concepts for their cross-cultural comparisons. For the studied, this pair was said to provide a common mode of assessment; for the anthropologists, it lent reality to their notion of moral community.

This over-rosy image of villages was picked apart from the 1970s onwards, for a variety of reasons. Many decried the structural-functionalist overemphasis on social stasis. Those inspired by Marx questioned the lack of social conflict in these studies; Davis, for example, exposed the ways honour did not bring people together but divided them in terms of social class (Davis 1977). Feminists in our ranks brought out the pervasive roles that gender division could play (e.g. Lever 1986). Very belatedly, some anthropologists began to rediscover the importance in their fieldsites of ideas about 'race' (Harrison 2002). And almost all, like other social scientists, were taken aback by the sustained rise of ethnic nationalisms, and the challenge of how specialists in social and cultural life should research them. 'Identity' became a key word for both the studied and those studying them. In the process anthropologists of Europe moved from the rural to the urban.

It seems much of our work is still framed by Barth's approach to identity which, though only a page and a half long and produced 45 years ago, is yet regarded as fresh today (Barth 1969: 14–15). Others might ponder: Is this an unwanted presentism or an even more unwanted recognition of the lack of ideas among Barth's successors?

Barth's transactional model is as now as infamous as it was influential. He stated that anthropologists of ethnicity should study 'the ethnic *boundary* that defines the group, not the cultural stuff it encloses' (ibid.: 14–15). What he meant by 'cultural stuff' was language, religion, traditions and laws, material culture and so on. As several have since counter-argued, his statement appears counter-intuitive. It is hard to believe that the constitution of the cultural stuff on which ethnic differentiation is grounded is largely irrelevant. Richard Jenkins comments:

> This surely cannot be true. For example, a situation in which the As and the Bs are distinguished, *inter alia*, by languages which are mutually intelligible for most everyday purposes – as with Danish and Norwegian – would seem to differ greatly from one in which the languages involved are, as with English and Welsh, utterly different. (Jenkins 1997: 107)

Sixteen years later Zenker put it more formally. For him, Barth's approach, which he terms 'pure constructivism', is 'empirically untenable because not all representations are equally viable for actors, and cultural variation may help explain how more or less successful processes of identity formation are shaped' (Zenker 2013: 26). He makes the good point that we need to discuss both actors' selection of cultural practices and their pretensions – that is, practices which they desire to have performed but are not yet practised. His key example of pretension is language revival, in his case Gaelic Irish in Catholic West Belfast (ibid.: 36).

In sociology, Stephen Cornell has similarly argued that we should attend to not just the boundaries of ethnic groups but to their content as well. He classes these internal factors in terms of interests, institutions and culture, and then focuses both on the variable content of ethnic identities, and on the role content plays in patterns of ethnic persistence and change. He argues that anything less produces an incomplete understanding of ethnic processes (Cornell 1996; Cornell & Hartman 1998: 86–9). In my multi-sited ethnography of Basque nationalism (MacClancy 2007), I argued in a comparable, though parallel fashion: unless we took seriously the cultural dimensions of identity, our understanding of those we study would remain forever partial, to an unjustifiable degree. In other words, if we do not attend systematically to what people say and do, we are acting in a thoroughly non-anthropological manner, with pretensions towards Olympian levels of condescension, tilting dangerously towards the patronizing and the neo-colonial.

Jenkins contends that identity is not an entity but an unstable process, the continuing interaction of self-identification, by identity-holders, and social categorisation, of identity-holders by others (Jenkins 1997: 51). This has led some to speak of 'modes of identification' rather than identity as a way to underline identity's nature, contingently grounded in place and time. What surprises me is that neither of these points seems to have been taken on board in a disciplined manner in subsequent ethnographies. To my knowledge, no one working in this sub-field has written any ethnography, whether a book or a paper, which goes beyond the separate analysis of self-identification and of social categorisation. No one appears to have dissected, in a detailed manner, the interaction between the two, and certainly not to have done so over time. I suspect that is because it is not easy to do; at the very least it needs an extended commitment to one fieldsite over years to do the job even adequately, as well as historiographical skills. The only exception I have learnt of comes from African studies and, significantly, is presented as an exercise in conflict resolution (see Schlee 2008).[1]

Furthermore, the degree to which one mode of identification prevails or one style of categorisation comes to dominate, for however short or long, is an eminently political question. Yet this crucial dimension of power, as far as I am aware, remains relatively understudied. With hindsight, I can today regard my Basque work as a fine-grained study of various cultural dimensions of Basque identity, and little more. One reviewer generously praised the book, but saved his spike for the final paragraph: why had I not incorporated analysis of the aims and work of the Basque government into my study (Itçaina 2009: 249)? This regional representative body is nationally notorious for the great efforts and money it has invested, since its creation in the late 1970s, in promoting a rainbow-wide diversity of Basque cultural aspects. I take my reviewer's point: by neglecting to examine the development of politico-administrative strategies towards Basque culture, my own study rarely strayed further than the wilder fringes of internal nationalist discourse and action.

Worse is yet to come: in my ethnography, I did not take into account the attitudes and opinions of non-Basques, whether resident in the Basque Country or elsewhere in Spain, whether Spanish nationalist or simply political centralist. Furthermore, I did not take account of Basque reactions to those attitudes. I do not know of any scholar of the Basques who has done any of that adequately. The sum result of these various exclusions or superficial treatments of topics integral to our sub-field is that the model of identity practised in my ethnography is historically grounded but not interactive nor appropriately sensitive to administrative policy and its effects. Indeed, I know of no nationalist ethnography which is, barring the possible exception of Urla's study of Basque language, nationalism and cultural activism (Urla 2012).

---

1. My thanks to Chris Hann for suggesting this reference.

In this chapter I wish to go further, to state that studies of identity in Europe (such as my own), and perhaps beyond, are fundamentally misdirected. Focusing on actors' bids to proclaim or manipulate identity, we run the real risk of forgetting that, given the evidence, most people are not much interested in identity. Indeed, the very opposite: they strive daily to uphold equality, commonality and a notion of humanity which usually tends towards the universal. They wish to connect, not divide. That's the main point I make here.

Let me demonstrate.

## THREE ETHNOGRAPHIC EXAMPLES

### County Fermanagh, Northern Ireland

In 2013 I supervised the undergraduate dissertation of Matthew Gault, on the expression of identity in his native region, the most south-western county of Northern Ireland. To outside audiences, 'the North' is almost always presented as an extreme example in Western Europe of the most deeply entrenched divisions, between a seemingly permanent Protestant majority and a large Catholic minority. The violent and murderous consequences of this division are all too well known. The results of Gault's fieldwork give us a very different portrait.

Rosemary Harris did fieldwork in an unnamed border county of Northern Ireland towards the start of the Troubles. Despite strongly voiced opposition across the sectarian divide, she found that hill-farmers 'recognised real obligations to their neighbours of "the other side" … and their relationships in all contexts were egalitarian' (Harris 1972: 184). Gault's work, forty years later, shows an even greater degree of contact and cooperation. He points out that locals claim they are 'naturally more tolerant', 'calmer', 'relaxed'; they do not 'take things too seriously' but 'keep things in perspective'. Instead of feeding division, they stress cooperation. Some explain this in instrumental terms: for small farmers to survive, certain agricultural tasks require their neighbours' assistance. Others make reference to tenets of Christianity which are so fundamental they bypass sectarian division, such as 'Love thy neighbour'. In fact Gault observes that in some cases there is more division between members of different Protestant denominations than between them and Catholics. Also, with the gradual decline of conflict in the North, it is only now becoming evident that, despite past avowals to the contrary, many people did maintain relationships with those 'on the other side': they just tended to keep quiet about them.

Locals tend to avoid open conflict. A very significant number of locals, from either religious camp, shy away from identification with one side or another. Organisers of cross-community drama workshops in the county town of Fermanagh discovered that participants were not keen to answer any questions about their identity or community background. Instead, they elected to emphasise the voluntary or community work they took part in (Jennings 2009). During the summertime marching season, when Protestant lodges parade through particular towns, there are remarkably few protests. 'It is more common for people who object to the parades in Fermanagh to avoid them' (Gault 2014: 26–7). Local Protestants uninterested or even uneasy about these performances may well downplay their religious affiliation during the marching season. On top of that, inter-village rivalries are not prominent. Indeed, 'Outside the village, ties to a particular village are more often used to find ways to include strangers into groups [*sic*] than exclude them, usually by finding out if they know someone you know from that village' (ibid.: 24).

The overall picture I gain from Gault's work, backed by my own 'halfie' knowledge as the son of an Irishman, is of a county whose occupants desire to stress mutual acceptance and the ability to work together over antagonistic division based on whatever mode of identity. This wish to connect rather than separate out is extended to immigrants to the county. One interviewee's rationale for the acceptance of incomers was that they became as tolerant as the locals were themselves avowed to be. In other words, the power of local ways was so strong that new arrivals came to act like the denizens, and so could be incorporated as part of the area. In this land, inclusion, rather than exclusion, is the order of the day.

### County Clare, the West of Ireland

In the early 2000s, I did brief but intensive fieldwork in the west of Ireland, specifically in County Clare, where my family comes from. I wanted to study the resident incomers, who immigrated in a series of waves from the late 1960s on, dubbed in turn 'hippies', 'crusties' and 'suburbanites' (MacClancy 2015). Locals classed all these people and other incomers as 'blow-ins'.

Both denizens and migrants stressed to me how very locally 'blow-in' could be defined. Not only was it applied to peace-loving Yanks and anti-Thatcherites from sink estates but to Irish on the move as well. The example several interviewees repeated to me was that, on marriage, a person might move from their natal village to that of their spouse a few miles away but could still be called a blow-in decades later, when on their death-bed. Even if an incomer's children integrated very successfully, they would always be known as 'the son/daughter of the blow from X'. This was often told to me with a smile, as though to acknowledge how ridiculous that might seem to outsiders. In a recent novel about contemporary rural Ireland, the author has a character ruminate:

> *Blow-in.* That phrase is used so derisively. As if to say it's a failing not to have been born and bred here, to have settled in a place outside of the place of your birth. Mam, doesn't mean anything bad by it, though. It's hard to shake your prejudices, I know. (Ryan 2012: 127, original italics)

At first glance, this appears a classic formulation of restrictive identity. To anthropologists obsessed with classification (perhaps a hangover from structuralism), it may even be viewed as an attractively extreme example. But I think this stress on categorisation would be to mischaracterise what is in fact going on. Focusing on a highly localised definition of 'blow-in' is perhaps to steer the discussion down an unproductive path, for the following reasons.

The more perceptive of 'blows' came to realise that they had entered small communities whose members were either all related to one another or had known one another since birth. Much of their conversation was about their kin, affines and personalities peppering familial and local histories. Like native Amazonians who when meeting a stranger seek a common (if fictitious) genealogical link in order to establish a social relationship (Riviere 1969: 101–2), locals in Clare would initiate conversations with a new person in their midst by engaging in a joint hunt for shared kin, in-laws or friends. The writer Niall Williams, a US blow-in, gives a good example of this. He married an Irish American and the two went to live in her late grandparents' house in south-west Clare. Not long after their arrival, the parish priest called round. 'Once he had inquired about our health, he moved the talk to that most important of subjects: "Who is it now are your wife's cousins?"' (Williams & Breen 1987: 124). When I started fieldwork in the area, 'blows' stressed how important it was I introduced myself to local interviewees by first talking about my grandfather.

Many interviewees who came in the first two waves stressed how welcoming the locals were. When I asked about their relations with neighbours, they spontaneously listed the unpaid labour locals gave to help rebuild their ramshackle homes, the tractors loaned, the furniture given, the repeated advice about farming freely provided, the parcels of food left out for them, the seemingly endless teas they were invited to and so on. One said she and her partner need never have gone shopping in their first three years if they had accepted all the invitations made to them. The question is, why were the natives so welcoming?

One 'blow' thought they amused the locals. With their seemingly strange ways and unusual lifestyle, they were good entertainment value: a potentially powerful consideration in a land where the gift of the gab is so esteemed. Others thought it because the denizens themselves were poetical, non-logical types, traditionally tolerant of the odd within their own number. In the words of one former hippy: 'When we came here first the locals accepted us in our eccentricity. I mean our immediate locals here are all completely mad in a lovely way. They'd talk to you for days non-stop about the fairies'. An alternative possibility came from a German ethnologist who studied the 'blows' in a north Clare village: he suggested the natives were so empathetic because of their 'primarily individualistic orientation' (Kockel 2002: 62). But if locals' desire for individualism has always been tempered by the pressures of community, then incomers' behaviour might well act as an educative demonstration of what could be. If so, the actions of incomers might not have been viewed as an already recognised idiosyncrasy, but as exemplary. A third possibility is that the locals' generosity was a genuine welcoming, an invitation to the new arrivals to engage in community by entering local networks of exchange: the gifts were instructive; they were meant to be returned in time, if not in kind. As one very well-established incomer said to me, long-term 'blows' who had a service they could provide, whether as builder, architect or fellow farmer, might not be seen as 'locals', but they could still be relied upon, and that was important for the indigenes. These prestations and counter-prestations have also an embedded ethical dimension, for here they are used to practise and to assert the primacy of a moral egalitarianism.

Of course, these three interpretations are not mutually exclusive. Taken together, they point to dovetailing social values: a high degree of tolerance, a qualified acceptance of individualism, the centrality of exchange and the performance of equality. Locals' upholding of these values for the sake of integrating the 'blows' could be regarded as the flipside of the more usual means they employ to connect with incomers. They cannot seek connection via consanguinity with these outsiders, but may hope to create it via action, leading to spasmodic but sustained interaction. Like the people of Fermanagh, across the border, the farmers and villagers of Clare actively downplay potentially divisive forms of identity, in this ethnographic case to extend their networks and prevent incomers from remaining strangers in their land.

### Navarre and the Basque Country

As a postdoctoral fellow, I did fieldwork in Pamplona for twelve months in total between 1984 and 1985. I spent all but three months of the following two years in Cirauqui, a village thirty kilometres to the south-west.

In the city I shared a flat with a man a few years younger than me. He had graduated from high school, then got a job in a bookshop, but was at the time unemployed. Every night he took me on his bar crawls, during which he gradually introduced me to his broad circle of friends and acquaintances. After a month or so, he grew tired of my repetitious questions about them and, somewhat peeved, instructed me: 'Don't keep asking me where they are from, what do they do, how do I know them. Just try to get on with them'. If I wanted to get on with people, especially him, I had to follow the local rules. I had to seek out what we had in common, as fellow human beings, I should not prematurely pigeonhole them into different categories.

Pamplona was then a place of apparently deep division and dedicated activism. I went there deliberately to study identity conflict, between revolutionary nationalists, who dominated leftist discourse in the area, and right-wing regionalist reactionaries, who were equally virulent in their claims. However, I eventually learnt there were limits to the behaviour of even the most deeply committed members of either side, who would, on occasion, put other loyalties before political kinship. During fieldwork it was suggested to me that members of an extended family, even if they were each professionally entrenched at opposite poles of the political spectrum, might put aside their differences at family gatherings, such as weddings, and might even quietly assist one another. When I tried to follow this up, some I spoke to acknowledged that cross-factional fraternisation did occur from time to time. But none wished to give further details; not surprising, given the great sensitivity of this information (MacClancy 2007: 41–2).

Most of my flatmate's drinking friends had learnt Euskera (the Basque language) as youths, in private classes. Many of them taught it as their job. Yet none ever discussed politics. I was very taken aback to learn later that not one of these teachers supported radical nationalism, but were critical of it. Most even rejected the nationalist message. Instead they stressed the need for *convivencia*, peaceful coexistence based on the tacit acceptance of difference. For example, once I had got to know them better, a few gently pointed out that though economic distinctions were never mentioned within the group, the different holiday destinations friends were able to choose were quietly noted.

On weekends I used to hitchhike out of Pamplona and into the countryside. It was a way to see the area and meet people I would not otherwise encounter. To spark conversation I would often ask the driver who picked me up about their political leanings: anti-nationalist or nationalist, and of what stripe. Once they had got over their surprise at my impertinence, many responded that they backed away from such pigeon-holing. They were, they said, *ciudadanos del mundo*, 'citizens of the world': people had to learn how to live together. One couple who gave me a lift started to complain about the recent rise in Pamplona of petty crime and burglaries, which was being blamed by many on gypsies. They stressed they were not *racistas*; long-resident gypsies in the city were upstanding members of their locale. It was the rootless gypsies who had recently moved into the area who committed these acts. Though concerned about antisocial petty criminals, the couple took pains to laud a broad-based *convivencia* which included law-abiding gypsies.

A few months after my arrival, a friend of my flatmate told me about two of our mutual acquaintances, the good chums X and Y. In what I understood to be a gentle, indirect admonition, he told me X was an avid birdwatcher. But when they went for walks in the mountains, sat under a tree and listened to the sounds, Y took great pleasure in the fact that he knew X was a learned twitcher, that X could immediately identify all the birds they could hear and where around them they were, that X would never mention any of this, unless prompted, and that X knew that Y would never so prompt him. Others in our conversation smiled with approval. In other words, part of the friendship of the pair was grounded on one not making any uncalled-for reference to his specialised knowledge. Any attempt at underlining a difference in learning between the two was anathema. I took the point.

Similarly, when I arrived in Cirauqui, villagers were extremely friendly when I was introduced to them. My aged landlord by my side, he would explain why I had come and what I wanted to do. One day, one villager replied, 'Goodness! So much education: you must be very bright!' I hesitated slightly, then felt a sharp dig in my back ribs from the old man, who was saying in a loud voice to the other man, 'Oh, but you're very bright too!' I quickly agreed in a lively manner. Later, when he heard me knocking back compliments, in an energetic but playful manner, he quietly commented to me, 'Good, Jeremy. You're learning'.

On the whole, while villagers were easily capable of categorising their neighbours in a variety of different ways, they tended not to do so. The only obvious exceptions to this generalisation were the deeply politicised, especially those on the revolutionary Left. What villagers were happy to discuss, in a good-natured manner, was individual idiosyncrasies, as though these personal quirks only enriched the social diversity of what they saw as their otherwise humdrum lives. Generally, they left labelling to one side and preferred to focus, within a broad, egalitarian and open-ended frame, on performance: mild eccentricities and people's level of participation in the public spaces of the village.

A further example: the *sociedades gastronomicas* ('dining clubs') are a well-known Basque institution which first arose in the 1900s. Today in the Basque Country, which has a population of 2.1 million, there are over 1,500 registered societies, over half established since the 1960s. In the province of Guipúzcoa, these societies are so popular that in some towns almost every adult resident is a member of one. Originally, women were prohibited entry, but in recent decades the rule has been progressively relaxed, and new societies formed from the 1980s onwards are open to both genders. Membership is not confined to Basques but may include labour migrants to the area. Incomers who move into a new housing block may well form their own building-based society and, if it proves successful, will seek registration as a fully fledged *sociedad gastronomica*.

The principles of these societies are few but clear. Each has its own premises, which contains a kitchen and an area for eating and relaxing. Each member of a society has a key to the premises and is free to use the kitchen, where they may cook a meal for a group of fellow members and their guests. At the end of the meal, money to cover the cost of the ingredients used is left in a box. There is no control over what is paid in other than the conscience of the members.

For the Basque sociologist Jesús Arpal, these societies present themselves 'as pure concelebration, in a pure production of elemental solidarity' (Arpal 1985: 147). They are seen to uphold cherished Basque values of good food, commensality and democratic conviviality (MacClancy 2007: 78–80). As many like to claim, a duke might sit next to a dustman, and both could expect to rise from the table, buoyed up by a good meal and good company. In this sense they are a much-used way to assert an ideal of joyous commonality where the quotidian divisions of work and class are shunted aside.

These societies are but one, peculiarly distinctive form among a diversity of socialising modes which together constitute a dense network in the Basque Country and the autonomous province of Navarre: taverns, bars, coffee shops, special-interest societies (mountaineering, folk-dancing and so on). The egalitarian nature of these spaces turns them into 'neuralgic centres of a true social network of communication and knowledge-sharing' (Homobono 2009: 71).[2] Moreover, many of the

---

2. On the toing and froing between bars in the Basque town of Irun, see Bray (2004: 111–26).

socialising modes are 'barely formalized' (Homobono 1994: 231), and are valued as such. A predominant mode is the *cuadrillas*, long-standing groups of friends, like that of my flatmate and his chums, who tour bars together, at least weekly, if not near daily (Gurruchaga 1985: 360–74). In Cirauqui and many neighbouring villages, socialising takes a slightly different form: on Saturdays villagers re-form into their age sets, each with its own premises, where pairs of members take turns to cook for the rest. The meal over, members of all *cuadrillas* then move to the bars in the village square where they mingle, sing and continue drinking.

In all these settings, whether Basque or Navarran, urban or rural, an active sociability was the general rule, grounded on a broad sense of equality, transcending the routine, divisive worlds of home and workplace. People worked hard to maintain *convivencia*, however fragile that might appear at times, and so strove to sideline disruptive difference, whether economic, social, occupational or political.

## IDENTITIES, COMMONALITIES

In the peaceful decades of the immediate postwar period, anthropologists of Europe underlined social harmony. Many of their successors, living among new forms of conflict, studied divisive modes of self-identification, and seemed to forget about local claims of commonality in the process. Why was this?

If identities are relational, they are by definition comparative. But comparison is rarely neutral. All too often, it is not 'We are different from you but equal', but rather 'We are different from you and better; you are different from us and worse'. Herzfeld goes further. He states evaluative judgement is a necessary component of identification, that there is no classification without hierarchy (Herzfeld 1989: 17). According to him, people cannot slot themselves and others into taxonomies without at the same time ranking those categories. Little wonder, then, that the more egalitarian-minded eschew classification.

One possible reason why anthropologists seeking components of identity may misconstrue their fieldsites is that they are waylaid by the easily identifiable. In other words, locals who wave banners may achieve their desired end: some people, ethnographers included, pay attention. To use a contemporary example, kilts, bagpipes, malt whisky and other folkloric items and events may be outstanding national symbols, but just how representative are they of modern Scots identities? A second example: a few years ago a Japanese doctoral student studying English identity asked me, to my surprise, how to obtain further information about Morris dancing. I suspect this is cock-eyed. There is a Morris 'side' (dance team) in the Oxfordshire village where I live: when asked why they participate, Morrismen stress the sociability and the drinking of their activity; almost all of these men-in-smocks push any question of tradition to the far margins of their concerns. For my neighbours, the Morris performances are agreeable but spasmodic entertainments, and nothing more, as far as I can judge. The word 'identity' is never mentioned. In sum, peoples studied, like the inhabitants of Cirauqui, the farmers in the west of Ireland, the city-dwellers of Pamplona or villagers in Oxfordshire, attend far more to everyday action and the non-verbal than to occasional but strongly marked performances and ticking lexical boxes.[3]

Tamara Kohn has discussed this well. In the course of her lengthy fieldwork on a Hebridean island in the north-west of Scotland, she came to realise that though locals could class people there into a neat set of categories ('locals', 'summer swallows', 'Glasgow cousins', tourists), observation of their quotidian reality uncovered other dynamics. She found that while everyday action might not be consciously equated with islander identity, it could be a far more revelatory and enduring marker of local identity than patently constructed symbolic markers such as ancestry, locality or consanguinity. Locals who openly manipulated these markers – for example, wearing kilts, recounting island history, celebrating public rituals – were only incorporated into the 'living and changing community' if they also engaged in 'appropriate everyday social action' (Kohn 2002: 143). One might be verbally classed 'incomer' but, thanks to their acts, be treated as more of an islander than some of those who stridently self-proclaimed that status. In this case, actions do speak louder.

Some anthropologists claim their colleagues, in the very exercise of fieldwork, exaggerate difference: it is an unavoidable component of our craft (e.g. Boon 1983: 3–26). If this be so, then it is only a short step for a fieldworker to focus on the studied group's own vaunted sense of distinctiveness. Here the anthropologist does not have to hunt for difference or to worry that they are imposing their own categories on others' ways: in these cases, the locals are themselves proudly promoting their own version of difference (MacClancy 1993). All that is left for the fieldworker to do is investigate who is using which style of this identity, when, where, why and to what effect. This is fieldwork at its most

---

3.  Mils Hills, in his study of multiculturalist policies in Mauritius, argues that though the national government seeks to balance the representation of, and the distribution of benefits to different identified groups, locals deliberately undercut this divisive identification and thus assert their humanity (Hills 2002).

seductively misleading, disciplinary dispositions blinkering the anthropologist to the breadth of what might be going on at their fieldsite.

Simon Harrison offers another clue as to why anthropologists may have passed over commonality. He highlights the ways ethnic groups that are remarkably similar in many ways to one another manage to distinguish themselves by the denial of resemblance (Harrison 2003). Commonality is masked for the sake of creating difference where little, it is argued, in fact exists. In a similar vein, Barth emphasised how much parents reproduced social class identity and socialised their children in class-consciousness by actively suppressing common behaviour (Barth 1994). In both these cases, commonality is not quietly masked, but actively expunged.

I am hesitant about adding the following, further possible reason for anthropologists favouring identity over commonality. The UK continues to be ill-famed as the home of a pervasive, steeply hierarchical social class structure, albeit now somewhat attenuated and transfigured. I suspect that some of my colleagues might be unwitting reproducers of the cultural bias of their own social class fraction. Research in Britain suggests that members of the less advantaged stress equality and common humanity, while the more moneyed socialise their children in the diverse dimensions of cultural distinction (see Anon. 2013). The consequence for such a middle-class activity as British academic anthropology is patent.

It is also possible anthropologists downplay equality and focus on identity because they are themselves products of a savagely competitive profession which rewards distinctiveness: the promotions and glittering prizes go to those who strive to stand out, to heighten their individuality as exceptional thinkers. What fat grants would they win for a project which investigates how people feel they are all the same, and spend their social time trying to connect with others? In this sense, there is an unattractive parallel between the strategies of successful anthropologists and the protagonists of the movements they study. Does this account for the lack of anthropological work done on people's avoidance of identity markers? One corollary is that perhaps the only way I claim attention for this chapter is by presenting my contention as a theoretical position.

Of course energetic contrarians, like myself, are but playing the same game as those they criticise: exploiting an underused argument to advertise their own independence of thought. The same ploy can also be seen in almost any discussion of anthropological ethics, where the loudest proponents of moral practice are suspiciously deaf to comments that they are using their platform to raise themselves up (MacClancy & Fuentes 2013: 19–20). What pleas can I mount in my own defence: a wish to correct academic distortion, or my own thirst for the juicy awards? At the very least I console myself that my own gambit is more open to scrutiny than that of those at whom I carp.

## THE MOTIVATIONS OF HISTORIANS, AND ANTHROPOLOGISTS

In the words of so many science-fiction films, we are not alone. Some historians have been making similar comments for some time about the practice of their colleagues.

In the 1980s, William McNeil, a distinguished exponent of a rigorous world history, underlined the major effects historians may have in the non-academic world, and thus the responsibilities they bear. He argued that by helping to define 'them' and 'us', historians play a significant part in steering love and hate. To McNeil, parochial history 'inevitably' enhanced conflicts; so he propounded an ecumenical version as a counterbalance. A veteran of the Second World War, he believed the production of an ecumenical history was the moral duty of the historical profession. McNeil wanted an intelligible world history which assisted individuals to identify with the success and failures of humanity as a whole. That, in his opinion, could lessen the lethal consequences of group encounters. For if readers came to recognise the complexity of human social life, they might learn to balance their loyalties 'so that no one group will be able to command total commitment. Only so can we hope to make the world safer for all the different human groups that now exist' (McNeil 1986: 7–8).

In 2013, David Cannadine, writing in a similar style of prophesy and moral exhortation, extended somewhat McNeil's line of argument. He contended that his colleagues' focus on the divisive consequences of religion, nation, class, gender, race and civilisation is misplaced, and that we need to be far more sceptical about the supposedly fundamental nature of those categories. He claimed to demonstrate that these vaunted, unbridgeable divides are in fact persistently breached by conversations which 'make a substantial, perhaps even preponderant, part of the whole human experience' (Cannadine 2013: 260). Cannadine worried that our present sense of the past has been distorted by 'an exaggerated insistence on the importance of confrontation and difference' (ibid.: 4). This was to disserve the cause of knowledge, and misrepresent the nature of the human condition, as well as 'misidentifying the best paths by which that condition has been improved – and may be further improved' (ibid.: 261). Instead of focusing on conflictual divisiveness, historians should pay equal attention to the human concerns and activities which transcend those divisions. Furthermore, according to Cannadine, this over-concentration on divided pasts shunts aside our just legacy: the knowledge that human societies are not constantly breaking down. 'Surely it is at least as worthwhile to take as our starting-point humanity's essential (but under-studied) unity as it is to obsess on its lesser (but over-studied) divisions?' (ibid.: 263).

If Marx and his followers have favoured conflict as the motor for change in capitalist society, it becomes easy to brand the ecumenical approach of both McNeil and Cannadine as politically conservative. In their otherwise laudable aim of dulling the edge of murderous conflict, they have run the risk of promoting the status quo. In other words, though they call for balance, they explicitly hope to rob firebrand ideologues of historical certainty. But, as Margaret MacMillan has argued, handling history with care may help us assess how much of a politician's words to believe (MacMillan 2009). She, like McNeil and Cannadine, is simply trying to undercut the power of rabble-rousers who misuse history for their own self-interested ends, no matter the political corner from which they fight. This trio is not arguing against the benefits of social change but the dangers of uninformed action.

McNeil wondered why his colleagues had shied away from an ecumenical view of human society. He opined that the career paths in his profession rewarded specialisation, which necessarily concentrates on minutiae (McNeil 1986: 8). Similarly, Cannadine asked why so few historians have attended to 'human association'. He thought it may be that this big story is as interesting to historians as good news is to journalists: a quotidian reality which rarely makes people open books or buy newspapers (Cannadine 2013: 262). Here we should remember the winning entry in the informal competition between journalists of *The Times*, for the most boring, still newsworthy headline: 'Small earthquake in China. Few dead'. How many extra copies would that sell?

## CANDEA'S CONUNDRUM

I do not wish to be misunderstood. I am not trying to set up an insurmountable opposition between commonality and identity. After all, it is well established that some peoples around the globe define humanity as 'us' – that is, themselves – and all others as non-humans or less than fully human. Commonality is not universal. What I am arguing is that despite such a rider, fieldworkers should expect to find commonality rather than not, in one or more of its many manifestations.

It is also well-known that identities are fluid, contested, negotiable, multiple and contextual, both ignored and vaunted depending on the moment and place. Of course, commonality may be viewed as merely a limited case of identity. But that move threatens to turn talk about identity into a trivially true, all-encompassing discourse, on an intellectual par with Freudian and evolutionary approaches. Either way, I contend that an open-ended commonality is more the norm than a virulent sense of identity, and fieldworkers who forget this do so to their own detriment.

This shift in perspective could have a radical effect on the way anthropologists of Europe do fieldwork and write their ethnographies: starting with commonality and then, and only then, seeing which identities began to emerge. Imagine, for example, a fieldtrip to the Basque Country which did not immediately focus on nationalist or anti-nationalist issues, but which commenced from people's associative networks: who spent time with whom, how, why, when; how welcoming were they to others, and on what grounds. What were the non-verbal activities valued by locals which incomers could perform; what difference could they make? If bars and cafes are lauded as spaces of spontaneous sociability, they should be spaces selected early by the fieldworker so as to see who interacts with whom, and how effective drink is in disinhibiting clients. As these points are established, one could then begin to track the contexts in which identity claims arise, their styles, their social and cultural effects. For example, Tone Bringa, in her Bosnian ethnography, underlines that before the Balkan conflict erupted, many schoolchildren in urban Sarajevo did not know 'their' ethnicity. In the mixed village she studied, locals, pre-conflict, lauded neighbourliness, and she could plot the contexts in which women followed ethnic lines, and the ones in which they transcended those divisions by acting as good neighbours (Bringa 1995). It was the arrival of war which changed all that.

One critic of this chapter stressed that not all incomers are accepted. To his mind, that fact confirmed the existence and boundedness of local identities. The ethnographic record obliges me to agree, somewhat. But my question would be: Are all incomers who are prepared to negotiate local ways and to work out how to participate ignored or brushed off? Just because not all incomers are accepted does not imply that none are or that many will not be over time. Shifting the fieldwork question means moving our initial focus from identity to commonality. To put it another way: fieldwork should start at a place for sociability, such as a popular bar, rather than a site for division, such as a noisy demonstration.

The rubric of the workshop on which these chapters are based is 'overheating': the idea is that uneven, accelerating globalisation leads, among other things, to a perceived threat to social integrities and the assertion of group identities. Maybe; maybe not. For in arenas where globalisation is all too evident, the natives may react not by reasserting a closed, local identity, but by emphasising their commitment to an open-ended commonality. We should not fall, either way, for easy sociological generalisation. It is up to us to examine what is going on in each ethnographic case. Another way to state my point is to acknowledge the parallels between commonality and vernacular cosmopolitanism – that is, people from different parts of the world deliberately pushing divisive identity markers to one side in order to celebrate their common interest, whether temporary or more enduring, in a particular behaviour or set of behaviours. Adam Kaul exemplifies the point well in his ethnography about music-making in a coastal village in County Clare. Visiting musicians from continental Europe, the USA and beyond gather there to play Celtic music, adopting and appropriating, enriching and developing the mix in the process (Kaul 2009). It is a salutary counter-example to those otherwise obsessed with identity.

A recent current within migration studies appears to be moving in the same direction.[4] Some working within this interdisciplinary space have begun to see 'conviviality' as the surprising flip-side to Vertovec's notion of 'super-diversity' (Vertovec 2007). In other words, ever increasing levels of multi-ethnic mix in urban areas do not necessarily lead to similarly rising degrees of xenophobia; rather, they enable the opposite. The call is thus for their colleagues studying migration to take off their ethno-focal lenses and look instead at how the common residents of a highly diversified neighbourhood learn to live together. For example, one research team investigating life in a highly diversified part of Antwerp uncovered that despite 26 per cent of its residents voting for an extreme right-wing, anti-immigration party, quotidian interaction between locals, of whatever background, was sufficient to create weak ties, which in turn generated 'a general sense of peacefulness, security and comfort in the area' (van de Vijver et al. 2015: 40). Similarly, a comparative study of internally diverse neighbourhoods in Lisbon and Granada found that though heterogeneity was common and experienced daily, this social intercourse did not reproduce otherness and could be transformed into a quotidian positive feature (Padilla et al. 2014: 632). In these cases at least, conviviality wins out over categorisation.

There is a further point to be made in all this: maybe we should not try to shunt identity aside for the sake of commonality or even conviviality, for the three are abstract nouns, which can all too easily suggest the existence of an underlying entity. Just as we prefer to speak these days of identity claims and modes of identification, so perhaps we should leave aside 'commonality' and 'conviviality' for the sake of 'strategies of connection' or 'bids to find common ground', however impoverished or marginal those tactics may at first seem.

---

4. I thank Thomas Eriksen for suggesting this avenue.

This is not a petty debate, for our words can have weight. As the historians mentioned above claim for their own discipline, there is a moral dimension to correcting this general misbalance in our studies. Anthropologists have long been aware how the potentially exoticising, sensationalist sections of their work may be manipulated by some of their own number as well as by others for their own self-interested ends (MacClancy 2002; Borofsky 2004). Closer to home, as an anthropologist of the recent Balkan conflict reminds us, our discipline's vaunted cultural relativism shares, most unfortunately, 'a rationale with political tendencies to celebrate and enforce exclusive nationalisms and ethnicities' (Bowman 2002: 219). Some anthropologists have engaged actively in those practices – for example, the great majority of German anthropologists who in the 1930s assisted the Nazi regime, some of them even participating in every stage of the Holocaust (Schafft 2007). Anthropologists are not just researchers of morality, but themselves moral agents as well.

When Matei Candea did fieldwork in Corsica, he noticed that first encounters between strangers usually excluded interlocutors' names. Though these anonymous introductions puzzled him at first, he came to realise that avoiding names enabled villagers to bracket personal identity and so allow interpersonal connections to emerge in the course of conversation. But at the end of his persuasive argument, Candea felt he was left with a question 'and this is very much an honest question, not a rhetorical one': if all is interconnection, how do we anthropologists classify people (Candea 2010: 135)? In other words, what is the status of 'culture' in our ethnographies? Is the underlying fear here that we are meant to act as E.M. Forster clones chanting in Dalek-like tones, 'Only connect. Only connect' and so on?[5]

Does this mean that, in the end (and I stress the qualifier), there might be a residual space for studies of identity as a categorical device for our essays and ethnographies? It is very important to note here that I am not suggesting a return to some notion of identity as being of primordial importance; rather, I am making acknowledgement of the role(s) that identity may play within a broader framing of commonality.

Perhaps Candea's question is off-beam, increasingly misplaced in a contemporary anthropology. For more and more ethnographies are problem-focused, where the problem is openly defined by the anthro-

---

5. The phrase comes from Forster's novel *Howard's End*: 'Only connect! That was the whole of her sermon. Only connect the prose and the passion, and both will be exalted, and human love will be seen at its height. Live in fragments no longer. Only connect, and the beast and the monk, robbed of the isolation that is life to either, will die' (Forster 1989: 1).

*Figure 2.1* Book-shaped piece of English Delftware, 1672. © Ashmolean Museum, reproduced by kind permission.

pologist, and the data deployed comes from several fieldsites, chosen by the ethnographer. In these scenarios, 'identity' may still be central but sharing centre stage in the resulting ethnography with a plurality of other foci.

### FEET OF CLAY? WE ARE ALL CLAY!

Sir David Cannadine likes to quote Angelou and Kipling, among other literary greats, to broaden the basis of his points. As an anthropologist, I prefer Anon.

In an Oxford museum is a book-shaped piece of English Delftware, dated 1672. Its cover is over-painted with four lines of memento mori verse. I take them as a sardonic comment on stereotyping and the denial of difference:

> Earth I am,
> It is most trew.
> Disdain me not,
> For soe are you.

## ACKNOWLEDGEMENTS

My thanks to Matthew Gault, for permission to quote from his dissertation, and to Kepa Fernández de Larrinoa, Chris McDonaugh and fellow participants, especially Chris Hann and Signe Howell, at the 'Overheating' workshop at the University of Oslo for their comments. Big thanks to Thomas Hylland Eriksen for inviting me.

## REFERENCES

Anon. 2013. Measuring Social Class in the UK: Bourdieusian Approaches. Fondation Bourdieu. Available at: www.fondation-bourdieu.org/index.php?id=20&tx_ttnews[tt_news]=52&cHash=e700bc3c82aa3ba35adda57144bc9bd9 (accessed 16 October 2014).

Arpal, J. 1985. Solidaridades elementales y organizaciones colectivas en el País Vasco: cuadrillas, txokos, asociaciones. In P. Bidart (ed.), *Processus sociaux, idéologies et pratiques culturelles dans la société basque.* Pau: Université de Pau and CNRS, pp. 129–54.

Barth, F. 1969. Introduction. In F. Barth (ed.), *Ethnic Groups and Boundaries: The Social Organization of Culture Difference.* Oslo: Universitetsforlaget.

—— 1994. Ethnicity and the Concept of Culture. Marett Lecture, Exeter College, Oxford, 29 April.

Boon, J. 1983. *Other Tribes, Other Scribes: Symbolic Anthropology in the Comparative Study of Cultures, Histories, Religions, and Texts.* New York: Cambridge University Press.

Borofsky, R. 2004. *Yanomami: The Fierce Controversy and What We Can Learn from It.* Berkeley: University of California Press.

Bowman, G. 2002. Comment on Robert Hayden's 'Antagonistic Tolerance: Competitive Sharing of Religious Sites in South Asia and the Balkans'. *Current Anthropology* 43(2): 219–20.

Bray, Z. 2004. *Living Boundaries: Frontiers and Identity in the Basque Country.* Brussels: PIE-Peter Lang.

Bringa, T. 1995. *Being Muslim the Bosnian Way: Identity and Community in a Central Bosnian Village.* Princeton: Princeton University Press.

Candea, M. 2010. Anonymous Introductions: Identity and Belonging in Corsica. *Journal of the Royal Anthropological Institute* 16: 119–37.

Cannadine, D. 2013. *The Undivided Past: History Beyond Our Differences.* London: Allen Lane.

Cornell, S. 1996. The Variable Ties that Bind: Content and Circumstance in Ethnic Processes. *Ethnic and Racial Studies* 19(2): 265–89.

Cornell, S., and D. Hartman. 1998. *Ethnicity and Race: Making Identities in a Changing World*. Thousand Oaks, CA: Pine Forge Books.

Davis, J. 1977. *People of the Mediterranean*. London: Routledge and Kegan Paul.

Forster, E.M. 1989 [1910]. *Howard's End*. London: Penguin.

Gault, M. 2014. Identity in County Fermanagh, Northern Ireland. BA dissertation. Oxford: Oxford Brookes University.

Gurruchaga, A. 1985. *El código nacionalista vasco durante el franquismo*. Barcelona: Anthropos.

Harris, R. 1972. *Prejudice and Tolerance in Ulster. A Study of Neighbours and 'Strangers' in a Border Community*. Manchester: Manchester University Press.

Harrison, F.V. 2002. Unravelling 'Race' for the Twenty-First Century. In J. MacClancy (ed.), *Exotic No More: Anthropology on the Front Lines*. Chicago: University of Chicago Press, pp.145–66.

Harrison, S. 2003. Cultural Difference as Denied Resemblance: Reconsidering Nationalism and Ethnicity. *Comparative Studies in Society and History* 45(2): 343–61.

Herzfeld, M. 1989. *Anthropology through the Looking-Glass: Critical Ethnography from the Margins of Europe*. Cambridge: Cambridge University Press.

Hills, M. 2002. The Formal and Informal Management of Diversity in the Republic of Mauritius. *Social Identities* 8: 287–300.

Homobono, J.I. 1994. Grupos y asociaciones amicales: la sociabilidad en Euskal Herria. *Inguruak* 8: 231–53.

—— 2009. De la taberna al pub: espacios y expresiones de sociabilidad. *La ortiga: revista cuatrimestral de arte, literatura y pensamiento* 87–89: 59–91.

Itçaina, X. 2009. Review of J. MacClancy, *Expressing Identities in the Basque Arena*, *L'Homme* 190: 245–9.

Jenkins, R. 1997. *Rethinking Ethnicity: Arguments and Explorations*. London: Sage.

Jennings, M. 2009. Playing Your Role: Identity and Community-Based Performance in Northern Ireland. *About Performance* 9: 103–25.

Kaul, A. 2009. *Turning the Tune: Traditional Music, Tourism, and Social Change in an Irish Village*. Oxford: Berghahn Books.

Kockel, U. 2002. *Regional Cultures and Economic Development: Explorations in European Ethnology*. Aldershot: Ashgate.

Kohn, T. 2002. Becoming an Islander through Action in the Scottish Hebrides. *Journal of the Royal Anthropological Institute* 8: 143–58.

Lever, A. 1986. Honour as a Red Herring. *Critique of Anthropology* 6(3): 83–106.

MacClancy, J. 1993. At Play with Identity in the Basque Arena. In S. Macdonald (ed.), *Inside European Identities*. Oxford: Berg Books, pp. 84–97.

—— 2002. Taking People Seriously. In J. MacClancy (ed.), *Exotic No More: Anthropology on the Front Lines*. Chicago: University of Chicago Press, pp.1–14.

—— 2007. *Expressing Identities in the Basque Arena*. Oxford: James Currey.

—— 2015. Fear and Loathing in the West of Ireland: The Blows of County Clare. In J. MacClancy (ed.), *Alternative Countrysides: Anthropological Approaches to Rural Western Europe Today*. Manchester: Manchester University Press, pp.143–68.

MacClancy, J., and A. Fuentes. 2013. The Ethical Fieldworker, and Other Problems. In J. MacClancy and A. Fuentes (eds), *Ethics in the Field: Contemporary Challenges*. Oxford: Berghahn Books, pp.1–23.

MacMillan, M. 2009. *The Uses and Abuses of History*. London: Profile Books.

McNeil, W. 1986. Mythistory, or Truth, Myth, History, and Historians. *American Historical Review* 91: 1–10.

Padilla, B., J. Azevedo and A. Olmos-Alcaraz. 2014. Super-Diversity and Conviviality: Exploring Frameworks for Doing Ethnography in Southern European Intercultural Cities. *Ethnic and Racial Studies* 38(4): 621–35.

Riviere, P. 1969. *Marriage among the Trio: A Principle of Social Organization*. Oxford: Clarendon Press.

Ryan, D. 2012. *The Spinning Heart*. Dublin: Doubleday Ireland.

Schafft, G. 2007. *From Racism to Genocide: Anthropology in the Third Reich*. Urbana: University of Illinois Press.

Schlee, G. 2008. *How Enemies Are Made: Towards a Theory of Ethnic and Religious Conflict*. Oxford: Berghahn Books.

Urla, J. 2012. *Reclaiming Basque: Language, Nation, and Cultural Activism*. Reno: University of Nevada Press.

Van de Vijver, F., J. Blommeart, G. Gkoumasi and M. Stogianni. 2015. On the Need to Broaden the Concept of Ethnic Identity. *International Journal of Intercultural Relations* 46: 38–46.

Vertovec, S. 2007. Super-Diversity and Its Implications. *Ethnic and Racial Studies* 30: 1024–54.

Williams, N., and C. Breen. 1987. *O Come Ye Back to Ireland: Our First Year in County Clare*. New York: Soho Books.

Zenker, O. 2013. *Irish/ness Is All Around Us*. Oxford: Berghahn Books.

# 3. Frozen Cosmopolitanism
## Coping with Radical Deceleration in Cape Verdean Contexts of Forced Return Migration

*Heike Drotbohm*

One of the most striking paradoxes of the contemporary phase of globalisation lies in the observation that our world is more and more interconnected through the flow of people, who regularly move to distant places for business, trade, political engagement, tourism or other types of leisure, while access to cross-border travel is more and more restricted for a large number of people. On the one hand, international mobility seems to be the key social capital of our time, reflecting individual capacity, success and worldliness; on the other hand, more and more people live in a wretched existence while waiting for things to improve. How many lives are fixed on the hope of a visa, for which there is little real chance? How many people get stuck during their journeys in places they did not choose? How many migrants live clandestine and confined lives in new countries of residence, where too much mobility might expose them to unwanted institutional contact? In fact, immobility and deceleration are as much part of our times as are mobility and acceleration – but these phenomena remain much less reflected in global studies.[1]

As I intend to show, the 'overheating effects, the tensions and frictions resulting from accelerated change' (Eriksen and Schober, this volume), can be studied particularly well from the perspectives of people whose sense of identity and belonging is fixed on the collective experience of mobility, but who are confronted with spatial confinement. In this chapter, I illuminate the experiences of migrants who have had access to international travel and had intended to make their lives in a nation-state different from their country of origin, but who were coercively removed from this territory through statecraft and have subsequently had to reintegrate involuntarily into their communities of origin.

In an age of anti-terrorism policies and the securitisation of international travel, the deportation of migrants is an increasingly common

---

1. For notable exceptions, see Hage (2009), Salazar & Smart (2011) and Khan (2016).

phenomenon (Peutz & De Genova 2010). Comparable to its historical antecedents of banishment and exile, the state-initiated return of migrants to their (alleged) 'home' countries is intrinsically linked to the organisation of state power and the territorialised organisation of citizenship (Drotbohm 2013). Especially in Europe and in North America, the attempt to secure state borders and to guarantee national security is increasingly connected to the territorial expulsion of unwanted foreigners, the growing severity of illegal immigration penalties and the administrative entanglement of immigration control, detention and deportation (De Genova 2007, 2009; Kanstroom 2012; Coutin 2015; Drotbohm & Hasselberg 2015).

Anderson, Gibney and Paoletti reflect on this nexus between deportation and the conceptualisation of citizenship, and underline the normative qualities of deportation:

> The act of expulsion simultaneously rids the state of an unwanted individual and affirms the political community's idealized view of what membership should (or should not) mean. Deportation thus shows the citizenry not simply as a community of law, but also as a community of value ... The deportee as criminal, bogus asylum seeker, trafficker, welfare cheat, un-integrated individual lacks the qualities that are necessary for citizenship in 'our' state. (Anderson et al. 2011: 548)

I will argue that this 'normativity of deportation' follows deported migrants back to their (alleged) 'home' countries. As will become clear, unintended and involuntary return disturbs the internal logics of transnational livelihoods and has particular consequences for both those who have been returned as well as those living in the country of origin who receive them. After presenting the particularities of Cape Verdean society, which has been 'transnational' since its beginnings, I will reflect on the moral meaning of being a returnee, which is based on a 'regular' and 'prepared' type of return. This lays the grounds for understanding how people perceive deported migrants in their country of origin. In the subsequent section I concentrate on the position of deportees in their communities of origin, where the paradox of hosting an immobile (and economically powerless) migrant has to be negotiated. Finally I show how deported migrants foster attachments to their former 'home' through self-exoticising narratives and particular patterns of consumption.

My account is based on twelve months of ethnographic fieldwork conducted between 2006 and 2008 on Brava and Fogo, two of the islands of Cape Verde, where I examined the impact of the legal regulation of transnational mobility on family lives and practices. I lived with my husband and five-year-old daughter among the residents of São Filipe and Nova Sintra, the two main towns of the islands of Fogo and Brava in the south-west of the archipelago. I concentrated my qualitative work on transnational households and carried out interviews with selected family members (Drotbohm 2009). Furthermore, I later visited absent members of these households living in Portugal (in Lisbon) and the USA (in Boston and Brockton) in order to incorporate their perspectives as well. While deportation was not initially central to my research project, its impact on transnational livelihoods was undeniable, and the precarious social position of deportees on the islands reflected the crucial significance of mobility and return for understanding the inner moral logics of this transnational social field.

The majority of the deportees I met had been returned from the USA, with only a few from Portugal and France.[2] My semi-structured interviews, most of them carried out in English, traced people's deportation experience, beginning with their living conditions abroad, next moving on to the moment of arrest and detention and the procedure of return, then to their experience of social reintegration, and finishing with a final reflection on their social condition in Cape Verde. While these cases cannot be understood as representative in any statistical sense, they do vividly illustrate the complex relationship between deportation and transnational livelihoods.

Approaching, interviewing and spending time with deportees proved not to be a particularly difficult task during my research. On the contrary, my status as a foreigner seemed to provide 'common ground' for sharing thoughts, not only about the deportees' particular situation, but also about recent developments in the Global North – be it the USA or Europe – as well as about the 'cultural particularities' of Cape Verde. I had the impression that our encounters and dialogues were appreciated as a way of 'making sense' of an often difficult and sometimes seemingly unbearable situation.

---

2. According to a statistical overview provided by Cape Verde's Instituto das Comunidades, the number of deportations has increased annually. Until 2002, there had been a total of 460 deportees in the entire country, 449 male and 11 female. Between 2002 and 2011, 857 Cape Verdean nationals were forcibly returned, 759 male, 98 female. Until 2002, the largest contingent of returnees came from Portugal, but since then the majority have been sent back from the USA. The majority of these had been convicted of violent crime (29 per cent), possession of and/or dealing narcotics (82 per cent), robbery (16 per cent) and lacking immigration documents (15 per cent) (IdC 2008; Neves 2012). It is important to note that only a minority of deportees are registered as such when they enter Cape Verde. Therefore, the actual number of deportees is likely considerably higher.

## BRAVA: A PLACE MADE BY TRANSATLANTIC CROSSINGS

Brava is the smallest of the islands of Cape Verde, lying in a rather isolated corner at the westernmost end of the archipelago, the last African territory before the Atlantic crossing. Like many island locales, Brava has beautiful, picturesque scenery. Everyday life on this hilly island of 70 square kilometres goes slowly. Most of the islanders have access to fishing and cultivate their own corn, legumes and vegetables in small garden plots. Occasionally they raise goats, pigs and, rarely, cows. The most important part of household income, however, reaches the islands from overseas in the form of migrant remittances. Cape Verde is a trans-nationalised place, its social, political and economic life spreads out not only over the archipelago's nine inhabited islands, but also among a large Cape Verdean diaspora, that is living in Africa, Europe, North and South America (Batalha 2004; Carling & Åkesson 2009).

This is the result of a phase of globalisation which commenced here much earlier than in many other parts of the world. Originally uninhabited, the archipelago was discovered by the Portuguese in the fifteenth century, and Portuguese sailors used the territory as a trading post for trafficking in sugar, cotton and especially slaves between the upper Guinea coast, Europe and Brazil (Carreira 1982; Meintel 1984; Halter 1993). Over the course of time, a creole society developed out of encounters between European colonists, African slaves and other immigrant groups, who established their existence on this barren archipelago and struggled against drought, poverty and political abandonment. The crucial meaning of ecological scarcity and severe famine for understanding the particular legacy of Portuguese colonialism in Cape Verde has mainly been examined from a historical perspective (Bigman 1993; Brooks 2006). According to these authors, the islands' spatial isolation, the absence of transport, especially during times of war, ecological scarcity as well as political neglect contributed to severe famines well into the 1940s. Indeed, George E. Brooks has commented that 'Cabo Verde during Portuguese rule was a gulag' (Brooks 2006: 101).[3]

Cross-border mobility and global networking thus became the cornerstone of the island nation's economic foundation from early on. Emigration, predominately involving men, and the support of family members from overseas, had already become the most important survival strategy within the archipelago by the early eighteenth century, when

---

3. According to Deirdre Meintel, the islands faced 58 years of severe famine between 1747 and 1979, during which approx. 250,000 people died (Meintel 1984: 55–72). Two of the worst famines occurred between 1941 and 1943 and in 1947/48, during which some 45,000 people died (Brooks 2006).

Cape Verdeans mainly migrated to the USA (Meintel 1984). After Cape Verde's independence in 1974, international travel diversified. Common destinations, especially in the context of labour migration, are the USA and Portugal, but also Luxembourg, France, Holland and Italy. Within the African context, Cape Verde's political stability is often seen as an exemplary case, and the country's strong connection to its diaspora as well as migrant remittances flowing back into Cape Verde's households are seen as crucially supportive elements of this politico-economic situation.

After centuries of Cape Verdean migration, the diaspora population now outnumbers the 550,000 inhabitants of the islands (Carling & Åkesson 2009), and transnationalism has become the dominant way of living. On the islands, social differentiation and inequalities are evident between non-migrants and migrants, non-mobiles and mobiles, and poor residents and wealthier *emigrantes* who return as pensioners from the USA or Europe and live comfortably on their social security checks (Carling 2008; Drotbohm 2009).

While Cape Verdean history can be summarised as one of transatlantic mobility and connectivity, and later as a combination of emigration and the establishment of transnational livelihoods, the situation changed considerably over the last decades of the twentieth century. Today, the gradual closing of European and North American state borders, the difficulty of obtaining visas, the increasing criminalisation of migrants, the rigid control and persecution of undocumented migrants as well as the forced return of migrants convicted of criminal offences, dominates the perception of migration in Cape Verdean transnational fields.

Given different migration patterns among the islands of Cape Verde, changes in immigration policy in different nation-states have had different consequences across the archipelago. Brava is the only Cape Verdean island with almost exclusive links to the USA; consequently, the vast majority of returnees arriving in Brava are deported from that country. Especially following the events of 11 September 2001, rates of deportation have increased annually (Neves 2012). Recent statistics put out by the Cape Verdean government show that almost every month since 9/11, migrants have been returned to Cape Verde against their will. To understand the situation and public perception of deported migrants, a look at the particular cultural meaning of return may prove useful.

## THEORISING RETURN IN TRANSNATIONAL SOCIAL FIELDS

While return migration has received more and more scholarly attention lately, it can still be stated that it remains an under-theorised part of the migration process. Especially with regard to the so-called migration–

development nexus and new forms of migration management, scholars have recently concentrated on government attempts to make use of return as a new tool for either improving living conditions in migrants' countries of origin (King 2000; Koser 2000; Åkesson 2011; Sinatti 2014) or as a means for repatriating 'unwanted' migrants, as can be currently observed in the context of the global financial crisis and rising rates of migrant unemployment (Bastia 2011; Boccagni 2011).

Irrespective of these trends, return migration has always been a strong part of the migration imaginary, as many studies confirm. Under regular circumstances, migrants preserve strong emotional ties with their country of origin, while fostering the illusion, or the 'myth', of return (Cohen & Gold 1997; Brettell 2003). Within transnational social fields, return migrants – both temporal and permanent – tend to enjoy a good reputation, since their return is perceived as an expression of loyalty, not only to kin and friends but also to the country of origin. Furthermore, as many migrants decide not to return, or are not able to return for different reasons (financial, legal and so on), return is also perceived as a kind of privilege or success. Hence, the accomplishment of return becomes a crucial means for articulating status hierarchies within transnational social fields, distinguishing the 'ordinary' migrant, who simply left and remained absent, from the 'mobile' migrant, who enjoys the freedom of continuous international travel (Drotbohm 2012, 2015).

According to Jean-Pierre Cassarino, the position of and reintegration of return migrants into their countries and communities of origin depends on several factors. He stresses the respective condition of return, also called 'preparedness':

> Preparedness pertains not only to the free choice of migrants to return home, but also to their readiness to return. In other words, to be optimally prepared, return is an issue of individual capacity to decide freely to return and to mobilise the tangible (i.e. financial capital) and intangible (i.e. contacts, relationships, skills, acquaintances) resources needed to secure return (i.e. readiness). (Cassarino 2014: 102)

This theoretical background regarding a 'regular' and valued type of migrant return is necessary for understanding the perceptions of return under involuntary and 'unprepared' conditions. In fact, several recent trends contribute worldwide not only to a diversification but also to a rising negative connotation of migrant return. More and more migrants, who do not manage to legalise their stay abroad, and who are confronted with xenophobia and with restricted access to education and employment, decide to return to their countries of origin prematurely and empty handed. Retired migrants, who have lost the security of their pensions due to the contemporary global financial crisis, may feel obliged to adjust their retirement plans and return to their countries of origin, where living costs are lower. Finally, a number of migrant-receiving states have resorted to the removal of unwanted non-citizens, such as undocumented migrants as well as those convicted of criminal charges, through forced or semi-voluntary return programmes, and these also contribute to a negative image of return migrants.

This increasing 'unpreparedness', the contingency and arbitrariness of return, is felt above all in those countries which depend to a large extent on the social and economic outcomes of transnational connectedness – the flow of migrant remittances in particular. Cape Verde is one of those countries, an island nation-state 'made' out of international travel and inter-continental connectedness. Return migration in general was and still is valued highly, both at the micro level of families and households as well as on the macro level, where the return of migrants is promoted through hometown associations, development programmes as well as policies on return and entrepreneurship (Åkesson 2011). As will become clear in the following, the ways in which deported migrants are received and manage to readjust their lives in relation to these unforeseen circumstances can be understood when interpreted in contrast to a regular mode of return.

### SENSING RADICAL DECELERATION

When interviewing, listening to or simply hanging around with deported migrants, it struck me how much they dwelled on their memories of the initial moment of arrival in Cape Verde. Especially those deportees who had left their country of origin during their childhood years and who had not fostered intensive contact with kin or friends remaining back on the islands during their years of absence had to cope with a veritable 'culture shock', that is the unfamiliarity of the place, both in its material and social sense, as well as with feelings of embarrassment and stigma caused by the unexpectedness of their return. Several biographical narratives centred on those very first impressions, when deportees were confronted with Cape Verde's dry landscape, its often poor aesthetics, its greyness and obvious poverty. Roberto, aged 45, who had returned six years ago after living in Portugal for 22 years, said:

> When I came here, I thought this was a war country. Everything was so rough, so grey, all these dilapidated buildings, everything run down. Cabo Verde! There is nothing *verdi*! [pronounced in an exaggerated

creole manner]. I did not expect this kind of poverty. I had my room, okay, but all this is grey concrete, *blocos* [bricks], you know. I mean, you get used to this, of course. But during these first weeks, I thought I would die.

In a comparable manner, other deportees reflected on their confrontation with the material and economic differences between their former living context and their alleged 'home country', which in many cases turned out to be rather unfamiliar. Roberto's younger friend Helder, who was in his thirties by this time, added:

At the very beginning, the first days, I hardly went outside. When I left the house, I just felt the wind in my face. There was so much wind. Man, this blows my mind away, I really thought this is absolutely crazy. I sat on the hill, this rocky landscape, the wind, the water, the salt in the air, and that's it. Wow! That's it. I was just sitting and staring down the hill, across the Atlantic. Wow. Man! This is a different century! I went back in time.

Helder was among those who had hardly any memories of the islands after he had been taken to the USA by his parents as an infant. In the above passage, the deportee remembers his confrontation with natural elements such as the wind, the salt, the ground, the water and the sun. He describes an extreme feeling of being reduced to the naked, somehow 'de-culturalised' conditions of human existence, facing the open, but absolutely inaccessible space of Cape Verdean maritime travel. In a comparable vein, other deportees described in detail their sense of having left everything they had been 'over there', that is, in the place from which they had been deported. Some, who had left Cape Verde very young, hardly spoke Cape Verdean creole and even lacked basic local knowledge for getting along in their everyday lives. This condition finds its parallel in a reflection on the intersection between deportation and mobility, understood as a basic human right, by Nicolas de Genova:

This intersection of the freedom of movement with the capacity for work, simply put, does indeed mark a 'zone of indistinction' (in Agamben's phrase) between naked (unformed, generic) human life and each historically particular configuration of social relations, or 'way of life', in which its distinct humanity is realized. That is to say, it marks the necessary and inescapable point of convergence between bare ('natural') human existence and any viable social formation as such. (De Genova 2010: 39)

Several of my interviewees suffered heavily from a particular feeling of confinement within these small island communities, where they had to readjust every aspect of their daily routines. During the initial phase of coping with these extreme feelings of unfamiliarity, some even tried to conceal the true reasons of their return, at least for some weeks. Toni, a small, energetic guy who owned a tattoo parlour on Brava, told me that he had at first tried to hold on to a mobile life, circulating between the islands. He remembered the first weeks after his arrival with an ironic undertone, telling me about 'the party' he celebrated together with his cousins and friends.

I simply did not tell them. They did not know the true reasons of my return. I had some hundred bucks in my bag and we just had a great time. We drank, the girls loved me, ah! This was heaven [*laughs*]. I was the big guy, once in my life. But after six weeks, they started asking me: 'When do you return [i.e. to the USA]?'

Being deported from the US on legal grounds for a minor offence, Toni will be restricted from entering the country for at least five years.[4] I asked him what happened when his friends discovered that he was unable to return back to the USA again. He answered:

I simply left, back to Praia [capital of Cape Verde] located on the neighbouring island, and stayed there for a while. But you cannot really hide on these islands. They will discover you. They found out, and two friends came over for telling me that they knew the true reason of my return. In a way this was good. I was able to go to Brava again. But I was never the boss again.

Toni's memories make clear how much his unexpected arrival was interpreted against the background of a 'regular' return, which supposedly confirms the status of the mobile traveller, who demonstrates and celebrates their upward social mobility and individual capacities for providing support. The question 'when do you return?' indicates others' sensing of Toni's (im)mobility, based on the understanding that only a returnee who returns once again (to the country of destination, in this case the USA) can remain a mobile person. The subject category *emigrante* in this context refers to a particular condition of existence: the capacity to continue to move and the respective social status, valued with

---

4.  Someone who has been deported from the USA cannot apply for admission to the country without complying with certain legal restrictions. The person must wait a certain amount of time (5, 10 or 20 years) before applying for re-entry.

high esteem, that one has not only to gain but also maintain and reaffirm. To cope with (or postpone) the stigma of an irregular, unprepared and unexpected return, Toni felt forced to perform mobility, at least within the islands, in order to correspond with islanders' expectations and enjoy temporarily the fruits of his former mobility.

## SOCIAL OTHERING IN TRANSNATIONAL HOUSEHOLDS

The option of concealment exists only for the first few weeks after the initial return. The majority of deportees lack the funds for performing an alternative, desired mode of return and immediately have to get in touch with their kin in the islands, who are expected to provide accommodation. Receiving a relative from abroad, deported or not, is perceived as a crucial family obligation in transnational networks. Under 'normal' circumstances – that is, under conditions of a regular return – the host will feel fortunate to receive a migrant, as this act demonstrates not only the functioning of transnational ties, but also a certain economic capacity. Unlike local Cape Verdeans, a migrant can expect being given a room of their own, and will be treated with particular attention. In return, the hosts can expect material and financial support: the migrant is expected to arrive loaded with gifts, and a financial contribution to compensate for the costs of their stay is also common. Hence, the islanders often celebrate the arrival of a migrant with a huge, often ostentatious welcome party (Drotbohm 2011).

Against this background it becomes clear that those who return involuntarily and empty-handed are often received in just the opposite manner. In Cape Verde, deportees are deprecatingly referred to as 'DPs', and are seen as 'useless' migrants who failed to secure their position abroad, eventually incurring debts and losing the capacity to support others – either by sending remittances or by sponsoring their kin's migration. Hence, those accommodating a deported migrant are often frustrated, feeling that in their view their returning kin should have supported them, not the other way round. Furthermore, the reputation of being labelled 'criminals' affects the reception of returnees in island households. Often 'crime rumours' circulate in the islands before a deportee's arrival, and every neighbour claims to have the more reliable information about the type of crime, conviction and years spent in jail (Drotbohm 2011). Obviously, deportees are aware of these tensions, which they interpret as a strong hostility against their return and stay, and struggle with the dependency that results from having to remain not only in a country, but also in a household, where they do not feel at home'.

Joseph, a deportee aged 25, who reached the islands three years before after living in the USA for ten years, remembers the first weeks he spent in his uncle's house, and employs a strong division between 'them' and himself in his recollections:

> They [his relatives who accommodated him] told me, 'Don't use too much *luz* [electricity], too much water'. They said, 'Don't take a shower every day'. They did not have any toilet paper! I mean, what is this? Jail [in the USA] has been the better place, I swear. There, I had my own money, I could buy my magazines, my sweets, but here, there is nothing.

As well as a critical reflection on material differences between Cape Verde and the USA, Joseph here describes his loss of agency within a household, where he feels isolated and stripped off his basic needs. Likewise in other narratives, deportees made use of 'they' to describe their kin's distance and often mischievous attitudes, and their own reluctant integration. Within these transnational households, cultural difference becomes obvious, dividing those who had once left the islands and returned from those who would like to leave but have not yet managed to do so. On both sides, patterns of consumption are used as a ground of mutual othering and as a way of distancing oneself from individuals who are part of one's own family, but appear to be rather unfamiliar.

In a recent article on people's perceptions of deported migrants in Afghanistan, Liza Schuster and Nassim Majidi describe the high level of stigmatisation that confronts deportees who have returned from Europe or North America. Interestingly, the level of stigmatisation seems to be higher in the case of deportees who have returned from further away, and less in the case of those who have been deported from neighbouring countries. Schuster and Majidi explain this

> in terms of the level of investment in the project by the family of the migrant who has been deported, but also the familiarity with conditions in the state from which one is being deported. In other words, stigmatisation may be seen as a way of punishing those who have failed to repay the family's investment and as a way of holding on to the dream of a better life in a distant destination, a dream challenged by deportation. (Schuster & Majidi 2015: 648)

In addition to the burden of involuntary return, they argue, this stig-matisation constitutes an extra pressure, which forces deportees to once again migrate (ibid.).[5] Unlike Cape Verde, where most deportees are unable to obtain a visa for travelling back to the Global North, many deportees from non-island countries manage to migrate again, and hence continue their existence as migrants, thus managing to comply with the expectations and role ascriptions articulated in their transnational social networks.

## FREEZING URBAN CULTURE FROM AFAR

Not all deportees described the experience of being returned involuntarily as traumatising and isolating as those quoted earlier. Others try to hold on to features of their former lives and their familiarity with an urban lifestyle. Some keep material traces of their former existence abroad – train or cinema tickets, bills, newspapers, magazines – while others showed me several times the paperwork produced in the course of their processing by the legal system. Those deportees who manage to maintain contact with kin and friends remaining in the country from which they were deported try to get consumer items sent from abroad – not only financial remittances, but also gifts and personal items constitute important and appreciated elements in the material flow connecting transnational migrants and their island kin. Deportees (to the regret of other islanders) make use of their ongoing connections to obtain the products they desire most.

Joseph, the ruturnee who complained above about the limitations his relatives imposed on him and about the magazines and sweets he missed, told me:

> It's so strange to be here. And then, the food! WTF! What the fuck! I had such diarrhoea. I cannot eat *catxupa* [a traditional Cape Verdean meal] every day, my body cannot digest that kind of beans-and-corn stuff. I need my French fries, my pizza, my Subway, MacDo, you get it? I am living on another planet here!

Joseph was lucky as he received huge packages containing canned food, sweets, cosmetics and clothes every couple of months. On the one hand, deportees use these products for creating a physical and affective environment they feel more familiar with. Some deportees meanwhile sell these gifts in order to improve their financial situation. In this regard, they are able to transfer their cultural capital from abroad to the new context: 'Our fashion is different', Nando, aged 28, told me:

---

5.  For a comparable case from Mexico, see Hagan et al. (2008).

I wear my baseball shirts, my hat, my jewellery, my Nikes. My *primos* [cousins] come and want to learn how things are in the US. I sell them a shirt for a good price, man. Then they look like us, then they learn how to walk like we do [*he laughs and exaggerates an 'urban' male youth walking style*].

Many deportees struggle with the obligation to create new social networks in the islands that extend beyond the group of other deportees. In order to impress their local, non-migrant peers, some build on the negative stereotype generated through deportation and reproduce the image of the 'brutal gangsta' in their own narratives. Their attitudes are also reflected in their outer appearance. While many islanders of the older generation complain about their physical appearance, their ostentatious baseball hats, oversized tee-shirts and baggy trousers, local girls are attracted to these tokens of mobility, inscribed in their movements, gestures and fashion.

While their criminal reputations may complicate social contact, especially with members of the older generation, their younger peers tend to admire and envy their crime-related experiences and the urban knowledge that presumably comes along with it. Therefore, deportees feel compelled to play the card of the urban outsider, especially in the presence of local girls, who admire their aura of having 'been there', where many of the 'immobile' islanders wish to go. In this transcultural context, the perception of an accelerated cosmopolitan culture of consumption, which is constantly in a state of innovation, is contrasted with a sense of Cape Verde's condition of persistent insularity, that is perceived as conservative, persistent and – in the voice of the young – boring. When 'DPs' tell or even invent narratives of criminality, they not only reminisce about their lost lives, but also refer to tropes of urban masculinity that are difficult to maintain under these exile-like conditions. Barbara Yngvesson and Susan Coutin describe a comparable situation in El Salvador, where deportees return with 'value added' (Yngvesson & Coutin 2006: 186). Deportees oscillate between attempts at social reintegration and rehabilitation on the one hand, and maintaining an exotic persona among their cousins and friends on the other. This puts them in a position where they constantly navigate between emphasising their innocence or victimhood while at the same time recounting their experiences of 'gangstahood' and violence.

## CONCLUDING THOUGHTS

In contexts of migration, processes of identification and re-identification are often challenged. As this chapter has shown, tensions and frictions can be caused not only by accelerated change generated by cross-border travel, but also by the confrontation with new places and the duty to readjust to new living conditions. When particular cultural values are attached to mobility and transnational livelihoods, the opposite may also hold true. For deported migrants, the experience of deceleration and unprepared return questions their status as migrants and forces them to search for alternative means for remaining the person they had chosen to be.

Deportees, like other types of displaced persons in general, are 'social constructions and moral imaginations' (Malkki 1996: 382), produced by society's encounters with mobility. Within these island communities, where mobility is a crucial element for defining the position of a person in their social landscape, categories such as 'DPs', 'illegals' and 'criminals' are powerful constructions of othering. Deported migrants grapple with these categories, and reproduce and revive them so as to orient their lives towards these social constructions, which in turn are a recognition of their former access to international travel as well as their formative years abroad. The position of deportees is not only evaluated on the grounds of their former access to international travel, but also on the grounds of the social and cultural values and expectations attached to mobility, such as access to a fast-changing urban lifestyle and its respective patterns of consumption and communication. In the attempt to hold on to these values, the cosmopolitan worldliness of deported migrants becomes essentialised and reduced to culturalised aesthetic icons. While Cape Verdeans usually celebrate the qualities of creole mixing in popular contexts such as food, music and the arts, deported Cape Verdeans practise just the opposite: they fix themselves on the products of their former mobility and freeze cosmopolitanism into an unchanging reference to distant and past places. Baggy trousers, pizza, Hershey's chocolate and Ziggy Marley's songs are perceived as sensory bridges to distant and inaccessible times and places and states of being.

The ethnographic details presented here illuminate the paradoxical outcome of deportation in a world shaped by accelerated mobility, rapid innovation and transnational connectedness. In a way, the common vectors and expectations regarding transnational mobility are reversed: when 'country of origin' and 'country of destination' switch position, when migrants are immobilised and receive financial support from relatives living in foreign places, the established norms and hierarchies of a transnational livelihood are turned upside down. Seen in this light, deportation can be understood as a side effect of an accelerated global mobility, in which mobile actors lose control over the direction and speed of their own movements. Therefore, a state's act of deportation not only refers to a spatial paradox of confinement and isolation in highly mobile spaces. It also contains a temporal paradox: seen from a transnational life-course perspective, deportation can be understood as a reversal of the gains of international travel (Drotbohm 2015). When life slows down in a world of high speed, social status is reduced or completely withdrawn. In this process, the regular and expected dynamics between spatial and social mobility come to an end and the actors experience a social standstill.

## ACKNOWLEDGEMENTS

The research on which this chapter draws was generously funded by a number of sources. My extended research in Cape Verde was funded by the Deutscher Akademischer Austauschdienst (DAAD). Subsequent phases of reflection, writing and academic exchange were made possible through fellowships at the International Research Centre project 'Work and the Lifecycle in Global History' (Re:Work) at Humboldt University, Berlin, the Freiburg Institute of Advanced Studies (FRIAS) as well as through a Heisenberg Scholarship provided by the German Research Foundation (DFG). In particular I thank the conveners and participants at the workshop on 'Identity and Accelerated Change', organized as part of the Overheating project at the Department of Social Anthropology, University of Oslo, who provided critical comments on the first draft of this chapter.

## REFERENCES

Åkesson, L. 2011. Making Migrants Responsible for Development: Cape Verdean Returnees and Northern Migration Policies. *Afrika Spectrum* 41(1): 61–83.

Anderson, B., M.J. Gibney and E. Paoletti. 2011. Citizenship, Deportation and the Boundaries of Belonging. *Citizenship Studies* 15(5): 547–63.

Bastia, T. 2011. Should I Stay or Should I Go? Return Migration in Times of Crises. *Journal of International Development* 23(4): 583–95.

Batalha, L. 2004. *The Cape Verdean Diaspora in Portugal: Colonial Subjects in a Postcolonial World*. Lanham, MD: Lexington Books.

Bigman, L. 1993. *History and Hunger in West Africa: Food Production and Entitlement in Guinea-Bissau and Cape Verde*. Westport, CT: Greenwood Press.

Boccagni, P. 2011. The Framing of Return from Above and Below in Ecuadorian Migration: A Project, a Myth, or a Political Device? *Global Networks* 11(4): 461–80.

Brettell, C. 2003. *Anthropology and Migration: Essays on Transnationalism, Ethnicity, and Identity*. Walnut Creek, CA: AltaMira Press.

Brooks, G.E. 2006. Cabo Verde – Gulag of the South Atlantic: Racism, Fishing Prohibitions, and Famines. *History in Africa* 33: 101–35.

Carling, J. 2008. The Human Dynamics of Migrant Transnationalism. *Ethnic and Racial Studies* 31(8): 1452–77.

Carling, J., and L. Åkesson. 2009. Mobility at the Heart of a Nation: Patterns and Meanings of Cape Verdean Migration. *International Migration* 47(3): 123–55.

Carreira, A. 1982. *The People of the Cape Verde Islands: Exploitation and Emigration*, trans. C. Fyfe. Hamden, CT: Archon Books.

Cassarino, J.-P. 2014. A Case for Return Preparedness. *Global and Asian Perspectives on International Migration* 4: 153–65.

Cohen, R., and G. Gold. 1997. Constructing Ethnicity: Myth of Return and Modes of Exclusion among Israelis in Toronto. *International Migration* 35(3): 373–94.

Coutin, S.B. 2015. Deportation Studies, Origins, Themes and Directions. *Journal of Ethnic and Migration Studies* (special issue) 41(4): 671–81.

De Genova, N. 2007. The Production of Culprits: From Deportability to Detainability in the Aftermath of Homeland Security. *Citizenship Studies* 11(5): 421–48.

—— 2009. Conflicts over Mobility, and the Mobility of Conflict: Rightlessness, Presence, Subjectivity, Freedom. *Subjectivity* 29: 445–66.

—— 2010. Theoretical Overview. The Deportation Regime: Sovereignty, Space, and the Freedom of Movement. In N. De Genova and N. Peutz (eds), *The Deportation Regime: Sovereignty, Space, and the Freedom of Movement*. Durham, NC: Duke University Press, pp.33–68.

Drotbohm, H. 2009. Horizons of Long-Distance Intimacies: Reciprocity, Contribution and Disjuncture in Cape Verde. *History of the Family* 14(2): 132–49.

—— 2011. On the Durability and the Decomposition of Citizenship: The Social Logics of Forced Return Migration in Cape Verde. *Citizenship Studies* (special issue) 15(3/4): 381–96.

—— 2012. 'It's Like Belonging to a Place That Has Never Been Yours': Deportees Negotiating Involuntary Immobility and Conditions of Return in Cape Verde. In R. Schröder and R. Wodak (eds), *Migrations: Interdisciplinary Perspectives*. Vienna: Springer Verlag, pp.129–40.

—— 2013. Deportation: An Overview. In I. Ness (ed.), *The Encyclopedia of Human Migration*. Chichester: Wiley Blackwell, pp.1182–8.

—— 2015. The Reversal of Migratory Family Lives: A Cape Verdean Perspective on Gender and Sociality Prior and Post Deportation. *Journal of Ethnic and Migration Studies*, (special issue) 41(4): 653–70.

Drotbohm, H., and I. Hasselberg. 2015. Deportation, Anxiety, Justice. *Journal of Ethnic and Migration Studies* (special issue) 41(4): 551–62.

Hage, G. 2009. Introduction. In G. Hage (ed.), *Waiting*. Carlton: Melbourne University Publishing, pp.1–12.

Hagan, J., K. Eschbach and N. Rodriguez. 2008. US Deportation Policy, Family Separation, and Circular Migration. *International Migration Review* 42(1): 64–88.

Halter, M. 1993. *Between Race and Ethnicity: Cape Verdean American Immigrants, 1860–1965*. Chicago: University of Illinois Press.

IdC (Instituto das Comunidades). 2008. Análise dos dados do recenseamento dos repatriados. Unpublished project report. Praia, Cape Verde: Instituto das Comunidades, Ministério dos Negócios Estrangeiros, Cooperação e Comunidades.

Kanstroom, D. 2012. *Aftermath: Deportation Law and the New American Diaspora*. Oxford: Oxford University Press.

Khan, N. 2016. Immobility. In N. Salazar and K. Jayaram (eds), *Keywords of Mobility. Critical Anthropological Engagements*. Oxford: Berghahn Books, pp.93–112 .

King, R. 2000. Generalizations from the History of Return Migration. In B. Ghosh (ed.), *Return Migration: Journey of Hope or Despair?* Geneva: International Organization for Migration, pp.7–55.

Koser, K. 2000. Return, Readmission and Reintegration: Changing Agendas, Policy Frameworks and Operational Programmes. In B. Ghosh (ed.), *Return Migration: Journey of Hope or Despair*. Geneva: International Organization for Migration, pp.57–99.

Malkki, L. 1996. Speechless Emissaries: Refugees, Humanitarianism, and Dehistoricization. *Cultural Anthropology* 11(3): 377–404.

Meintel, D. 1984. *Race, Culture, and Portuguese Colonialism in Cabo Verde*. New York: Maxwell School of Citizenship and Public Affairs, Syracuse University.

Neves, S.R. 2012. Critical Analysis of the Deportee Integration Project of Cape Verde. Unpublished report. Praia, Cape Verde: Instituto das Comunidades.

Peutz, N., and N. de Genova. 2010. Introduction. In N. De Genova and N. Peutz (eds), *The Deportation Regime: Sovereignty, Space, and the Freedom of Movement*. Durham, NC: Duke University Press, pp.1–32.

Salazar, N., and A. Smart. 2011. Introduction: Anthropological Takes on (Im)Mobility. *Identities* 18: i–ix.

Schuster, L., and N. Majidi. 2015. Deportation Stigma and Re-migration. *Journal of Ethnic and Migration Studies* (special isssue) 41(4): 635–52.

Sinatti, G. 2014. Return Migration as a Win-Win-Win Scenario? Visions of Return among Senegalese Migrants, the State of Origin and Receiving Countries. *Ethnic and Racial Studies* 38(2): 275–91.

Yngvesson, B., and S.B. Coutin. 2006. Backed by Papers: Undoing Persons, Histories and Return. *American Ethnologist* 22(2): 177–90.

# 4. 'We Are All Strangers Here'
## Transforming Land and Making Identity in a Desert Boomtown

*Astrid B. Stensrud*

Majes, beloved land,
Who shelters the men of Peru,
Men of all the bloods,
Pride of Caylloma and of Peru.

You forged yourself between stone and stone,
And grew with a view to triumph,
Transforming the desert into beautiful fields,
With hope, love and freedom.

Great men are your strength,
Ranchers and farmers,
Who are cultivating the furrow of progress,
With the effort of Villa el Pedregal.

Populated centres (settlements, urban centres), agribusinesses,
La Colina, El Alto and El Pedregal,
They were witnesses of the New District,
They are the pride of Arequipa and of Peru.

—Ing. Edgar Zamalloa Bravo, 'Himno de Majes'

### 'A PLACE OF OPPORTUNITIES'

'This place is unique in Peru, there is no other place like here; it is a *sui generis*!' Julio told me enthusiastically one morning in January 2014, outside the municipal building in Villa El Pedregal, the urban centre of the Majes Irrigation Project, which is also a boomtown growing at a fast pace. Located between Arequipa City and the Pacific coast in southern Peru, Majes is growing in the middle of the desert where the water arrived three decades ago, and has been populated by people from all over the country ever since. The Majes Irrigation Project was made possible by the construction of a 100 kilometre-long irrigation canal bringing water from a dam in the Andean highlands. It was planned in detail by state engineers who designed both the urban centres and the infrastructure for 40,000 inhabitants. Today's population, an estimated 120,000, is spreading out in the surrounding desert. Majes is a bustling place of farming, engineering, industry and business; it is called a 'place of opportunities' that attracts new people every day who come in search of work and business. Julio was eager to point out that 'Here everything is yet to be done, to be founded. [...] Here we are working to emerge'. The newcomers can allow themselves to imagine a fresh start and strive for social mobility. Some look for fast money to be made from temporary jobs, trade or various business ventures, and others dream of a permanent home and a future for their children. However, rapid population growth also creates concerns. The director of the municipal social work office, Pablo Cornejo, said in an interview later that day that this district had disproportionately more incidents of domestic violence and child abuse than other districts in the province. He then complained to me that the people here 'have no cultural identity', because 'they come from all places and they all come with their own culture'.

'We are all *forasteros* [foreigners, strangers] here', Edgar Zamalloa said, when I visited his seed shop in Villa El Pedregal some days later. Mr Zamalloa is the writer of 'Himno de Majes', a song that won a contest organised by the municipality and was declared the official hymn of the Majes district in December 2003. Mr Zamalloa is an engineer by profession and came to Majes to work on the construction of the irrigation project in 1985, two years after the first settlers had arrived. A self-taught historian, he has written a book about the local history of Majes, which he sold in his seed shop (see Zamalloa 2013). The book tells the story of how the Majes Irrigation Project came into being. Illustrated with photographs and maps, the book is full of technical data about irrigation systems, soil, seeds, infrastructure, buildings, urban planning and institutions, and praises Majes for being a 'generous and friendly land of singular beauty ... considered the promised land where milk and honey flow, thanks to the arrival of the water and the effort of the first settlers who came to these pampas' (ibid.: 1). The book also contains a chapter on 'traditions and customs', with descriptions of dances and bullfights, where Zamalloa praises the cultural diversity of Majes, yet argues for the need for creating a dance that is particular to it. When I asked Zamalloa about the new generation of young people who are born here, he said that their parents still inculcate them with their own old habits: 'I teach my son my way of being, my customs from Apurímac, and those from Cusco and Puno do the same thing'. He continued heartily, 'the children are the new population and they have to create their own Pedregalean identity (*identidad pedregaleña*), a Majes identity (*identidad majeña*), and feel for this land'. Then he suggested that I, as an anthropologist, could contribute with some ideas to help create a new cultural identity for Majes. As tempting as this might be, this is not what I intend to do in this chapter. Instead, I look into what it means when people in Majes say 'There is no culture here', or 'We have no identity', while others claim to be 'extremely *majeños*'.

The Majes Irrigation Project is emblematic of the kind of state-driven modernisation that took place during the later half of the twentieth century, and it is also connected to global exchanges of finance, knowledge and products. In today's world of accelerated change at a global level, the strengthening of unique local identities becomes more important than ever (Eriksen 2007; Comaroff & Comaroff 2009). In the literature on globalisation, local cultural diversity is generally imagined as a form of resistance to the proliferation of global capitalism (Tsing 2000: 339). In Majes, however, there was no existing 'local culture' before the construction of the irrigation project and the influx of international corporations, development agencies, settlers and migrants from all over the country. The inhabitants of Majes are building a new society in a desert without previous settlements, where one of the challenges is to create a local identity for people who come from different positions and backgrounds in Peru's hierarchical and racialised society. Some of them are poor Quechua-speaking peasants from the highlands, others are middle-class families from the city; some are illiterate while others have higher education.

A basic premise in this chapter is that identities – whether linked to ideas of culture, ethnicity, race, class, gender, place or nation – are not given, but produced through practice and encounters with others. As Stuart Hall has argued, identities are constituted within, not outside, representation, and they relate to the invention of tradition:

> identities are about questions of using the resources of history, language and culture in the process of becoming rather than being: not 'who we are' or 'where we came from', so much as what we might become, how we have been represented and how that bears on how we might represent ourselves. (Hall 1996: 4)

These identities are produced in specific historical and institutional sites and within the play of specific modalities of power, Hall argues. Hence, it is important to examine the contingent and particular circumstances in which identity is invented (whether this is done consciously or not), produced and negotiated.

In this chapter, I ask how sentiments of belonging and affinity to land and people are made in a new place that is undergoing accelerated change. Based on ethnographic field research among farmers, entrepreneurs, engineers and workers during a stay in the area from November 2013 to March 2014, I explore narratives and performances of different forms of identity. I argue that in spite of the supposed lack – or clash – of 'cultural identity', other identities that hinge on labour and entrepreneurship are made through everyday work and relations. This in turn produces a sense of ownership and belonging to Majes as a place, while also generating new hierarchies between settler farmers and landless labourers, successful businessmen and street vendors.

## THE MAJES IRRIGATION PROJECT: A DREAM COME TRUE?

At the entrance of Villa El Pedregal – the main urban centre of Majes – you are met by the impressive statue of General Juan Velasco Alvarado. Although the idea of building an irrigation canal from the Colca River to the arid pampas of Majes and Siguas was conceived in 1912 and planned in the 1940s, it was Velasco who started the execution of the Special Project Majes–Siguas in 1971. The pampa of Majes – situated between the Andes in the north-east and the Pacific Ocean in the south-west, and in between the narrow river valley of Majes in the west and Siguas River in the east – used to be arid and barren. Since the beginning of the last century, 'it was a dream to colonise these pampas', a dream shared by politicians, engineers, farmers and the government.

As part of Velasco's reformist government's efforts at bringing Peru out of feudalism and poverty and into an era of modernity and progress, the irrigation project was seen as a programme of regional development aimed at creating agricultural and industrial production and employment. The international consortium MACON built the Condoroma Dam,[1] situated 4,158 metres above sea level and with a storage capacity of 285 million cubic metres, as well as 88 kilometres of tunnels and 13 kilometres of open canal in order to bring water to the Majes pampa situated at an altitude of 1,000 metres, where a stable and warm climate would secure good conditions for agriculture. Some 11 years and US$700 million later, the water arrived in the pampa in 1982, and the first group of 592 settlers (*colonos*) started to work on their land (Zamalloa 2013). After having applied for the programme, they had been distributed among different

---

1. El Consorcio Majes MACON consisted of five companies from five countries: Sweden, the UK, South Africa, Canada and Spain. Design and supervision was by an Italian consortium, in addition to two Peruvian companies.

categories: smallholding farmers, landless peasants, agricultural workers and professionals (mostly agronomists, but also doctors, lawyers and engineers), and then a certain number of applicants were selected randomly from each category. Each *colono* got to buy 5 hectares of land, which was considered a standard family unit, made available through a loan scheme by the state-owned Agrarian Bank. Today, there are 2,600 farmers, who are organised in the Water Users' Organisation, and a total area of 15,800 hectares has been irrigated during the first phase of the project. There are also some larger areas that are owned by companies, for example the Pampa Baja Group that produces avocado and citrus fruit for export on their 1,244 hectares of land, and where 2,000 workers are currently employed.

Between 1984 and 1992, the settlers of 'Section A' of the Majes Irrigation Project were supported by the European Economic Community, and received financial help, technical assistance, technology, equipment and machinery, reproductive animals and training (ibid.: 57). Settlers often talked with pride about the modern irrigation technology from Israel, and the genetically improved cows from Holland and Germany. The settlers started to sow alfalfa, called the 'colonising seed' because it prepares the land by giving it nitrates, and which is used as cattle fodder. Today, most farmers still have alfalfa fields and cattle, and they sell their milk to the plant run by the Gloria Group, one of the largest companies in Peru, whose owners are among the few Peruvian billionaires that have made it onto the Forbes lists. Other crops are sold to middlemen or directly to one of the agro-export enterprises, like the Peruvian company Open World Export and the Danish–Peruvian company Danper, which produce canned artichokes and red peppers for export. During my interview with the elected district mayor, Elard Hurtado, he boasted of the quantities of milk produced (800,000 litres daily), and the commerce and 'economic movement' that this production stimulates. He highlighted the existence of four banks and twelve financial institutions as an indication of a booming local economy: 'We are a pilot centre of economic development [...] The monthly movement here is 30 million US dollars. This place has the highest economic growth rate on a national level. Or maybe in the whole world'.

However, the president of the Junta de Usuarios Pampa de Majes, the farmers' irrigation organisation, pointed out that the quality of life had not improved much, except for the gains made by each farmer on their own, 'through his own effort'. Neoliberal deregulation since the Fujimori regime in the 1990s has led to new differentiations between those farmers who have increased their wealth, and those who have lost their land to the bank because they could not manage their loans. Since crop prices vary according to market supply and demand, the farmers describe their economic reality as a lottery where you can either win or lose. This experience fits the neoliberal ideology that valorises the figure of the risk-taking entrepreneur, which has been heavily promoted in Peru over the last two decades. In fact, according to Zamalloa, one of the principal achievements of the development of the Majes project is 'the change in attitude and mentality of the settler: that they stop working in a traditional way and transform themselves into entrepreneurs (*empresario*)' (ibid.: 343).

However, there is a great deal of ambivalence concerning this ideal. The overall plan behind the Majes project was to develop an industrial export-oriented agriculture, yet many – especially engineers and politicians – complain that this has not happened. Some blame the farmers, as did one engineer who had worked in Majes for 30 years and who argued:

> Who benefits from milk production? Gloria! And the farmers? Instead of taking risks and orienting the crop to exports (*cambiar de cultivo para la exportación*), they continue with alfalfa and cattle, and they are satisfied with what Gloria pays for the milk every two weeks.

Although the cattle farmers complain about and protest against Gloria and its low rate of payment, they also see milk production as a stable and reliable income.

Today, the majority of the population no longer consists of farmers: new people move in every day in search of work, business and land. Most

*Figure 4.1*   Cows and alfalfa fields on a typical family farm in Majes.

of them come from poor villages in the southern Andes. According to the census of 2005, there were 35,334 inhabitants in Majes. The population has boomed since then, and today's population is unknown since no new census has been undertaken. In 2014, the municipality considered the annual population growth to be between 10 and 13 per cent (in Peru as a whole it stands at 1.3 per cent), and the number of inhabitants to be somewhere between 100,000 and 120,000. The majority of non-farming inhabitants of the area live in the extensive Ciudad Majes, a desert area without infrastructure, and they make a living as land labourers and factory workers, in mechanical workshops or in the service sector, where many are self-employed as taxi drivers or food-and-drink vendors at small restaurants, in the streets or in the marketplace.

## 'NONE OF US ARE FROM HERE':
### PIONEERS AND CULTURAL ENTREPRENEURS

In one of the three marketplaces in the centre of Villa El Pedregal, Martina and her husband Freddy own a stall where they sell fruit juice, sandwiches and cakes, and also CDs and DVDs of popular Peruvian music and music videos.[2] DVD recordings of fiestas and rituals from different provinces – like celebrations of saints, carnival dances, bullfights and ritual fist fights (called *takanakuy*) – are especially popular. Whenever the couple received a new DVD, they screened it on their TV in their juice shop, and small crowds of people often assembled on the pavement to watch. Examples of the most popular recordings are the *wititi* dance from the Colca Valley (where Martina comes from), the *takanakuy* fights from Chumbivilcas in the Cusco region (from which Freddy comes), and the Candelaria fiesta in Puno. People from these different places are recognisable by their dresses and hats, and by the music and dances.

One day over breakfast I talked with Martina and Freddy about the upcoming carnival celebrations in February. Martina said that most people celebrate with the *yunsada*,[3] and each group did so according to the style of their place of provenance. Many people in Majes are organised in cultural associations based on their provinces of origin, like Chumbivilcas or Espinar. As Martina said, 'each person will always be pulled towards their place'. Freddy said that there are no fiestas in El Pedregal; the only celebration of Majes is the anniversary on 21

---

2. Names of persons are anonymised. Exceptions are persons holding public offices.

3. *Yunsada* is a ritual where people drink and dance around a tree decorated with balloons and gifts. Couples take turns in cutting the tree with an axe, and the couple that gives the final cut before the tree falls down is in charge of organizing next year's *yunsada* and filling the tree with gifts.

December, where all the groups present their typical dances in the main plaza. 'None of us are from here', he said, and 'there are no customs here'. I often heard this claim in Majes: people from different walks of life – farmers, merchants, workers, lawyers, engineers and municipal employees – told me that 'there is no identity here'. They often went on to explain that there is 'a struggle of cultures', 'a clash of cultures' or 'a crossing of cultures and races'. A more positive comment I heard was that 'we drink from all the cultural sources', as one municipal social worker stated.

This apparent contradiction between 'many cultures' and 'no culture' is reminiscent of the seeming paradox that Clyde Mitchell (1956: 9) found in the Copperbelt of former Northern Rhodesia (present-day Zambia), where the Kalela dance tended to emphasise tribal differences, while songs and dresses were drawn from an urban existence that tended to submerge these differences. Mitchell argued that in the Copperbelt, where people from many ethnic groups had come to live together in towns to work in the copper mines, 'tribalism' became a significant category of day-to-day interaction and provided 'a mechanism whereby social relationships with strangers may be organised in what of necessity must be a fluid social situation' (ibid.: 31). As Zoila Mendoza (2000: 38) has pointed out, Mitchell's work was pioneering in suggesting the importance that dance-forms might have in redefining socio-cultural categories that shape relationships between groups in the context of migration and radical social change: dance helps mediate the polarities of 'modern' migrant life. The expressions of local identities in the boomtowns of the Copperbelt led the anthropologists of the Rhodes-Livingstone Institute to shift from a *detribalisation* perspective to one of *retribalisation*, or what was later labelled urban ethnicity.

I mentioned to Martina and Freddy that I had been told that the municipal authorities wanted to create a proper Majes identity. Martina then wondered how they would design the hat and the skirt. 'They would have to mix all the instruments!' she contemplated. By 'instruments', she was referring to material objects, especially clothing, since particular dresses, skirts, hats and ponchos are visible signs and markers of regional belonging and/or ethnic identity in Peru. Martina was born in a village in the Colca Valley of the Caylloma region, known for its Collagua-Cabana culture and as where women's dresses consist of embroidered skirts and hats (Femenías 2005). Participating in the *wititi* dancing during the fiestas of Colca Valley requires investing time and money in acquiring the latest fashion in skirt designs, which recently has changed every year. While Martina does not care to spend money on these fashions, others consider this an investment in the maintenance of relations with kin and friends, and they attend celebrations in their home villages as often as they can afford to.

Many of the region's cultural associations also organise their *fiestas* in Majes. The ritual dances, where participants dance for their patron saints, are of key importance in these fiestas. The most impressive dance performance in Majes happens in the first week of February, when thousands of *puneño* dancers fill the streets of Majes to celebrate their patroness, the Virgin of Candelaria, with processions, huge brass bands and colourful dance groups of different styles. The dances from Puno are very distinct from other regional dances in southern Peru, and similar to Afro-Bolivian dance, with its origins in the slavery of the colonial era. The Saya Caporal dance is associated with youth, sensuality and strength because of the fast tempo, the shoulder shaking, hip swinging and short skirts of female dancers and the athletic jumps of the male dancers. The Saya style is also associated with modernity and urban lifestyles, because of similarities with Afro-Caribbean styles of cumbia and salsa that are popular all over Latin America (Mendoza 2000: 211–12). The Morenada is seen as a more traditional and dignified dance, and the dancers are usually older, married people (Lazar 2008: 136). However, they are no less spectacular, with men in ponchos and hats and women in brightly coloured long *pollera* skirts and colourful bowler hats. The Diablada dance, with origins among the indigenous miners of the Bolivian highlands, is the most outstanding, as it features extravagant devil costumes in vivid colours and elaborate horned masks. According to the leader of the Puno association in Majes (which has 1,800 active members), around 60 per cent of the current population in Majes are *puneños*. They are known to be very 'visible' for several reasons: they are known to be hard workers and good businesspeople; they often work as vendors in the streets and markets; the women are easily recognised because of their peculiar bowler hats and layers of petticoats and skirts (*pollera*); they are well organised, and they tend to spend an impressive amount of resources on public *fiestas*. As Mendoza has shown in her study of Cusco, identity is not merely expressed through the dances, but the performance of dances is a crucial context in which identity is publicly defined (Mendoza 2000: 4). In fact, dance performance has been a site of confrontation and negotiation of identities since the beginning of the Andean colonial period (ibid.: 5). No wonder Zamalloa draws attention to the significance of creating a new dance in his book about Majes:

> Given that the population of Majes is made up of men of all the bloods (*sangres*), coming from all parts of deep Peru, who have come and/ or have brought or are introducing dances and customs from their

different places of origin, which are taking root in our district of Majes, it is a challenge for the future and our future generations to obtain an authentic and traditional dance and/or customs according to our reality and life experience. (Zamalloa 2013: 347)

The reality of life in Majes is made from diversity. It is no coincidence that the official slogan of the district municipality of Majes was chosen to emphasise the productive strength of cultural diversity: 'With the force of all the bloods [sic]' (Con la fuerza de todas las sangres). The phrase is taken from Edgar Zamalloa's 'Himno de Majes'. Coming from the highland region of Apurímac, Zamalloa was inspired by his compatriot José María Arguedas, the anthropologist who authored the novel *Todas las sangres* ('All the bloods'), a title that refers to the cultural diversity of Peru. The plural form of blood reflects an essentialist discourse of identity in which conceptualisations of culture and 'race' overlap. From the colonial era to today, differences in culture and class have been – and are still – racialised in Peru, based on an imagined 'racial' distinction between Spanish conquistadors and heterogeneous native populations. The mixed offspring were called interchangeably *mestizos* or *cholos*, and these categories have been either romanticised or used pejoratively in different discourses (Weismantel 2001). After the conquest, a spatial segregation based on conceptions of class and race took a hold, based on the idea that indigenous people belonged in rural communities and should stay there, whereas the cities and coastal areas belonged to the whites and *mestizos* (Degregori 1994). However, from the 1940s onwards, there has been massive migration from the poor rural highlands to the coastal cities, and today the majority of urban Peruvians identify as *mestizos*. Ethnic and racialised categories in Peru are intrinsically linked to social class and place, which in practice means that a person from a Quechua-speaking rural community who moves to the city, acquires formal education, learns Spanish and adopts an urban lifestyle is no longer considered to be 'indigenous' but *mestizo* (van den Berghe 1977; de la Cadena 2000; Stensrud 2011).

Since the creation of the municipal administration in 1983, the mayors of Majes have been keen to create and promote symbolic events, objects and performances that show the uniqueness of Majes and that simultaneously evoke patriotic feelings among the predominantly *mestizo* population. In his book, Zamalloa places great emphasis on the importance of these symbols:

The symbols are what distinguish and particularize a determinate territory, whether it is district, province, department or nation, and it is there our own identity of love for freedom and for our land, and especially for our people, is born. (Zamalloa 2013: 345)

In 1993, the municipality ran a public competition to create a coat of arms and a flag for Majes. The coat of arms that was chosen depicted soil, irrigation systems, green fields, agricultural products and the horizon. The winning flag had two colours: green, representing the green fields and crops, and white, representing freedom, justice and peace (ibid.: 346). The 'Himno de Majes' quoted above was chosen in 2003, and

*Figure 4.2  Witti* dancing in Chivay. Many people in Majes go home to their villages to take part in celebrations.

other songs and poems have also been written in honour of Majes, such as '*Ofrenda Lírica a Majes Tierra de Promisión*' ('Lyrical offering to the promised land of Majes') authored by Raul Castillo, a professor originally from Puno (ibid.: 356). Monuments have also been built: the Settler Monument (*Monumento al Colono*), which is a statue of a farmer holding a milk can, and the Cow Monument (*Monumento a la Vaca*), depicting a cow being hand-milked by a milkmaid with a bucket. What is apparent in these objects is how they all stress the importance of hard work, especially of the settlers, who are depicted as pioneers and frontier folk who have overcome the harsh desert environment.

## 'THERE WAS NOTHING HERE':
### STORIES OF SACRIFICE AND HARD WORK

'Ouff, it was terrible!' Helen said when I asked her how it was to come here as a little girl with her parents 27 years ago. 'Everything was earth and dust. When you were eating, you had to cover your plate because of the strong winds. There were no cars, and we had to walk to school'. Her answer fits neatly into the narrative told by all the settlers and their children that I interviewed; a shared story of stones, dust, wind and hard work to make the land fertile. Those who came as small children and have grown up in Majes both express a sense of sacrifice and a sense of ownership of the place, as they have lived through its transformation and made it part of themselves. The leader of an organisation called Hijos de Colonos ('Sons of settlers'), for instance, has lived in Majes since he was ten years old, 'when there was nothing here, just stones and dust'. He told me that he and the other sons of farmers who had grown up in Majes felt more *majeños* than their parents because they had invested their childhood and youth in this place: 'this is one of the reasons that we feel extremely *majeños*'. When I asked what he meant by that, he said:

> Because we have this heart, this soul, of having invested everything here. Many of us who are children of settlers, we left our studies and professional careers. Why? Because we dedicated ourselves to the transformation of the arid land to what it is now; totally productive land. Thanks to this effort, this sacrifice, many people have at least some bread to put in their mouth.

The settler families started out from very different backgrounds, previous experiences, knowledge and expectations. Market vendor Martina came from Colca Valley as a ten-year-old girl in 1990, when her parents settled into a new farm in 'Section C'. Having imagined and anticipated the green fields and prosperity of Majes, it was hard to accept that the reality was different. She had to walk far through unknown arid land to school and to the store. People lived in houses made of straw mats, the tap water was warm and tasteless, and they had to eat dried food, since fruit spoiled easily in the heat. She soon learned that life in Majes meant hard work. Her parents woke up every day at 3 AM to put out the irrigation sprinklers and milk the cows by hand; her mother's hands grew stiff from this labour. Martina's parents had extensive experience from farming in the highlands, but the seeds and cattle were different in Majes, and Martina observed that in retrospect they should have received more training and technical support. Her father bought good cows, of a 'good race'. They had a big cow named Antonia and her udder was so huge that it touched the ground. But her first offspring died:

> We didn't know how to do it; it was different from the highlands. When the cows were ready to give birth, they [Martina's parents] were supposed to help getting the offspring out, but they didn't know that. In the highlands the cows give birth by themselves; they don't need any help. But these did not [do that], that's why the first calves died. Only one calf survived. If not, we would have had more good cows.

As I had been talking to people in the highlands about Majes, I told her that people in Colca Valley, where she is from, think that the people in Majes are rich. 'Yes, there they think that we have money [...] They don't know that we also suffer. I live from my work!' Martina started her juice-vending business by herself in a market stall ten years ago; since then it has grown little by little.

José's family was very poor when they lived in his home village. His grandparents only had a tiny piece of land and a couple of cows, and they mostly worked as labourers on other people's land. They were the poorest family in the village and had nine children. When the Majes project opened, they all registered, and four brothers – José's father and his uncles – got farms there. José says that they were all dreaming about their new lives in Majes; 'they had high hopes of coming here and changing their lives; to earn another way of being'. The four brothers talked proudly about how they were always united and worked together. Instead of hiring help like others did, they joined forces; one day they would all work in one field, and the next day they worked in the field of another brother. As the oldest son of one of these brothers, José had to help with the farm work. He was eleven years old when they came to Majes in 1983, and every day he had to get up at 4 AM to herd the cattle.

In 1998, José's grandmother was buried in a cemetery in the arid outskirts of Majes, where the number of graves was steadily growing. Each year, her husband, children and grandchildren visit the grave on her birthday, and I was invited to join them in 2014. After cleaning the grave and decorating it with flowers, they brought a case of beer and sprinkled some drops on the grave, for the grandmother, and on the ground, for the earth mother. Then they sat in a circle around the grave, sharing bottles of beer, drinking, talking, joking, laughing and advising each other. One of the women commented that the grandmother was watching her children and that she would be glad to see that they were happy and united. When people bury their loved ones in a place, they also acquire a past in that location, in its very soil. Burying and remembering the dead make affective connections to the land and a hinge between the past and the future. Visiting the graveyard and acknowledging the presence of the ancestors' souls and the earth mother as a sentient being creates a sense of continuity amidst accelerated change.

### 'WE WILL GROW HERE': AMBIVALENT FUTURES

'The population of Majes is increasing by leaps and bounds', one of my interlocutors in Majes said. Every day new people arrive, and most of them find work as land labourers on a day-to-day basis. The structural inequalities that cause people to leave their villages and search for a better life in the city are reproduced in Majes, yet there is a strong narrative of Majes as the 'land of the free', providing equal opportunities for social mobility. Many of the landless workers yearn for a piece of land on which to build a house of their own. With the creation of Majes as a new district, ownership over desert land and several responsibilities were transferred from the state entity AUTODEMA (Autoridad Autónoma de Majes) to the district municipality, for example the provision of infrastructure and drinking water. These are challenges that increase in importance with every passing day, as the population grows faster than the municipality is able to plan and execute infrastructural work for. Earlier, AUTODEMA distributed plots of land at subsidised prices, but today, many of these plots are sold rather expensively. For those without money there are, however, alternative ways to get property, and many join squatters (*grupos de invasores*) to occupy desert land collectively. The situation was often described as chaotic, conflictual and at times violent, because of illegal land trafficking, lack of control and corruption.

Formally, a person can present a claim for ownership if they can prove that they have taken 'possession' of a place – that is, that they have built a house (many use straw mats, which is the cheapest material) and have lived there for a certain amount of time. Neighbourhoods that have been invaded collectively often organise meetings to discuss strategies. The goal is to formalise ownership and obtain property title deeds, and then eventually to get piped water, electricity, roads and other infrastructure. In February 2014, the Municipal Office of Formalisation had 20,000 case files with applications for title deeds. Alfredo was the leader of a housing association in a neighbourhood that was legal, yet lacked infrastructure. Once a week, a truck brought water, and at night the children lit candles to study. Alfredo was persistent in his fight to obtain electricity and water, and his wife Lucía supported him: 'We should make an effort; if one doesn't insist, nothing happens'.

People desired to own a piece of land and a house because they saw a future for themselves in Majes. The anticipation of a future was also heightened by the promise of progress that arrived with the second phase (*segunda etapa*) of the irrigation project, which was inaugurated on the pampa of Siguas on 6 February 2014. In his inauguration speech, Peru's president Ollanta Humala said that this project is important for 'the country's development'. Once the construction of the Angostura Dam of 1,000 million cubic metres is finished in a few years time, 38,500 new hectares in the pampa of Siguas will be irrigated. This land will be sold in units of 200, 500 and 1,000 hectares each, which makes the farmers in Majes fear the dominance of big agribusiness corporations, possibly even foreign companies. President Humala was keen to promise work for everyone: 'all the productive forces in Arequipa should dive into Majes–Siguas II, to create a modern agriculture, an agriculture that can be exported and that will generate 200,000 jobs [...] And it will benefit 300,000 families who will live off our agriculture, off our export agriculture'. Many of the farmers in Majes were sceptical, however, like the leader of the irrigation organisation, who said:

> With Majes–Siguas II it will be hard for the small farmers to get access to fields. It will not benefit us. If it fosters more jobs, it would be good. But it will harm us because we will have to pay the same for the water as the big firms; the tariff will increase.

Juan Rondón, who was the very first settler to arrive in Majes in 1982, put it matter-of-factly: 'The future will be according to the agreements that are made. The price of the water will increase, the corporations will dominate. There will be no market [for farmers], and the prices [of their products] will not increase'.

Most people in Majes look towards the second phase in Siguas with ambivalent expectation: they look forward to becoming part of a 'metropolis', but they know that the big companies will benefit most from the progress made, while they will provide the labour. Many of the families that I came to know in Majes are eager to support their children in getting an education as engineers so that they will become part of the professional workforce and not blue collar workers in fields or factories, or part of the multitude of informal vendors and taxi drivers. When I asked Martina about the future, she said:

> We will grow here. As there is industrialisation everywhere, it will be the same here. In Siguas there will be companies like Danper and Pampa Baja, and we will be employed by those companies. That is why

I want my children to study and become professionals and technicians, so that they will not be just [unskilled] labourers.

*Figure 4.3*  Future plans for Majes–Siguas II, the second phase of irrigation in the Siguas desert.

### LIVING, WORKING, BELONGING: CONCLUDING REMARKS

When I asked Mario about how he had experienced growing up in Majes since he came here 32 years ago as a four-year-old child, he replied:

Practically it is part of my life, because I have been brought up here – and well, it's like ... now we have got used to this place and I think that now our life has been made here, my family, my children ... Everything has been made here, it's practically my life.

The generation that has grown up here have grown *with* this place, and got *used to it* as a part of their lives. Hence, they express a strong identification with the land, a connection that they have forged for themselves through work, both in the sense of labour and relational work. People also make their stories in the land through working it. Relations to the past and to the land generate a sense of belonging and affective connections. This feeling of belonging is articulated through narratives of sacrifice and suffering, and through the effort involved in making something productive out of nothing. They have made Majes part of themselves and in such a way they have become a part of Majes.

When people in Majes say that there is 'no identity', they refer to a specific thing or institution called *identidad cultural*, which they associate with a package of dance, music, dresses, hats and rituals. These material things and practices undergo processes of constant change; they can be inherited, but can also be deconstructed, reconstructed and altered, especially in new urban contexts like Villa El Pedregal. *Identidad cultural* might mean different things for different persons: a patron saint, a colourful dance performance or a tasty local dish that one can be proud of. The municipal authorities invest a lot of time and resources in creating symbols, slogans and monuments, and organising public events such as singer-songwriter contests and anniversary celebrations, and generally demonstrate a great concern for constructing unity and local identity. There seems to be persistence in the notion that every place needs culture; every territory needs to be culturalised (cf. Gupta & Ferguson 1997). Stuart Hall argues that the fictional nature of the invention of identity in no way undermines its discursive, material or political effects. Precisely because identities are constructed within and not outside discourse, we need to understand them as lying within specific discursive formations and daily practices. Moreover, they emerge within the play of specific modalities of power, and are thus the products of the marking of difference and exclusion (Hall 1996).

One of the things that make Majes a special place is the non-existence of a pre-existing population, and the diversity of its population, coming as it has from all places and classes. If we think of people, groups, policy makers and culture makers as engaged in 'class projects', where class is an object of desire (or repulsion) (Ortner 2003: 13), then the Majes Irrigation Project can indeed be seen as a modernising and standardising project to create a class of successful *mestizo* entrepreneurs. The fostering of an entrepreneurial spirit and the importance of hard working pioneers is materialised in 'the Settler Monument' situated in the centre of Villa El Pedregal, and is also acclaimed in the speeches in every anniversary celebration or inauguration ceremony. Majes was designed as a modernising project where people from all over the country were allowed a 'fresh start'. Every family was allocated the same amount of land and given the opportunity to make a livelihood and try to achieve social mobility. Yet social differentiations are already emerging, and in the second phase of the irrigation project, larger inequalities can be anticipated, as big corporations will be allowed to buy huge areas of land. In pre-designed development projects like Majes–Siguas, there will always be unintended consequences and the future of this large-scale endeavour is still uncertain. There is a potential contradiction between egalitarian cultural identities and emerging social hierarchies. On the one hand, the cultural intimacies and commonalities emerging from growing up and living together, in addition to the explicit efforts of strengthening a new Majes identity, create place-based identities and a feeling of shared history and destiny. On the other hand, competition between farmers and the introduction of new companies and industries will lead to capital accumulation for some and dispossession for others, and new hierarchies will emerge based on the division of labour and the increasing impact of large-scale corporations. The new generation that is growing up in Majes will have to deal with contradictory forces of unity and division of different scales and negotiate these tensions in everyday life, and in local, regional and national struggles about the direction Peru takes as a country in the future.

## REFERENCES

Comaroff, J.L., and J. Comaroff. 2009. *Ethnicity, Inc.* Chicago: University of Chicago Press.

Degregori, C.I. 1994. Dimensión cultural de la experiencia migratoria. *Páginas* 19 (130): 18–29.

De la Cadena, M. 2000. *Indigenous Mestizos: The Politics of Race and Culture in Cuzco, 1919–1991.* Durham, NC: Duke University Press.

Eriksen, T.H. 2007. *Globalization: The Key Concepts.* Oxford: Berg.

Femenías, B. 2005. *Gender and the Boundaries of Dress in Contemporary Peru.* Austin: University of Texas Press.

Gupta, A., and J. Ferguson. 1997. Beyond 'Culture': Space, Identity, and the Politics of Difference. *Cultural Anthropology* 7(1): 6–23.

Hall, S. 1996. Introduction: Who Needs 'Identity'? In S. Hall and P. du Gay (eds), *Questions of Cultural Identity.* London: Sage Publications, pp.1–17.

Lazar, S. 2008. *El Alto, Rebel City: Self and Citizenship in Andean Bolivia.* Durham, NC: Duke University Press.

Mendoza, Z.S. 2000. *Shaping Society through Dance: Mestizo Ritual Performance in the Peruvian Andes.* Chicago: University of Chicago Press.

Mitchell, C.J. 1956. *The Kalela Dance: Aspects of Social Relationships among Urban Africans in Northern Rhodesia.* Manchester: Manchester University Press.

Ortner, S.B. 2003. *New Jersey Dreaming: Capital, Culture, and the Class of '58.* Durham, NC: Duke University Press.

Stensrud, A.B. 2011. 'Todo en la vida se paga': Negotiating Life in Cusco, Peru. PhD dissertation. Oslo: Faculty of Social Sciences, University of Oslo.

Tsing, A.L. 2000. The Global Situation. *Cultural Anthropology* 15(3): 327–56.

van den Berghe, P., and G. Primov. 1977. *Inequality in the Peruvian Andes: Class and Ethnicity in Cuzco.* Columbia: University of Missouri Press.

Weismantel, M.J. 2001. *Cholas and Pishtacos: Stories of Race and Sex in the Andes.* Chicago: University of Chicago Press.

Zamalloa Bravo, I.E. 2013. *Reseña histórica del distrito de Majes.* Lima: Corporación Grafical.

# 5. Identifying with Accelerated Change

## Modernity Embodied in Gladstone, Queensland

*Thomas Hylland Eriksen*

In the busy industrial hub of Gladstone, Queensland, most of the people you meet are likely to express optimism about the future, and they are not worried about change. Although the current economic boom was predicted to end soon after my fieldwork there in 2013/14, there was widespread conviction that 'something new will come up' and little overt anxiety about a possible recession. This, at least, was the general view among the participants at a workshop held at Central Queensland University in February 2014, featuring the presentation of the main findings of a report on the likely and assumed prospects of small and medium-sized businesses. Commissioned by the Gladstone Chamber of Commerce, which organises the small and middle-sized businesses of the city, the survey had been carried out by the local consultancy firm Amarna (see Amarna 2014). And although the picture was mixed, the general outlook for the city, the report concluded, was positive.

In spite of a projected loss of 5,000 local jobs (plus another 5,000 fly-in-fly-out jobs) by the end of 2015, few of the local businesses surveyed expected a dramatic downturn, although many expected having to lay-off a few employees. This may seem surprising, given that many of the companies in question did brisk business supplying goods, maintenance and miscellaneous services to the huge construction site where activities would soon cease. When asked, many of the business owners answered that they expected the city to go into temporary decline, or a lull, over the coming years, but that they believed this would not affect their own activities adversely.

At the workshop, attended by representatives of the business community, the consultancy segment and local government – about 40 persons altogether – various issues concerning the near future of Gladstone were discussed, and the strengths and weaknesses of the city, seen in a wider competitive space, were pointed out. For example, a local business leader stated that it was not easy to FIFO (fly-in-fly-out) to Gladstone, since virtually all flights from the small airport went to Brisbane. Another predicted that with the end of construction on Curtis Island, a big vacancy rate was more likely than mass unemployment, since most of the people who stood to lose their jobs were likely to search for employment elsewhere. An executive from QGC (Queensland Gas Company), one of the big investors in the region, mentioned 'community spirit' as a form of capital that might alleviate problems arising with the imminent cooling down of the local economy.

Of those business owners who saw a downturn coming, the main issues mentioned were a decrease in work, staff issues (a blanket term), high costs and people not buying locally. The term 'Gladstone tax' was invoked by one, referring to the high cost of living and producing in this thriving, booming industrial city. Three quarters of the respondents to Armana's survey said that they had seen an increase in their customer base owing to the construction boom, but more than half (52 per cent) said that they had felt negative effects.[1] To them, the economic boom had not led to an increase in their turnover, only increased traffic, a strain on local services and deterioration of the shared infrastructure.

According to the Amarna researchers who presented the report, there had been 'a couple of comments about the environment being sacrificed', but on the whole, the respondents were concerned with growth, change and the possibilities of making a good living in Gladstone after the construction boom. One civil servant nevertheless pointed out that recent environmental problems resulting from dredging and emissions, which had been widely publicised in the Australian media, might have 'damaged the Gladstone brand'. When a spokeswoman for GAPDL (the Gladstone region tourist association) spoke about future prospects in her field, a young woman who had just moved to the city from Noosa on the Sunshine Coast said that the first thing she had noticed were 'the coal trains moving along the seafront. So perhaps tourism is not the first thing I'd think about'.

The mayor, Gail Sellars, a cheerful woman in her fifties, smiled and brought attention to the fact that Northern Oil had decided to build a plant in Gladstone recently. 'This has not led to much attention in the media, but it is an example of the positive things happening here'. During tea, the mayor confessed to me that 'people say to me, "Gail, take off your rosy glasses and face the problems!" But that is not what we need around here right now'.

---

1. A total of 212 owners of small or middle-sized enterprises had responded to the survey, a response rate of 67 per cent.

One of the board members of the Gladstone Engineering Alliance suggested to 'change the term "boom" to "growth", and get rid of "bust"'. The mayor agreed. Another emphasised the importance of being proud of being an industrial town and that people should not pretend otherwise. In order to attract new investments, he said, it was important to change the negative perception of Gladstone. (I made a note to self on my laptop: 'Change negative perceptions, fine; but changing reality – more difficult'.) The 2013 success of the musical *Boomtown*, which mobilised hundreds of volunteers and was performed for large audiences on three consecutive nights, was invoked as a kind of event that might 'raise the pride and give positive attention'.

The participants at the seminar also spoke about building clusters, the role of charities and black-tie events, the synergy effects of having many industries and a large skilled workforce in a small region, and the problem of high costs. Many shop owners complained that lots of people seemed to go to Rockhampton (an hour's drive to the north) or elsewhere to buy things. But, as an industry leader said: 'Obviously, if you can get it more cheaply elsewhere, you'd do it. Even business owners do. So why are they whinging about people going elsewhere?'

The word 'whinging' has a strongly negative connotation in Australia and Gladstone. It is used about people who complain for no good reason and wait for others to solve their problems. As a sentiment, it is the opposite of resilience, a term used by many of the speakers at the conference.

After the event, I had a chat with Lyndal Hansen of Amarna about the term 'resilience'. Lyndal said that Gladstone had 'always been a boom-and-bust town', and that new investments had ensured continued growth and precluded mass unemployment in the past. Indeed, the Gladstone region has a somewhat lower unemployment level (below 5 per cent) than Queensland as a whole (above 6 per cent). She was confident that the city would continue to grow and prosper in the foreseeable future. There are two main reasons that this view, shared by business leaders and local politicians, deserves attention. First, as mentioned, the city stands to lose 5,000 local jobs very soon. Secondly, its lifeblood, the source of its confidence, growth and prosperity, consists of fossil fuels from the rich coal fields and burgeoning gas fields in the interior of Queensland, and in a world with a growing desire to shift to renewable energy, total dependence on coal may be a difficult adaptation to maintain in the long run.

Gladstone has grown in spurts, but quickly and significantly, ever since industrialisation of the town started in the 1960s. New suburbs continue to be built, new industrial estates are established, while the existing ones prevail or, in some cases, are demolished. An industrial and industrious town, Gladstone may give the European or North American visitor the feeling of a time lag or a déjà vu: It represents a confident, optimistic vision of industrial modernity, with its sprawling bungalow suburbs, smoking chimneys, swivelling cranes and thundering truck traffic, its streets lined by drive-through bottle-shops and patrolled by 'utes' (utility vehicles) driven by men in phosphorescent, high-visibility work clothes – all held together by the numerically dominant class of the city, a prosperous, male, white middle class. Its vibrant, masculine, industrial ethos and upbeat optimism leads one to make associations with cities such as Detroit or Cleveland in the 1950s, which were then beacons of modernity and symbols of the future.

This chapter discusses the implications of fast change for the sense of collective self, belonging and identity among Gladstonites. It is often assumed, not least in the social-science literature, that belonging is mainly based on memories and reminiscences, and that personal identity is connected to a sense of continuity with the past and predictability, with two influential contributions here being those of Halbwachs (1950) and Connerton (1989). Gladstone represents, in some important ways, an intriguing contrast.

## A SHORT HISTORY OF ACCELERATED CHANGE IN GLADSTONE

Gladstone is the undisputed industrial hub of central Queensland, but it began to develop as an industrial town only in the 1960s, leading its population to grow from about 5,000 in 1950 to 26,000 in 1979 and 65,000 (including the greater council area following an amalgamation) in 2015; the Queensland government anticipate a doubling of the population by 2036 (QGSO 2013). However, until the 1960s, the city was by and large perceived, by residents and outsiders alike, as a stagnant backwater. The most authoritative history book about the city, by Laura McDonald, has the telling title *Gladstone, City That Waited* (McDonald 1988). It was named after William Gladstone at its foundation as a fledgling port settlement in 1853. As colonial secretary some years earlier, Gladstone had proposed that Port Curtis should be populated by a mixture of 'expired convicts' from Van Diemen's Land (Tasmania) and newly arrived convicts from England. It was going to be the capital of Northern Australia, including present-day Queensland and the Northern Territory. Nothing came of it, Gladstone remaining a forgotten country town for more than a century, languishing in the shadow of more glamorous neighbours.

To the immediate north were Rockhampton – 'the meat capital of Queensland' – and Mount Morgan, the site of the gold mine that was at one time the world's largest; the mine operated from 1882 to 1981, contributing substantially to the Australian economy for decades, and leaving behind it a toxic wasteland. To the south were the sugar and rum capital Bundaberg and the thriving fisheries of Hervey Bay, a further couple of hours south of the city that did become the state capital of Queensland in 1859, Brisbane. Gladstone, its main natural asset being its excellent, sheltered deep sea port, shipped modest quantities of meat, cereals and miscellaneous produce, and its largest economic enterprise from 1893 until its closure in 1963 was Swift's Meatworks, an abattoir and cannery. Swift's, which flourished especially during the great spam boom of the Second World War, when it supplied allied forces with tinned meat, offered good work, but it was seasonal and required people to find other sources of income for more than half the year. Apart from a number of medium-sized cattle farms, especially in the Mount Larcom area to the west, the Gladstone region also produced fruit and vegetables for the regional market, especially in the fertile volcanic soil of Targinnie to the immediate north. Fishing was also a significant economic activity.

When Swift's closed and was demolished, the plot and some adjacent land had already been purchased by the mining company Comalco (later Rio Tinto), which immediately set about building what would become the world's largest alumina refinery. It opened in 1967, followed almost immediately by the opening of a railway extension connecting the port of Gladstone to the Moura coal fields in the interior of Queensland, and an expansion of the port itself with the construction of a coal terminal at Barney Point in the city. The unevenness of the fast growth of the town was already very visible during the construction years of the mid to late 1960s, when thousands of contract workers lived in tents, caravans and temporary housing on cricket fields and the showgrounds. The local infrastructure was incapable of keeping up with the influx of workers. It has been calculated that a quarter of Gladstone's population lived in temporary housing in the early 1970s. An elderly woman who now lives in a retirement village on the outskirts of the city remembers the time as a chaotic one:

And there was turmoil, I can tell you. People lived in caravans – *families* lived in caravans. We were incredibly lucky in that we got a five-bedroom house for [A]$20 a week. It was through [local politician and port administrator] Bill Golding's wife. Later, we bought the house from them at a very good price. But you can imagine [the main street]

Goondoon Street on a Saturday night, the drinking and fighting ... This is returning now with the FIFOs.

There have been several later periods of industrial expansion as well. The Gladstone Power Station, now the largest in Queensland, produced its first kilowatts in 1978, and was later expanded on several occasions and privatised in 1994. The Boyne Island Aluminium Smelter was completed just south of QAL (Queensland Alumina Limited) in 1982. The city's second coal terminal opened in 1997; the largest cement factory in the country is Cement Australia's operation at Fisherman's Landing, just north of the city; Orica has a cyanide factory in the same area, and a second Rio Tinto-owned alumina refinery was opened at Yarwun, 10 kilometres north of Gladstone, in 2004. In addition, the city has many smaller industrial enterprises, as well as a broad range of auxiliary activities directly or indirectly associated with the industry (from scaffolding to the construction of new suburbs). In a word, Gladstone has, in the space of just a few decades, experienced a succession of industrial developments that have led to a continuous growth in size, population and prosperity, thus fully justifying the use of the past tense in McDonald's book title: it no longer is a city that waits; it is rather at the epicentre of contemporary, carbon-fuelled industrialism, with its high-intensity electricity production, alumina works and expanding coal port.

The expansion continues. Since 2011, massive amounts of construction have again taken place in Gladstone, bringing money, infrastructural changes, environmental protests and temporary workers into the city yet again. On Curtis Island, just across a narrow strait from Gladstone, three large liquid natural gas (LNG) terminals have been constructed by the American engineering firm Bechtel. The gas terminals themselves are owned by three distinct conglomerates. Plans to build a fourth LNG terminal were finally cancelled, or perhaps postponed, in early 2014, owing to the uncertainties in the global market for gas. In addition to the LNG terminals themselves (which are located on an island that forms part of the Great Barrier Reef Conservation Area), thick pipelines connect the terminals with the gas reservoirs in the coal seams of the interior of Queensland. Simultaneously, a third coal terminal has been built at Wiggins Island, a few kilometres north of Gladstone, in a bid to increase coal exports, as international coal markets have been booming, especially in East Asia. Although coal prices fell in 2013/14, the logic of expansion and economies of scale continues to apply. If the mining companies and Queensland Government are to make reasonable profits in a future characterised by unstable coal prices, it will be necessary to increase the production capacity and expand the ports.

Living in Gladstone does not merely entail living amidst the din, smells and possible health hazards of industrial activities. It also requires an acceptance of change, not least regarding the composition of the population. Only a minority of adult Gladstonites were born and bred in the city. Many long-standing residents admit that they had never planned to stay, but rather envisioned living there for a few years to work hard and save money; they eventually stayed. Many adolescents and young adults express a wish to leave. Reasons may be that 'there is nothing to do here' (referring to leisure activities, compared to larger cities), few institutions of higher education, a limited job market outside industry and a somewhat drab and polluted environment. Among the elderly, there has been a marked tendency to leave Gladstone since 2011, and the trend is sometimes spoken of as a 'grey exodus'. One retiree in his seventies, who would soon be moving elsewhere, stated that he would ideally stay in Gladstone, where he had lived since his thirties, and he had family and friends there; however, there was no retirement village in the city other than for ex-employees of certain corporations, so he saw few other options than moving to a serviced retirement village elsewhere in Queensland. Other pensioners have left for economic reasons. If they owned their house, they were in a position to make a large profit selling it during the recent boom; and if they rented, they might no longer be able to afford to live in Gladstone. A couple of my acquaintance – she was not working, and he had just retired – sold their house in early 2014 (when prices were already declining) and moved to the Sunshine Coast near Brisbane, about 400 kilometres south. Just a week after they had left, I received an e-mail from her waxing lyrical about the natural beauty and healthy air of their new environment, as opposed – implicitly – to the grittiness of Gladstone.

Most of the newcomers to Gladstone have resettled there from other parts of Australia, but a fair number are foreigners employed by one of the corporations, typically on a temporary '457' visa. There is an NGO, Welcoming Intercultural Neighbours, which holds meetings and organises events introducing foreigners, many of them Asians, to the Australian way of life, giving language classes when needed and teaching necessary skills, from Queensland's traffic rules to the Australian tax system. For Australians who move to Gladstone, no formal introductions are made, and an obvious research question was how newcomers assimilate, and how the population of Gladstone, seen as a whole, copes with the fast and abrupt changes in their social surroundings.

For the purpose of the present analysis of local identity, temporary workers and FIFOs are bracketed, and the focus is on settled Gladstonites. As noted, they are usually not born in the city, but in most cases they have spent most or all of their adult life there. They tend to be married and to own a house located in a more established area than the newest suburbs off Kirkwood Road, a ring road that was opened in 2012 to facilitate further urban expansion. The men have steady jobs or are self-employed, and they have one or several children. Discourse about accelerated change and its effects on local identity among Gladstonites who identify with the city tends to waver between the pessimistic, the optimistic and the ambivalent. Of course, people do not hold identical views, but they take part in a shared discursive universe.

Some of the most salient changes concern population growth and changes in the composition of the population. Although foreign immigration has hitherto been modest, mobility into the city from other parts of Australia is significant and leads to a skewed gender and age balance compared to the national average. Settled residents perceive change every day. They observe the greatly increased traffic in the harbour, they see cranes building new industrial enterprises, infrastructure or dwellings; they notice the incessant traffic along the Port Access Road transporting FIFOs back and forth to building sites; they notice changes in the rush-hour traffic, in the cost of living, in the structure of civil society and in volunteering.

### FIFOS

In Queensland, fly-in-fly-out work is largely associated with mining and construction. According to the Queensland Resources Council, about 1,000 miners live on the Sunshine Coast, 800 on the Gold Coast, 3,700 in Mackay, 2,000 in Rockhampton and 2,850 in Townsville.[2] In Gladstone, about 5,000 of the 10,000 workers employed temporarily in construction on Curtis Island are FIFOs, mostly living permanently in another part of Queensland. In the local daily, the *Gladstone Observer*, in various Facebook groups and in everyday discourse, there has for years been vivid debate about the way in which FIFOs relate to the city. In fact, most FIFOs rarely enter the city. They have to pass through it in order to get onto boats to Curtis Island, but when they do, they travel on the Port Access Road, which, although it intersects the city, is physically segregated from it. When this road was completed in 2010 in order to facilitate heavy and frequent traffic to and from the main port area,

---

2. *Gladstone Observer*, 4 December 2014, p.3.

houses were demolished and the city was effectively cut in two. There were local protests, but to no avail. In 2016, the road was being expanded westwards to further facilitate fast access to the growing port.

Every day, buses move workers from Port Central to the airport, or to the jetty at Fisherman's Landing, or to and from Bechtel's main offices and induction centre just west of the city. On Sunday evenings, buses take workers who have spent half of Saturday and/or Sunday in Gladstone down to the port in order for them to get back to work.

One frequently mentioned topic concerns littering in public places. A woman of my acquaintance said that Red Rover Road, which is mostly used by Bechtel buses taking workers from A to B, was strewn with rubbish, mostly food wrappers, beer cans and soft drink bottles. 'You don't see this anywhere else in the area', she said, adding that 'it's obvious in a way, isn't it, that FIFOs care less about the local environment than people who live here permanently. They have no attachment'. A study nevertheless seems to indicate that FIFOs express less concern about littering than locals, but that there is no apparent difference in actual practices (Campbell et al. 2014).

Another largely negative discourse about FIFOs concerns their role as customers in Gladstone shops. Several shopkeepers complain that FIFOs scarcely enter town and rarely shop (they stick, allegedly, to the pubs). One owner of an independent, specialised shop claimed that he had experienced no positive effect whatsoever from the influx of a large and well-heeled group of workers in the immediate vicinity. He went on to explain that representatives of Bechtel had entered his shop some time ago to get quotes for a large number of products. He then spent some time calculating prices and giving them an offer, only to discover that they would use his prices as a benchmark for negotiating discounts with a larger, Australia-wide chain. They ended up buying nothing from him. He said that he had felt no positive effects from the presence of FIFOs. Similar views were expressed by other independent shopkeepers.[3]

The hospitality business, from hotels and the caravan park to inns, pubs and restaurants, express very different views. They have seen a steady increase in business since construction on Curtis Island began, and have been in a position to raise prices. A new, upmarket apartment hotel was opened in central Gladstone in February 2014, and others report few vacancies since the beginning of construction on the island. The exception, oddly for hotels, are the holiday periods, which are quiet.

Local politicians tend to express more equivocal views about FIFOs. They point out that FIFOs work for companies that pay local council

---

3. See Eriksen (2016a) for a theoretical approach to these clashing scales.

rates and which also create local jobs (positive), while at the same time they allegedly lack local engagement and do next to nothing for the community (negative). A more unanimously negative view is often expressed by Gladstonites engaged in voluntary work. To them, the FIFOs are mainly a burden on the community; they use the infrastructure, but spend little and contribute nothing.

There are also widespread murmurs about other negative effects of the FIFO phenomenon. Many locals claim that prostitution has grown perceptibly in Gladstone over the last few years following the influx of thousands of male workers in the region. Others claim that drunk and disorderly behaviour, sometimes involving drunken driving and violence, has become more widespread recently, since, as an elderly woman points out, 'you have to remember that a large proportion of the workers are young men far from their families, far from their mothers, with nobody to look after them'.

There is much about Gladstone that recalls something Bauman said about projects of identity in the twenty-first century, 'avoiding fixation and keeping the options open' (Bauman 1996: 18). The city relies on continuous change to such an extent that continuity would be perceived as an aberration. Growth implies change, and prosperity depends on growth. Therefore, change is widely accepted as a necessary fact of life. As an environmental activist in Brisbane explains, Queensland 'can't do without it [mining]', and in order to keep unemployment down and the resources boom up, 'they need big things to build'. Partly for this reason, she adds, new large projects will be started in the state as soon as construction is finished in Gladstone (in 2015), so that the workers can move on to the expanding coal port of Abbot Point further north or to the new coal fields in the Galilee Basin.

Compared to regular employees, temporary contract workers live according to a different rhythm. They work hard for several weeks before leaving for their week off. They need temporary lodging, are unstable and impermanent, and the constant mobility of large numbers of people in the city creates a sense of flux and restlessness. Not only the workers, but many of the managers fly in and out. Even the director of QAL lives in Brisbane.

A local journalist partly confirms, and partly contradicts, what other informants say:

Obviously, FIFOs have no sense of belonging to a community here, they've got their families and commitments elsewhere. If they have a garden, they tend it in Bundy [Bundaberg] or the Gold Coast, not here. I guess there isn't a heck of a lot of respect either. On the other hand, many businesses have expanded; contracting services do good business with FIFOs after all.

His colleague adds:

The advice you get about work in Curtis Island is that you should leave your brain on the ferry. I heard about one bloke who was disenchanted already after three months. It is an artificial community, you know; well paid, but empty and somehow meaningless. You have 28 days on and nine days off. But they stop work at 2 PM on Saturdays, and some come into town then. You'd have noticed them, I guess, the drinking, the noise, a bit of fighting.

Many FIFOs arrive at the airport, are shuttled off in a bus waiting for them, drive down to Port Central or Fisherman's Landing, and are taken straight out to the island from there. They engage minimally with Gladstone as such, and locals observe this with a mixture of relief and resentment. The FIFOs do not contribute much to the local community, and they are widely seen as alien, a necessary evil.

## INDUSTRIAL DEVELOPMENT

Discourses about industrial development – and I here mainly have the construction projects on Curtis Island in mind – are more complex than those about FIFOs. While FIFOs are by definition not locals, many permanent residents of Gladstone, of both genders (but mostly male), have found well paid temporary employment on the island. Stories are told about cleaners who earn $120,000 a year (roughly equivalent to the salary of a full professor), although this rumour was refuted or at least modified by several informants who have worked as cleaners on the island. Indeed, many Gladstonites have abandoned their steady jobs in town for a better paid temporary job on the island, with some doubling or even tripling their income. This nevertheless has its costs. The work regime on the island is strenuous, and family life suffers when the head of household has to leave home at 4.30 every morning, to return only after dusk. Women with husbands who work on the island tend to be ambivalent. Their husbands earn good money, but their participation in family and married life has become limited.

Many local employers react negatively to the accelerated change affecting Gladstone. It is difficult, they point out, to find reliable, good staff when one cannot compete with the wages on Curtis Island. Many kinds of employment have been available on the island, ranging from regular construction work to driving, engineering, canteen work, dredging and piloting the many boats shuttling people back and forth to the mainland. In a single month in 2013, the number of movements in Gladstone harbour was 33,000 (compared with an average of 3,000 before construction began).

This greatly increased activity has driven up wages, making it difficult even for the largest local employers, such as QAL, to compete with Bechtel; but residents also complain about deteriorating public services. A typical complaint concerns the municipal hospital, which has a reputation for being below the standards of neighbouring hospitals (it is mainly compared to the one in Rockhampton); and this situation is often explained through a shortage of qualified medical staff. City councillors confirm this, and they also admit that there have been difficulties in recruiting staff in the police and educational sectors. A popular rumour, later refuted, had it that even the local McDonald's flew employees in and out for a while at the height of the construction boom.

There is a very widespread negative discourse about industrial development in Gladstone, but it is rarely heard locally. Councillors may complain that 'Gladstone is too often in the news for the wrong reasons'. Say 'Gladstone' to an environmental activist anywhere in Australia, and you will hear about the destruction of the Great Barrier Reef due to local activities, notably dredging and ship traffic, but also large-scale processes, notably the contribution of the fossil-fuel industry to climate change. However, this particular discourse is by and large absent in the city itself, where environmental concerns tend to be specific and locally anchored (Eriksen 2016b). The main local critique of the dredging of the harbour (which eventually led to a major scandal publicised in the national media) concerns not the reef, but the negative effects on local fisheries. Only a handful of my informants were categorically negative about the construction of LNG terminals on Curtis Island, but many held that the environmental destruction had been devastating because the Gladstone Ports Corporation had opted for cheap solutions rather than sustainable ones – specifically, that they had not secured the toxic dredge spoil properly, allowing it to spill into the harbour. A main discourse about the dredging can thus be described as ambivalent: dredging as such was acceptable, since Gladstone had to develop in order to keep up; but it was not executed in the right way.

Yet to some, the combined effects of several simultaneous, new industrial projects had severe impacts on their identification with the city. One person concludes: 'They have demolished the old [shale oil] plant and built a new one. Coupled with the destruction of the harbour,

Curtis Island and the surrounds from the gas projects, our town is not such a nice place anymore'.

## HOUSING AND CIVIL SOCIETY

Many locals have profited economically from the shortage of housing resulting from the boom. Those with units or houses to let have made good money during the period of construction on the island; those in a position to sell have similarly profited. However, as alluded to above, the housing situation has led to a change in the demographic composition of Gladstone, destabilising important institutions in civil society. Many of those who have left are pensioners, who either could no longer afford the rent, or who were tempted by the prospect of selling in Gladstone and buying a similar house at a lower price just a couple of hours further south, in a healthier and prettier environment. As a result, it has become increasingly difficult to recruit people for voluntary and charity work, which largely depends on retirees. Moreover, as many fathers are absent working on the island, and as many pensioners have left the city, organising children's sports events at weekends has become a challenge, as these activities also depend on the voluntary work of parents and grandparents. As a woman in her forties told me, she had never done football refereeing in her life until construction on Curtis Island began, but she was now 'getting the hang of it', since mothers had to take on the tasks typically assigned to fathers.

Other complaints about the effects of accelerated change on the infrastructure are also heard. Some mention increased traffic during rush hour and difficulties in finding parking spaces in the shopping areas. Others talk about the alleged deterioration of manners in a city where many do not feel a moral responsibility and where social control is uneven. A woman in her forties, who habitually took long walks as her main exercise, told me that 'in some of the new housing estates, you don't get the feeling that people belong at all'. As an example, she mentioned how men who shared a house might, upon moving in, remove shrubs and even trees planted on the front lawn, in order that they could all park their cars in front of the house.

On the other side, few complain about the de facto growth of Gladstone, where the new ring road, opened in 2012, is already the central artery connecting several brand new housing estates to the city and the suburbs directly to the port. The typical view would be that in so far as people who move in pay their rates and support themselves economically, they are welcome. At a ceremony in the Gladstone Entertainment and Convention Centre on the eve of Australia Day (26

January), new Australian citizens living in Gladstone were invited to take the citizenship oath. Some 57 did so, perhaps roughly half of them of European origin (mainly British and New Zealanders). In her speech, the mayor joked that Gladstone welcomed all new residents since they kept the council afloat through paying rates, and gave them, as a symbolic gift, a small potted plant 'that you can plant outside in your garden, and if you don't have one yet, put it in a large pot and plant it when you get your garden'. The assumption was that people were settling and not temporary residents, and would have gardens. This is what the local council wants.

Many small and middle-sized local businesses have profited from the recent boom (Amarna 2014). Some deliver goods and services to Bechtel, from scaffolding to transportation, while others have increased their turnover as a result of a larger customer base. An example is a man in his fifties who sells and installs top-end car stereos; but the largest shopping mall is also expanding. Many locals also appreciate the increase in consumer choice; for example, three new restaurants opened in the city centre in the first half of 2014. Likewise, the expansion of the local mall was met by and large with enthusiasm.

The mobility, flux and growth characterising both the infrastructure and the population of Gladstone places demands on the sociability of residents. 'You have to be fairly outgoing to thrive here', said a fairly recent arrival from another English-speaking country, and mentioned his wife, 'who is a bit shy, who doesn't like meeting new people too much, who dislikes large functions ... she's had real difficulties adjusting to life here, and for a while, she didn't even go to the supermarket on her own'.

A well educated woman in her late thirties, who had lived in Gladstone for a few years but was about to move abroad with her young family, had misgivings about the uneven rhythms of change in the city. While certain things change fast, she implied, others do not, and as a result, the system as a whole gets out of sync. As she says:

> The hospital isn't great, the shopping is terrible. We have a five-year-old, and it has been very hard to find a place for him in a kindergarten. When they start school, of course, that problem is gone. We were hoping that the industry would fund an early childcare centre, open 24 hours in order to accommodate children of shift workers, but that did not materialise.

In spite of the rapid changes affecting everyday life in often unanticipated ways, there are also ways in which society is being reproduced regularly and routinely. Some institutions of civil society, such as the Gladstone Chamber of Commerce, the three local chapters of the Rotary

Club, charities such as the Salvation Army and Caritas, sports clubs, as well as annual public events such as the Eisteddfod talent competition (which is very popular in Gladstone) and Australia Day, many of them involving overlapping key personnel, ensure both regularity and continuity. In addition, public institutions, notably schools, the health sector and regular public services such as rubbish collecting and postal delivery, provide a structural framework enabling the reproduction of central features of everyday life amidst change.

From the foregoing description of change as the norm, coal as the fuel, and mobility as the precondition, a garden of forking analytical paths appears. There are many ways in which optimism concerning change and progress in Gladstone can be analysed. In the present discussion, I have focused on the uncompromising modernity of Gladstone. Lacking the preconfigured social and cultural patterns of tradition, but also unperturbed by the ambivalence and uncertainties of postmodernity, Gladstone is fundamentally committed to the central values of modernity, and it is a modernity characteristic of the early twenty-first century, which also has a distinctly Australian flavour. Change is accelerating as the past vanishes rapidly in the rear mirror, competition intensifies and the city is glued together in a modular way which facilitates the absorption of new arrivals and provides cues for discourses about future directions. Let me explain.

### ACCELERATED STRUCTURAL AMNESIA

In an industrial, transient town such as this, there are scarcely any old and venerable families, and the sense of continuity with the pre-industrial past is weak. Although third-generation Gladstonites exist, they are few.

Jake, a welder in his late thirties who recently moved to Bundaberg with his family, says: 'The sense of community is different. Here, I go into a pub, and there'll be ten, fifteen, twenty blokes I know'. When I asked if some of them would have moved here from Gladstone, Jake replied: 'Yeah, but it's mostly people simply living here. There is more community, more stability here I guess. Gladstone is all work and moving'.

Recall the statement at the beginning of this chapter about Gladstone *always* having been a boom-and-bust town. Other informants occasionally remark that the city 'has been industrialised for generations'. As a matter of fact, the industrial history of Gladstone goes back only to 1967, less than fifty years as I write. Statements of this kind seem to suggest that 'the past' was in fact quite recent, and that social memory is generally shallow. This is not, strictly speaking, accurate. Two museums, the Calliope River Historical Village and the Gladstone Maritime Museum, both depending on volunteers owing to limited funds, display objects, pictures and buildings enabling the visitor to create a genealogical narrative stretching back to the mid nineteenth century. Visitor numbers are nevertheless modest. Moreover, local amateur historians – foremost among them Paulette Flint and Betty Laver (sister-in-law of the famous tennis player Rod Laver, from Rockhampton) – publish locally distributed books and pamphlets about different aspects of the city's history. Finally, the closed Facebook group 'Gladstone: Remember When', where old photos, historical details and anecdotes are continuously being posted and discussed, has more than 6,000 members.

In other words, there are many in Gladstone who feel attached to the city's history, volunteer in the museums and actively discuss the link between the past and the present. Gladstone has eleven listed buildings – that is, of importance in terms of heritage, and which thus cannot be legally demolished – dating from the late nineteenth and early twentieth centuries. It should be noted here that compared to many other societies, 'the past' in Australia is recent. The *longue durée* of the continent, which is Aboriginal, is poorly known by most white Australians and rarely identified with by them. The continent's total population was less than four million as late as 1901, the year of Australian independence, when the Federation was founded. Gladstone's population was less than a thousand when the rail link from Brisbane was completed in 1897, and it doubled from 7,000 to 14,000 between 1960 and 1970, the first decade of industrialisation. With a 2015 population of over 60,000 in the greater council area, it is easy to surmise that most of the inhabitants do not have a deep genealogy connecting them to the Gladstone area. The close relatives of my informants (parents, siblings, adult children) in very many cases live elsewhere, but often in Queensland. And in spite of the efforts of enthusiasts, the council and civil society associations devoted to social memory, knowledge of and interest in local history tends to be limited. Year Zero, to many Gladstonites, was 1967, the year that Comalco, soon to become QAL, fired up its carbon-intensive ovens.

Among long-settled immigrants in Gladstone, there are some recurrent standard narratives about Australia in general and Gladstone in particular. During conversations with Eduardo, a Latin American married and settled in the city for five years, it often transpires that he is frustrated with the 'lack of substance' in the city. And upon asking Rosa, a single mother in her fifties from another South American country, who had moved from Sydney a few years ago, whether she missed the art and culture scene in the larger city, she responded, slightly dismissively, that 'nothing in Australia has any depth anyway'. Confirming this view, but from a different perspective, a young Italian man who had studied for several years in Australia, confessed that he felt bogged down in history at home. 'Here, everything is new. Back there, everything is old', he said.

In a word, *newness* is celebrated in Gladstone. Apart from the listed buildings and a few 'old Queenslanders' (wooden houses built on stumps, mostly from before 1950), most of them dilapidated and awaiting demolition, the city comes across as new, and this is the case with both the CBD (Central Business District) and residential areas. A house is considered old if the owner grew up there as a child when it was new in the 1970s.

As Connerton says, in a discussion of speed, architecture and obsolescence, a 'powerful source of contemporary cultural amnesia ... has to do with the nature and the life history of the material objects with which people are customarily surrounded', adding that today 'it is we who observe the birth and death of objects, whereas in all previous civilisations it was the object and the monument that survived the generations' (Connerton 2009: 122). The *frozen moments* described by Neumann (this volume) thus become marginal relics useful for occasional commemorative ceremonies, but uninteresting in the ongoing swirl of everyday life. As Anna, an ex-resident of Gladstone, said when we were discussing the FIFO phenomenon:

> Probably, the most widespread disease is not related to dust or respiratory problems, or even environmental poisons, but mental health. I'm thinking about stress and the side-effects of the emptiness of lives devoted to making as much money as possible as fast as possible.

Accelerated structural amnesia was the topic of an art installation displayed at the annual Rio Tinto Alcan Martin Hanson Memorial exhibition in 2013. Created by the local amateur artist Vicki Johnson and titled *Crime Scene*, the installation consisted of shards of glass, pieces of wood, rusty nails and odd bits and pieces left behind at demolition sites where houses with generations of history had been unceremoniously torn down in order to make way for something new and shiny (see Figures 5.1, 5.2 and 5.3). Displayed in sealed transparent bags, labelled and captioned, the objects told a story of accelerated change where any sense of continuity was lost, where fast profits took pride of place and where the past was deemed worthless because it was inefficient and paid nobody's salary. Discussing her motivation for creating this installation, Vicki told me that she had been struck by the brutality with which fragile, old wooden structures were crushed to oblivion and replaced with anodyne blocks or office buildings, all in the name of progress.

She was angered and saddened by this ruthless development, sensing a fundamental contradiction between the profit seeking of the developers and local needs, but she says that 'people are mostly too afraid, or perhaps just too apathetic, to speak up against this kind of thing'.

Mary, a woman in her forties who lives in a caravan park near Calliope, west of Gladstone, reacted in a similar way to changes in her immediate surroundings, although her concern was not with attachment to a built environment but to nature. Since 2012, several housing estates have been built in the area, requiring the removal of large swathes of bush, and leading to a situation where wild animals can be seen more often than before near and inside the caravan park. Possums, wallabies and kangaroos have become a common sight, as have snakes. Mary is critical of the development because no consideration is given by the developers, or the political authorities, to the needs of the ecosystem and the

*Figure 5.1* Vicki Johnson, *Crime Scene*, installation (detail). Photograph by the author.

*Figure 5.2* Vicki Johnson, *Crime Scene*, installation (detail). Photograph by the author.

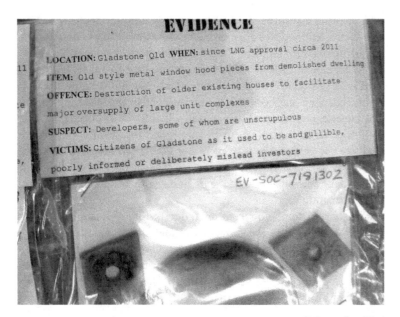

*Figure 5.3* Vicki Johnson, *Crime Scene*, installation (detail). Photograph by the author.

animals that inhabit it, but she adds that the quality of life in the caravan park has also deteriorated. One of its main assets was its proximity to relatively unspoilt nature, which is now gone; and the animals, now squeezed into a shrinking space, are stressed and can be a nuisance to people.

Vicki and Mary are not alone in resenting the ways that the rapid loss of memory can create a sense of detachment and alienation, but the only recent development project that has led to visible protests was the construction of the Port Access Road, which intersects central Gladstone in a very noticeable way. Demolition of the old and the construction of the new are generally accepted almost as a law of nature.

## A MODULE-BASED IDENTITY

In which sense is Gladstone a place? Have its residents entered into a Faustian pact whereby they sacrifice soul for profits? Its continuity with the past is tenuous, its roots thin and fragile. Its population generally takes a pragmatic view of their physical location. Young people tend to want to leave. Their parents plan their retirement in the healthy climate and beautiful surroundings of the Sunshine Coast. You can belong, but you would be hard pressed to grow deep roots. As a middle-aged couple told me, they had lived in Gladstone nearly all their adult lives. Now that their livelihood was gone owing to some unintended side-effects of infrastructural development, they were planning relocating to Tasmania. 'Why Tasmania?' I asked; 'Does either of you have a connection there – family, close friends?' 'No', they responded, they didn't know a soul in Tassie, but they had been there once on holiday and liked the climate and lifestyle. So they were prepared to sell out, buy a convenient house in Tasmania and move there permanently. The facility with which Gladstonites relocate is worthy of consideration, given that human identity is so often associated with place. The changes to which they so easily adjust encompass changes in their own physical location as well as in their surroundings.

The short history and recent migration history of Australia provides part of the answer. In a country where mass immigration is seen as a necessity, which has been the case in Australia for two hundred years, it is necessary to develop mechanisms of fast inclusion. The entrance ticket could not be too expensive; people had to be turned into Australians quickly.[4] This situation contrasts with that of a farming society or city

---

4. 'People' here refers largely to English, Scottish and Welsh immigrants before the First World War, a sprinkling of other Protestant North Europeans between the wars,

with a long continuous history and a long established population, where the inclusion of new arrivals may be far more cumbersome, and where mobility is much less common.

The cheap entrance ticket requires informality in casual interaction (for which Australia is famous) and a common cultural grammar which can easily be acquired by those who move into a community. In Gladstone, the required cultural competence can be likened to a highway code. Apart from knowledge of English and following the law, economic independence (most likely through wage work) is most frequently invoked as a requirement for being accepted.[5]

The vast majority of the residents of Gladstone are Australians (with New Zealanders the second largest group), and there is a pan-Australian comparative language for talking and thinking about communities. In any community beyond a certain size, there must be schools, sports teams, voluntary associations, churches and a hospital. The services offered by the council are comparable – and are actively being compared – with the same services elsewhere. Typical Australian leisure pastimes – fishing, barbecuing, going to the beach, sport (as performers or spectators), various forms of entertainment – are comparable from city to city, and are being compared. The Eisteddfod (a talent competition of Welsh origin) is especially well organised and popular in Gladstone compared to other cities in central Queensland. However, the high street is less enticing than the one in Bundaberg, the shopping far worse than in Rockhampton, the harbour less charming than the one in Hervey Bay. But on the other hand, the new Spinnaker Park at the marina is really quite nice, and Awoonga Lake a few miles up the road is really good for barramundi fishing compared to what is on offer elsewhere.

The elements that create a local identity in Gladstone are spoken of in a comparative, generic language. They could be seen as interchangeable modules, like mobile homes transported on trailers. When, in mid 2014, a *Gladstone Observer* journalist ran a private survey asking his Facebook friends what kind of services or establishments they missed in Gladstone, a surprisingly high number of the respondents mentioned a brand. They did not say 'a good steak and seafood restaurant', but 'a Sizzler's'. Some wanted 'a better Target' (a chain of budget clothing and homeware stores). Some said that it was 'about time that Gladdy got its Myers' (a chain of upmarket department stores). In private conversation, Gladstonites have said to me that it is significant for the city that it now

---

immigrants from other parts of Europe (such as Greece and Italy) after the Second World War, and today, increasingly, East Asians, especially in the big cities.

5.   There is more to be said about this, but this is not the occasion.

has a Ribs'n'Rumps, a second Coffee Club and a Hog's Breath (three popular restaurant chains) on Goondoon Street, because it helps build the city's identity as a place where you can belong and live, not just a place to sleep and work. In this city, which is an embodiment of modernity in one of its purest forms, even its identity as a unique place in the world is made up of interchangeable modules. As the world changes, so must Gladstone change.

## REFERENCES

Amarna. 2014. Boom or Bust? Survey of Small and Medium-Sized Businesses in Gladstone. Consultancy report. Gladstone: Amarna.

Bauman, Z. 1996. From Pilgrim to Tourist; Or A Short History of Identity. In S. Hall and P. Du Gay (eds), *Questions of Cultural Identity*. London: Sage Publications, pp.18–36.

Campbell, M., C.P. de Heer and A. Kinslow. 2014. Littering Dynamics in a Coastal Industrial Setting: The Influence of Non-Resident Populations. *Marine Pollution Bulletin* 80(1/2): 179–85.

Connerton, P. 1989. *How Societies Remember*. Cambridge: Cambridge University Press.

—— 2009. *How Modernity Forgets*. Cambridge: Cambridge University Press.

Eriksen, T.H. 2016a. *Overheating: An Anthropology of Accelerated Change*. London: Pluto Press.

—— 2016b. Scales of Environmental Engagement in an Industrial Town: Glocal Perspectives from Gladstone, Queensland. *Ethnos*. Pre-publication March 2016. http://dx.doi.org/10.1080/00141844.2016.1169200

Halbwachs, M. 1950. *La mémoire collective*. Paris: Presses Universitaires de France.

McDonald, L. 1988. *Gladstone, City That Waited*. Gladstone: Boolarong Publishers.

QGSO (Queensland Government Statistician's Office). 2013. Projected Population, by Local Government Area, Queensland, 2011 to 2036. Available at: www.qgso.qld.gov.au/subjects/demography/population-projections/tables/proj-pop-lga-qld/index.php (accessed 18 January 2015).

# 6. Guarding the Frontier
## On Nationalism and Nostalgia in an Israeli Border Town

*Cathrine Thorleifsson*

### NEOLIBERAL CHANGE IN A SETTLER COLONIAL STATE

The State of Israel was founded in 1948 based on a vision of the nation-state as an ethnic entity, and mass immigration was considered key to ensure a Jewish majority over the Palestinians. During the 1950s, the government embarked on a massive immigration program aimed at bringing Jews from the Middle East and North Africa to settle in the new state.[1] Around 900,000 Jews from Arab and Muslim countries emigrated, and almost 600,000 of them went to Israel. The disintegration of the Jewish populations in Arab lands was almost total.[2] Before the genocide of European Jews, the Zionist movement, whose members were for the most part of Eastern European origin, had taken little interest in the Jews from Middle Eastern countries. Israel's motivation, as expressed by a leading Israeli politician, was 'not the need to save them, but to create a Hebrew majority in Israel' (Shafir & Peled 2002: 77). The notion of *aliyah*, physical and moral ascent to the land of Israel, epitomised by the story of Exodus, inspired the Zionist movement.[3]

The Israeli state apparatus was dominated by Ashkenazim (Jews of European descent) who tended to hold Eurocentric attitudes towards Mizrahim (Jews from Arab and Muslim countries). The Ashkenazi authorities viewed Mizrahim as essential members of the expanding settling nation. At the same time, they marked Mizrahim as racially

---

1. The Law of Return gave the entire Jewish collectivity, including non-resident and non-citizen Jews of the Diaspora, the right to settle in Israel and obtain full citizenship.

2. The reasons why Jews emigrated is a question of much academic debate. However, both Zionist immigration campaigns and growing anti-Semitism in some Arab and Muslim countries after the establishment of the State of Israel were contributing factors.

3. The term *aliyah*, literally meaning ascent, was borrowed from traditional Judaism and has been used ever since the first wave of immigrants arrived in Palestine. The term is associated with the synagogue, as reading the weekly Torah on Saturdays is also called *aliyah*.

and culturally different from the national identity (Shenhav 2006: 192). Their peripheral position within the Zionist nation-building ethos was further solidified by spatial planning policies. In the 1950s, Mizrahim were disproportionately placed by the government in 28 semi-urban development towns, in peripheral regions to the south and north for economic, security and settlement reasons.[4] Like other new settlements, the development towns were often built on the ruins of villages in which Palestinians once lived and worked, and from which they were violently expelled. The construction of Jewish communities, all built against Arab opposition and hostility, was depicted culturally in terms of national revival, territorial repatriation and historical redemption (Ram 2003: 228). Mizrahim were sent to remote districts in order to prevent the return of the displaced Palestinian population, and created a human militarised frontier against the neighbouring Arab countries considered hostile to the new state. They supplied the Ashkenazi-dominated *kibbutzim* (communal farms) with cheap labour. Mizrahim became entrapped by settler colonialism on the geographic and socio-economic margins of the state, positioned between the dominant Ashkenazi elite and the Palestinian population. The *kibbutzim* settlements constituted a major cultural symbol of the new modern, egalitarian, Western-oriented Zionist national identity (Tzfadia 2007: 58). The state thus allocated more and better land to the *kibbutzim* than the development towns due to their perceived contribution to nation-building, generating a wide ethno-class disparity. To reduce the high unemployment rate amongst Mizrahim, the government provided loans and other incentives to promote textile manufacturing and food processing, as well as metal and chemical industries in the peripheral towns. Starting in the late 1980s, several processes of accelerated change altered the socio-economic and demographic landscape of Israel. Neoliberal restructuring of the Israeli economy negatively affected Kiryat Shemona and other peripheral towns. Reforms of the Histadrut (Jewish Federation of Labour) weakened organised labour, and the towns lost several tax benefits and social services previously provided by the state. State-owned enterprises, particularly in the textile industry, were closed down or outsourced to countries like Egypt and Jordan, where labour was cheaper. The border populations of Kiryat Shemona missed out on the economic growth witnessed in Tel-Aviv and other urban regions, experiencing a crisis-laden cooling

---

4. Mizrahi Jews, the majority from Morocco, constituted 63 per cent of all immigrants during the 1950s and were expected to become a part of the working class in rural areas. By 1963, the development towns had a total of 170,000 inhabitants, of which 71 per cent were Mizrahim (Shiblak 2005: 12).

down of the economy, including rising unemployment and the creation of a 'precariat' (Standing 2014).

Beginning at the same time, mass immigration of around one million Jews and non-Jews from the former Soviet Union brought about a significant change in Israel's demographic landscape.[5] Around 130,000 immigrants from the former Soviet Union, mostly from lower socio-economic backgrounds, settled in development towns where they were offered cheap public housing. Israeli planning policies served to consolidate Israel's ethnocracy and its hierarchy of social, economic and ethnic stratification between different categories of belonging: Ashkenazim, Russian-speaking Jews, Mizrahim and Ethiopian Jews.[6] At the time of my fieldwork, the development towns were far below the national average in terms of employment, education and income. Despite social mobility, research shows an extensive overlap between ethnic background and socio-economic position cutting across generations (Yiftachel 2006).

Today, Kiryat Shemona has a population of around 25,000 inhabitants, of which the majority is Mizrahim followed by a small Russian-speaking minority. The main sources of employment are manufacturing, labour-intensive industries, the neighbouring *kibbutzim* and the security apparatus. Kiryat Shemona serves as a commercial centre for the surrounding settlements and soldiers stationed at the Israeli Defence Force's command base located in the city centre. The town is publicly perceived as an unsafe place. Since the 1960s, more rockets have hit Kiryat Shemona that any other Israeli city.

Taken together, the neoliberal restructuring of the economy coupled with fast demographic change and cross-border violence constitute an *overheating* effect (Eriksen 2016). The most notable response to accelerated change has been the overheating of exclusionary identity politics. Together with the ultra-Orthodox Russian speakers and settlers, Mizrahi residents of the periphery make up the majority of the right-wing constituency in Israel.[7] Israeli citizens, who are vulnerable to the impact and loss of the welfare state, are at the same time opposed to the dilution of the religious and national components of Jewish identity

---

5. The largest *aliyah* occurred between 1990 and 1996, when over 600,000 immigrants arrived.

6. Today, 18 per cent of the Israeli population resides in development towns, of which about two-thirds are of Mizrahi origin, and the remainder are predominately migrants from the former Soviet Union, with a smaller number from Ethiopia (Yiftachel 2006).

7. The results of the 2014 elections show that the various forms of mostly exclusionary populism (Likud, Shas and Yisrael Beiteniu) constitute the framework of the current right-wing government.

for the state and its citizens (Lehmann & Siebzehner 2006). While voting tells us about large-scale patterns, it tells us less about the hopes, needs, longings and interests of ordinary people. A focus on lived experience can provide a richer and more nuanced understanding of identity dilemmas caused or heightened by accelerated change, rather than the static group approach which has informed much scholarship of Mizrahim.[8] Scholars have noted how borderlands are not only a zone of state domination and control, but also represent creative negotiations over meanings of nationhood (Lavie 1996: 90; Donnan & Wilson 2001). With this insight in mind, I turn to a discussion of how settler colonialism intertwined with the consequences of neoliberal globalisation affect identity and belonging among Mizrahim in Kiryat Shemona.

## GUARDIANS OF THE FRONTIER

Geographical peripheries should not always be considered marginal. Despite living far from the centres of national governance, border populations are often a key element in the nation-state's imaginary. Those who inhabit the borderlands represent the frontier myth, and the ambiguous relation of that territory to the centres of political and economic power (Norton 1993: 58). Zionist leaders have for a long time idealised the frontier settlements as essential for both Israeli security and nation-building. During the 1950s, Ashkenazi state officials tried to inspire in Mizrahi immigrants a Zionist spirit and convince them about the importance of living on a frontier. Baruch Bez, a police commander posted in Kiryat Shemona in 1952 to monitor immigrant absorption noted: 'There, in those villages and *kibbutzim*, Jews have settled on the border, and have been there for many years. They work by day and guard by night for their homes and families ... and for us, as they are defending us too' (quoted in Tsipman 1953: 56–57).

The idealisation of the frontier populations continues today, and within the national imaginary, Kiryat Shemona epitomises frontier towns due to its proximity to Lebanon and the fact that it is frequently hit

8. In previous studies, Mizrahim have been portrayed as having little agency beyond the collective appropriation of the Mizrahi label to negotiate nationhood. During the 1990s, the term Mizrahi emerged as a political category that implied rejection and resistance of both past and present practices exerted on Jews who arrived from Arab and Muslim countries and their children to make them inferior. The Israeli scholar and activist Sami Shalom Chetrit (2000) explores the emergence of Mizrahi resistance through an analysis of social and political movements such as the Black Panthers, Tami, Shas and the Mizrahi Democratic Rainbow. All, although through different means, have challenged the hegemony of Ashkenazi Zionism.

by rockets fired from across the border. This image of Kiryat Shemona has also been internalised by its residents, including local state officials and religious leaders seeking to attract visitors, supporters and residents. The chief rabbi of Kiryat Shemona, Zephaniah Drori, is the founder of the Yeshivat Hesder, an institution combining three years of military service with Torah studies. In the institution's promotional video, Kiryat Shemona is referred to as a sacred frontier and the institution's students as its guardians. It starts off with the Talmudic phrase of 'the guardians of Israel neither slumber nor sleep':

> Kiryat Shemona is on the frontline of battle [*sic*] for Israel's survival and Yeshivat Hesder is the heart and soul of that community. The self-sacrifice exhibited on a daily basis, to be that safety zone, to be that buffer from its Arab enemies that would like to see Israel wiped off the face of the map, is a normal way of life. You're three kilometres away from Hezbollah. You can look at the Golan Heights; it is the foremost position to safeguard Jerusalem. Kiryat Shemona is what keeps Ahmadinejad and Assad out of Tel-Aviv and Jerusalem. The students are Israel's secret weapon. They are ready to put down the book and pick up the gun.[9]

This statement emphasises the strategic importance of the border town as a guardian for the whole country. The rhetoric of a 'safety zone' as a 'normal way of life' resonates with the desire for security rooted in Israel's settler origins. Particularly in moments of cross-border violence, Kiryat Shemona becomes a central margin, a place that is crucial to imagining the Israeli nation. In times of emergency, the town is strategically used by the state to mobilise support and create a moral identity. At the end of 2008 and beginning of 2009, the Israeli Defence Force (IDF) conducted a three-week-long attack on Gaza, the first major Israeli military offensive since the second Lebanon war. Operation Cast Lead was presented as retaliation for Hamas's repeated rocket attacks on towns in southern Israel. In the months leading up to the war and in the midst of it, national politicians, the media and religious leaders created a strong public awareness of Mizrahi-dense border towns facing the Palestinian-fired rockets in a manner that validated their place in the frontier ethos.

On 23 September 2008, Israel's former prime minister, Ehud Olmert, revalorised the role of the town in providing security (*bitachon*) for the centre. 'Your patriotism is a source of security for all of us', he claimed

---

9. From *In the Footsteps of Heroes*, 6 mins 20 secs. Available at: http://wn.com/Kiryat Shemona (accessed 25 February 2015).

in an emotional speech held at the local football stadium. Benjamin Nethanyahu's election campaign promised to provide security and jobs. The leader of the right-wing Likud tapped strategically into local anxieties and disillusionment, promising to favour military response over 'soft diplomacy'. This seemed to be a powerful formula for the residents of Kiryat Shemona, who felt threatened by external attacks and a pervasive sense of deprivation. The idealisation of the periphery by state officials moved Mizrahim symbolically from the margins to the centre of a national frontier, thus blurring the image of a periphery.

The Zionist ideal of steadfastness was nurtured through public schooling. Sylvia Parto (aged 38), the former principle of the largest high school in town, Dancinger, welcomed me to her home. Coming from a Moroccan Jewish family, she had been born and raised in Kiryat Shemona. 'Although I have lived through difficult times, I have never become used to war. Children should get used to ice-cream, but not to rockets', she said. The economic deprivation and frequent rocket attacks, combined with public stigmatisation, had made Kiryat Shemona a particularly challenging place to grow up for youngsters. She taught schoolchildren national spirit (*roach etnam*) so that they could remain strong when faced with suffering. Sylvia believed that the periphery could teach the centre much about strength and endurance, particularly since the frontier had moved further south during the war with Lebanon in 2006, during which rockets hit Haifa. Like other research participants she stressed the importance of remaining steadfast and patriotic when faced with hardship; otherwise Jews might be confined to the Diaspora again. 'It is important to remain strong. When you're in a survival mode, you don't fall apart'.

State officials' Zionist concepts of national strength and steadfastness were appropriated by Mizrahim in Kiryat Shemona to cope with borderland anxieties and to empower themselves as essential members of the nation. Like elsewhere in Israel, everyday life in Kiryat Shemona is saturated with security rituals and technologies (Katz 2007). Banal spaces such as malls, bus terminals and public buildings are sites of surveillance and risk-assessment. Everyday life was affected by nationalist sentiments because existential insecurity was not a relatively transitory condition but perceived as ordinary. Strength as a spoken and behavioural code (Sa'ar 2006) was a key element of self-nationalisation, a process where people fashion themselves into nationalised subjects, using distinctive narrative actions and embodied practices in the intimate register of work, neighbourhood, family and household (Jean-Klein 2001: 90).

My neighbour Esther Zakay welcomed me mockingly to 'Kiryat Katyusha' ('Katyusha town'), named after short-ranged rockets. We walked around Esther's neighbourhood and she painstakingly pointed towards places that had been hit by rockets during the second Lebanon war of summer 2006.[10] An apartment building, a house, roads, streams and trees – all seemed to bear damage from the war. While eating lunch with her family a few months later, all of a sudden we heard a loud yawning sound. Esther immediately put down her cutlery and the look on her face turned anxious. She paused for a moment and stood stock-still, looking around as if waiting for the alarm announcing incoming rockets. After a few minutes she seemed to relax and exhaled with a sigh of relief. 'Oi va voi, I thought for a moment it was a Katyusha rocket!' Esther claimed that going through war and hardship had made the residents of the periphery particularly strong.

> We try to live a normal life. We have learned to live with fear (*pachad*). It has become like a habit. Whenever a Katyusha falls, you go to the shelter, then afterwards life continues. You can't be afraid all the time. A new war will meet those with weak nerves. I'm no hero, but it's important to remain strong. There is no town in the world that will face hardship as Kiryat Shemona. In the face of the next war, we will also stand upright.

During the weeks the war lasted, over half of Kiryat Shemona's residents fled southwards. Some research participants were proud that they had remained in town. Shlomo (62), a factory owner who would have had the financial means to relocate, claimed that only devoted and strong residents had stayed put. 'I felt I was on a mission to defend the country. The people here are very strong and enduring'. Shlomo turned his ability to live and remain in an exposed frontier town into a sign of strength and steadfastness, rather than ethnocratic exclusion.

For Benny and Revital Chackotay, a couple in their mid 50s, living in the Galilee region had become an important part of practising religious Zionism. When discussing the Palestinian presence in Israel, it did not take long before sentiments of colonial anxiety surfaced:

> We will not be surprised if our city becomes Arab in the future. We hope that our country remains ours, that it remains Jewish. If we move, the Arabs will quickly take over the rest of the country, from Golan in the north to Haifa, Jaffa and Jerusalem.

---

10. During the second Lebanon war of summer 2006, over 4,000 missiles, mainly short-range Katyusha rockets, were fired into northern Israel. More than 1,500 houses were destroyed or damaged (Shindler 2009: 345).

For Benny and Revital, the existence of external and internal enemies was central to their sense of self and community. Both Russian-speaking Israelis and Palestinians were routinely marked as a demographic and cultural-religious threat to the Jewish nation. Benny noted ironically that Russian immigration had made Israel less Jewish in religious terms and more Christian. 'We came for the love of Judaism. The Russian immigrants came for the money!' he said, accusing the new Israelis of being non-Jewish or not Jewish enough.[11]

The Chackotay family perceived it as their sacred obligation to stay put in the north and to protect national territory against threatening Arab others and the West more generally against Islam. The belief in the 'Eurabia' conspiracy theory, alleging Arabisation and Islamisation of Europe, strengthened their perception of the threat posed by Muslim others.[12] Benny, who had not left Israel since his arrival as a child, believed that the Turks would soon outnumber the Germans and that the Moroccan and Algerian communities were a threat to France. He wanted to know the size of the Muslim population in Norway and whether my country was also in danger of Islamisation. Such anti-Muslim sentiments in Israel are produced in part by a transnational flow of ideas concerning Muslims who are perceived as an imagined collective with certain inherent features thought to be threatening to 'our way of life'. By believing in a radical external Muslim enemy, the perceived threats, from domestic difference and anxieties such as ethno-demographic fears relating to the presence of Palestinians or non-Jewish citizens, can remain in 'their place'.

To cope with the (un)intended consequences of settler colonialism and neoliberal globalisation, residents created a local identity around heroic steadfastness that was routinely expressed in speech and practice. Nationalist identifications were overheating during critical events such as during the build-up to or in the midst of war. A heightened sense of national unity was felt in the town, and residents invested more emotional energy in the symbols of nationhood. Both individuals and representatives from the municipality decorated the town with banners adorned with slogans such as 'We love Tzahal' (the Hebrew acronym for the IDF), idealising the warrior image of the soldiers and boosting their morale. Blue and white Israeli flags were flown on balconies, in streets and in social media profiles. Members of Yeshivat Hesder moved

---

11.   Paradoxically, this sentiment towards Russian immigrants resembles the precarious status of Jews in Russia as mistrusted others (Remennick 2007: 9).

12.   The 'Eurabia' concept was coined by Bat Ye'Or (2005), claiming a conspiracy led by French and Arab powers to Islamise and Arabise Europe.

their prayer ceremonies from the synagogue to the town square so that residents could join the congregation in public. National authorities invoked the courage of the steadfast people who remained in the towns and felt they had a moral right to continue fighting. The self-national-isation processes moved the Mizrahi ethno-class symbolically from the margins to the centre of the national frontier, thus blurring the image of a periphery. The war meant that residents of Kiryat Shemona ignored, avoided or forgot the structural conditions that divided the periphery from the centre. In the aftermath of war, self-nationalisation practices cooled down. Mizrahim in border towns faded from the national agenda and sank back into their multiple and competing loyalties of family, class, religion and region.

## TRANSNATIONAL LONGINGS

Marilyn Strathern (1995: 111) has noted how nostalgia can function as a potent source of social reconnection and identity in turbulent times. The representation of memory, even when mythologised, can salvage a 'damaged' sense of identity and re-territorialise Mizrahi experience (Halevi-Wise 2001: 2). While expressing strong nationalist fervour to deal with existential insecurities, my interlocutors simultaneously identified with places outside the nation's border, partly in response to the same processes of accelerated change. Mizrahim from the older generation who had experienced another home within their lifetime particularly compared Israeli landscapes in relation to that other world. The following ethnographic vignette shows how one of my interlocutors, Mazal Salma, invoked the past to cope with existential insecurity.

Following the death of her husband ten years ago, Mazal had been employed at the Gibor textile factory, a job she had lost when the factory recently shut down. To support herself and her three children, she had found part-time work as a tailor in the appliance and giftware store, *kol-bo-tal. Kol bo* means 'everything is in it', and that was true for the eclectic mix of items you could find in the shop: from textiles and kitchen utensils, to synagogue and liturgical items.[13] I visited her on an October morning in 2008. Mazal sat in the modest sewing room attached to the shop. A few customers had entered to be measured and fitted, bringing pattern books and materials with them. As the customers left, Mazal sat

---

13. *Kol bo* is the mainstream Hebrew term for a small department store that sells everything from food to clothing to small electrical appliances. Like many Hebrew words, it does have Biblical origins but has become more secularised as Hebrew itself has become more secular.

down in front of a sewing machine surrounded by colourful threads and fabrics, sharing her story.

Mazal grew up in a moderately well-off Jewish home in Istanbul, the city her ancestors had settled in after fleeing the Inquisition in Spain. 'They received us with open hands', Mazal said admiringly. In Turkey, Jews and Muslims took care of each other and the rich would give to the poor and needy. Mazal romanticised Turkey as the most beautiful country in the Middle East, protecting its Jews and assisting Israel when 'they ran to Turkey for help'.

> In our daily life, I hardly thought of who was Jewish and who was Arab. We got along fine, and some of my best childhood friends were Muslim or Christian Arabs. We had excellent relationships with our neighbours. Jews formed a part of the Turkish government. It was only after the establishment of the Israeli state that all the trouble (*balagan*) began. My mother used to run a small laundry service for mostly Turkish Muslim women. The customers loved my mother and used to give her money and food in payment for her services. They loved her so much that they told her: 'Don't go to Israel. We want you to stay here with us, in Turkey'.

Mazal's mother told her customers that she wanted to leave for Israel, where relatives had already resettled. She contacted senior officials and sheiks to ask for permission to leave. She would have only been allowed to leave when she had reached 80, but she was only 36 at the time, so she emigrated in 1956 against the will of the authorities.

For Mazal's family and many others with them, migration to Israel, *aliyah*, had been characterised by loss and downward social mobility. Tough conditions in the *ma'abarot*, the tented immigrant absorption camps, were part of collective memory. Mazal contrasted the greed and self-seeking individualism of the present with the togetherness of the past, constructing a positive narrative around traditional values such as modesty and moderation.

> Israel is not what it used to be. Before, people cared more about each other. We did not have much, but at least we were together. It was a time of modesty. If Israelis used to do everything for their country, today they do everything for themselves. I wish I could have my childhood back. Or that I could move to Turkey. I have asked my son. With God's help I can leave before I die.

In Mazal's case, nostalgia seemed to be the outcome of accelerated change caused by migration and the neoliberal restructuring of the economy. She experienced a sense of being constrained by both cultural dispossession and socio-economic and geographic entrapment. By retelling her mother's memories of an open and inclusive Turkey and narrating a period of modesty in Kiryat Shemona, she articulated values that no longer existed for her in Israel. Her experience of great economic distress might have strengthened her nostalgia and wish for a better life in Turkey. Israel became a place of partial loyalty and belonging without fully accepting its status as her definitive homeland. Through defiant memory and longings for a future return, she projected aspirations outside the boundaries of the nation.

During the 1960s, Shosa Ezra, a 60-year old woman of Iraqi decent, had worked in a *kibbutz*. She remembered how the *kibbutznikim* (people from a *kibbutz*) used to look down upon the inhabitants of Kiryat Shemona. 'I used to work in the kitchen of Kibbutz HaGoshrim. They asked us to work all the time and we were not even allowed to take a break. What is this? Work all day, without a break?' Clearly upset, when I asked how she thought the relationship was today, Shosa replied in a firm voice:

It is worse! They are even nastier today. They still have their noses in the air. But now the *kibbutznikim* are also facing difficult times due to the economic crisis. Finally they also have to work as we have done our entire life. Finally they also feel what I have felt.

Shosa's almost hostile attitude toward the Ashkenazim reflects the tensions that the economic dependence between the development town and *kibbutzim* has generated. Shosa seemed to distance herself from the historical and current discrimination she had experienced from Ashkenazim by invoking transnational connections. Sitting in the Chackotay's store one warm August afternoon, she bragged about her son's hope of opening an electronics store in the USA. Shosa gesticulated enthusiastically. With jewellery-covered hands, she took his passport photo out of a worn leather wallet. Proudly lifting the image towards me and then turning it towards other customers present, she continued to boast about his success:

Ten years ago my son said he was considering leaving Israel. I would protest loudly and say, 'How can you leave our country?' Now I am glad he left. Thousands of Kiryat Shemonim live in Miami! I have gone through difficult days in this country, but times have changed.

The entire political system is corrupt. Today there are only liars (*shakranim*) and thieves (*ganavim*) left. The Arabs can sleep safely, because we [the Jews] are creating enough trouble for ourselves.

Shosa's changing attitude toward *yeridah*, emigrating from Israel, was shared by the majority of my interlocutors who expressed disillusionment with the Israeli government. For them, the state had broken its ideological promise of providing jobs and security for Israel's citizens, and particularly those living in the borderlands. Thirty years ago, during the previous financial recession in Israel, those who considered or thought about emigrating from Israel were generally condemned. Most Israelis would consider emigrants weak Zionists who left the homeland for the shallowness of material gains. Just as *aliyah* was a more permanent decision, emigrating from Israel was considered an all-consuming total break with the homeland and a threat to national cohesion. However, the stigma attached to emigration is changing. Israel's shift towards being a neoliberal state, while perpetuating the marginality of Mizrahim in development towns, has at the same time created opportunities for participation in large-scale 'flows' of information, capital and people (Appadurai 1996; Nitzan & Bichler 2002).[14] The pervasive sense of hardship coupled with a precarious security situation encouraged residents in Kiryat Shemona to invest in transnational connections as potential 'emergency exits'.

Shosa's cosmopolitan orientation coincided with a strong sense of national identity and nostalgia. A month after our initial meeting, I visited Shosa at home. Excitedly, she showed me old family photos her sister had brought from Ashkelon. Flicking through the carefully preserved black-and-white photos, she commented on the clothes worn in them. 'That is my mother', she said, pointing to a woman wearing a necklace depicting the four-fingered hand of Fatima, a popular sign of protection again the evil-eye and used throughout the Middle East and North Africa. She paused, took a deep breath and started talking, in long emotional sentences:

Sometimes I watch documentaries with stories from the countries we came from. I know that my mother made uniforms for the British soldiers in Iraq in the 1920s. Some of my mother's sisters married soldiers that brought them back to England. I don't know whether they were Jewish or not. If my mother was still alive I could have asked her.

---

14.   One reason for this is the large number involved: an estimated 700,000 Israeli citizens live abroad.

I am sure I have distant relatives in England. The similarity between Jews from Iraq, Iran and Morocco is that they guarded their Judaism. Because they were living in Arab countries, they had to guard their religion. They did not marry a *goy* [a non-Jewish person], no way. Paradise (*Gan HaEden*) was close to the Euphrates and Tigris, where the tastiest fruits were. I tell my children that according to the Bible, the border of Israel runs from the Euphrates and Tigris to Lebanon in the north and the other border to Jordan.

Shosa expressed nostalgia for a specific place and time. Living in Iraq, her family had engaged in previous global 'flows' and cosmopolitan networks, while protecting their religion against external influence. Shosa seemed confident that her son would not abandon his Jewish identity even though he lived the American dream. The references to relatives in the USA and England, invoking an idealised past in Babylon and exaggerating about her connections to an outside world, perhaps indicated a need to downplay the structural impact of the Israeli ethnocracy on her own position in Israeli society. Faced with both hardship and mobility caused by neoliberal globalisation, Shosa fashioned herself as a nostalgic yet cosmopolitan guardian of the expanding settler state.

## CONCLUSION

The development towns of its frontier regions have been glorified by the Ashkenazi elite since the founding of the State of Israel for they function as part of a spatial practice of controlling territory and peripheral populations. The peripheral yet central position of Mizrahim in the national project is an outcome of settler colonialism and has intensified with changes caused by neoliberal globalisation. In Kiryat Shemona, the shift from a socialist to a neoliberal society, the salience of immigration and the Jewish–Arab Palestinian conflict have created an 'overheating effect' that has heightened the precariousness of identity, resulting in increased nationalist fervour, nostalgia and cynicism, all of which are typical responses to accelerated change. In times of crisis, border Mizrahim were moved by state officials from the margins to the centre of the Israeli nation in the image of frontier guardians. The marginalised position of Mizrahim in Israel's ethnocracy, yet their central importance to a militarised frontier ethos, might explain why Mizrahi critiques of the effects of neoliberal policies and the Ashkenazi elite have in some cases veered toward an embrace of ethno-nationalism. In response to ordinary insecurity, residents created a local identity around heroic steadfastness, fashioning themselves into resilient guardians of the nation's borders.

Simultaneously, several research participants felt strongly connected to the country where they were born or from which their ancestors came, thus challenging the image of rootedness emphasised in the Israeli state's rhetoric. Mizrahim emphasised global connections both as a form of cosmopolitan capital, emphasising connections to the outside world, and as a strategy to reduce a sense of entrapment. Transnational orientations were not necessarily accompanied by the weakening of national identity, but rather by challenges to that identity's dominant nature. Identifying with the nation or other places beyond its borders through talk or practice allowed Mizrahim to negotiate their structurally entrapped position within Israel's ethnocracy. Moreover, it seemed to counter the tension between Zionism's esteemed valuation of frontier settlements and their actual deprivation. The (trans)national identity responses to insecurity both challenges and sustains ethnocratic boundaries.

In one way, the Mizrahi residents of Kiryat Shemona have very much internalised the national project. There is a strong commitment to the project of Israel as a Jewish state, and suspicion of non-Jews and those who are questionably Jewish. At the same time, nostalgia for places of origin and belonging and inclusion outside Israel contain elements of a critique of the state project. One strand is a critique of the Ashkenazi elite; one is of other sorts of relationships with non-Jews; another is a longing for the earlier socialist political movements characterised by greater egalitarianism, entailing a critique of the economic policies of the central government. Taken together, these are subtle forms of critique of the status quo embedded in discourses and practices that in many respects remain nationalist and exclusionary.

## REFERENCES

Appadurai, A. 1996. *Modernity at Large: Cultural Dimensions of Globalisation.* Minneapolis: University of Minnesota Press.

Chetrit, S. 2000 Mizrahi Politics in Israel: Between Integration and Alternatives. *Journal of Palestine Studies* 29(4): 51–6.

Donnan, H., and T.M. Wilson (eds). 2001. *Borders: Frontiers of Identity, Nation and State.* Oxford: Berg.

Eriksen, T.H. 2016. *Overheating: The Anthropology of Accelerated Change.* London: Pluto Press.

Halevi-Wise, Y. 2001. Ethics and Aesthetics of Memory in Contemporary Mizrahi Literature. *Journal of Israeli History* 20(1): 49–66.

Jean-Klein, I. 2001. Nationalism and Resistance: The Two Faces of Everyday Activism in Palestine during the Intifada. *Cultural Anthropology* 16(1): 83–126.

Katz, C. 2007. Banal Terrorism: Spatial Fetishism and Everyday Insecurity. In D. Gregory and A. Pred (eds), *Violent Geographies: Fear, Terror, and Political Violence*. New York: Routledge, pp.349–61.

Lavie, S. 1996. Blowups in the Borderzone: Third World Israeli Authors' Gropings for Home. In S. Lavie and T. Swedenburg (eds), *Displacement, Diaspora, and Geographies of Identity*. Durham, NC: Duke University Press, pp.55–96.

Lehmann, D., and B. Siebzehner. 2006. *Remaking Israeli Judaism: The Challenge of Shas*. London: Hurst.

Nitzan, J., and S. Bichler. 2002. *The Global Political Economy of Israel*. London: Pluto Press.

Norton, A. 1993. *Reflections on Political Identity*. Baltimore: Johns Hopkins University Press.

Ram, U. 2003. Postnationalist Pasts: The Case of Israel. In J. Olick (ed.), *States of Memory: Continuities, Conflicts, and Transformations in National Retrospection*. Durham, NC: Duke University Press, pp. 513–45.

Remennick, L. 2007. *Russian Jews on Three Continents: Identity, Integration and Conflict*. New Brunswick, NJ: Transaction Publishers.

Sa'ar, A. 2006. Feminine Strength: Reflections on Power and Gender in Israeli-Palestinian Culture. *Anthropological Quarterly* 79(3): 397–431.

Shafir, G., and Y. Peled. 2002. *Being Israeli: The Dynamics of Multiple Citizenship*. Cambridge: Cambridge University Press.

Shenhav, Y. 2006. *A Postcolonial Reading of Nationalism, Religion and Ethnicity*. Stanford: Stanford University Press.

Shiblak, A. 2005. *Iraqi Jews: A History of Mass Exodus*. London: Saqi Books.

Shindler. C. 2008. *A History of Modern Israel*. Cambridge: Cambridge University Press.

Standing, G. 2014. *The Precariat: The New Dangerous Class*. London: Bloomsbury.

Strathern, M. 1995. Nostalgia and the New Genetics. In D. Battaglia (ed.), *Rhetorics of Self-Making*. Berkeley: University of California Press, pp.97–120.

Tsipman, H. 1953. *Al HaDerech Sheli* [On my road]. Unpublished manuscript, Museum of Local History, Kiryat Shemona.

Tzfadia, E. 2007. Public Policy and Identity Formation: The Experience of Mizrahim in Israel's Development Town. *Journal for the Study of Sephardi and Mizrahi Jewry* 1(1): 57–82.

Ye'or, B. 2005. *Eurabia: The Euro–Arab Axis*. Madison, WI: Fairleigh Dickinson University Press.

Yiftachel, O. 2006. *Ethnocracy, Land and Identity Politics in Israel/Palestine*. Pittsburgh: University of Pennsylvania Press.

# 7. Cultural Wounding and Healing

## Change as Ongoing Cultural Production in a Remote Indigenous Australian Community

*Amanda Kearney*

Recollections of frontier violence resonate through the trauma narratives of ethnic groups across the world. For those Indigenous populations that have survived colonial violence and found their social and cultural geographies existing within the contact zone, the experience has triggered varied cultural responses. Ranging from simmering agitation to overheating in the most aggressive of cases, responses often bring with them a realisation that things will never be the same again. Rapid cultural change or the slowing down and discontinuation of long held cultural practices can trigger profound reflexivity. With quiet and individual reflection or public and political group dissent and resistance, there emerges a mindfulness that agonises over the threat or reality of cultural change and its implications for group identity. Realising that one is undergoing a process of change raises questions as to what the group might now be and how they progress into a future that can safeguard the lives and hopes of their descendants.

The speeding up and slowing down of culture that comes with cultural wounding and the anxieties of survival as both a sadness and a joy is vividly illustrated through Indigenous Australian cross-generational narratives of cultural change born of the contact moment. The 'overheating' effect of cultural wounding is such that wounding acts are often cataclysmic enough as to demand identity reconstitution if not remaking for those who suffer harm. At the very least they prompt shifts in the cultural habit of the group, as expressed through the epistemological, ontological and axiological structures of life. Change may be imposed upon the cultural group as they are drawn into contact zones, yet it may also be what ensures ethnic and cultural survival, thus complicating the notion that all change is necessarily enforced in contact spaces. Accepting change can be part of an accommodating project or a creative response to the present needs and future desires of the group. This complicates a vision of violence and wounding as catalysts for cultural decline and inevitable fracture.

In this chapter, I hope to unravel this complication further, through a discussion of cultural wounding and healing, raising the possibility that change is not only the difficult consequence of culture contact and inter-ethnic tension but may also be a vital part of ongoing cultural productions when living in frontier zones and across contested spaces. Change is envisioned as a form of motivated action, a glittering indicator of ongoing cultural production and dynamic habitus in the everyday. So too it may be indicative of control, in which degrees of change are modulated and interacted with, not merely passively received. Approached in this way, we might inch closer to realising the implications of change (accelerated or not), and more importantly might begin to appreciate the ways that people themselves not only respond to change, but might be in control of its pace and impact.

Methodologically, this chapter concerns the experiences of those who are historically and structurally oppressed after generations of 'cultural wounding'. Collaborating with Indigenous groups in Australia I have witnessed the effects of cultural wounding, listened to the form it takes in narratives of personal and group experiences and watched it manifest itself in lifestyle and cultural changes. Alongside the experience of hardship has persisted the condition of survival, marked by a capacity to 'get on with things'. Through collaborative research with Yanyuwa families in the south-west Gulf of Carpentaria, northern Australia, I have explored the condition of being a 'saltwater person', reflecting on how this might have changed over time, and in light of cultural wounding and healing in a settler colonial context.

Travelling through saltwater country[1] with younger and middle generation Yanyuwa has revealed that relationships to Indigenous law and homelands are sometimes marked by conditions of fear, nervousness and uncertainty. Not classically held to be dispositions of a 'proper' saltwater (or Indigenous) person, these reveal the process by which generations differentially go about placing themselves into country and healing in the aftermath of cultural wounding. These anxieties, whilst certainly

---

1. 'Country' is a term used by many Indigenous Australian language groups to refer to their homelands as made up of land, sea, bodies of water, kin and resources. It is a holistic term. Rose describes it further as an 'Aboriginal English term', an 'area associated with a human social group, and with all the plants, animals, landforms, waters, songlines, and sacred sites within its domain. It is homeland in the mode of kinship: the enduring bonds of solidarity that mark relationships between human and animal kin also mark the relationships between creatures and their country' (Rose 2014: 435). The term 'country' is often used by Indigenous Australians to refer to their homelands. These land and sea territories were created by ancestral beings and are inscribed with the bodies, markers and laws of these creation beings. 'Country' and 'homelands' are the preferred terms throughout this chapter as they convey Indigenous ownership and authority.

linked to the overheating effects generated by settler colonialism, must be read as more complicated in their origins and cultural significance. Undeniably, settler colonialism brings with it agents of change that often go unmitigated in their assault on Indigenous lives and cultures. Yet, what I hope to highlight here is that cultural habits change not only as a result of cultural wounding, and the changes which do occur need not be detrimental to group survival and well-being. This will be illustrated by reference to the shifting terrain that supports a sense of being Yanyuwa and a 'proper' saltwater person. Even when triggered by the overheating effects of settler colonialism and when the pace of change is unprecedented, Indigenous groups still culturally modulate the effect, and continue to configure relationships with one another, and with their homelands and ancestors, on distinct epistemological and ontological terms.

## CULTURAL WOUNDING AND INDIGENOUS AUSTRALIA

Australia is a settler colonial nation with a history of cultural wounding against the Indigenous nations that predate and have survived British settlement. The nations that make up Indigenous Australia include distinct ethnic groups that claim ancestry along linguistic and ancestral lines. Prior to the arrival of the British in 1788, there were over 250 distinct Indigenous languages mapping onto as many diverse ethnic groups (McConvell & Thieberger 2001: 16). Acts of cultural wounding have significantly diminished this number, and been directed at the social fabric that holds these groups together, as well as the biological relations that have allowed populations to endure. That the legacy of this wounding is felt today is undeniable. As an anthropologist I began working with Indigenous Australians in the late 1990s. I arrived in a remote community at a time when languages were already classified as dying, where land had been alienated and day-to-day life was vastly different to the ethnographies of the past fifty years. Young people had more interest in hip-hop than songlines and ceremony. Cross-generational tensions were awash and elders struggled to find conversational partners to speak of the world in their own language. Since that time I have seen children become adults, adults become elders and elders sadly pass away. For each generational group there is a clear sense of what it means to be Yanyuwa. Whilst elders may speak of the loss of culture, few middle or younger generations feel that the future lies in salvaging its remnants. Most recognise that life today is different, yet some things are non negotiable and must remain an omnipresent part of life. The nexus of ancestry, country, kinship and law holds every Yanyuwa in a web of meaning, yet the effects of cultural wounding have shifted the

*Table 7.1*   Examples of cultural wounding. Adapted from Kearney (2014).

| Kinship, Biogenetics and Cultural Wounding | Kinship, Social Fabric and Cultural Wounding |
|---|---|
| Genocide, including child removal | Cultural genocide and ethnic cleansing |
| Forced sterilisation | Individualism and neoliberalism |
| Enslavement and possession | Forced relocation, population transfer |
| Rape and sexual violence | Theft of land and sea territories |
| Anti-miscegenation law | Designification of home |
| Institutionalisation and imprisonment | Enforcing universal family and societal law |
| Blood quantum, chromatic inventories of skin colour, genetic testing | Constitutional and prescriptive erasure of social and political presence |
| Epidemics | Criminalising identity and cultural expressions |

There is significant crossover in terms of the effects of cultural wounding. Wounding enacted on biogenetic kinship will have an impact on the social fabric that holds ethnic groups together, and potentially vice versa. The distinction made here does not diminish this relational impact but rather aims to highlight the initial target for wounding.

way this nexus is understood across generations and how it is embodied in everyday life.

In an attempt to better understand the conditions of everyday life in a remote Indigenous community I have turned to the concept of cultural wounding (Kearney 2014). Cultural wounding, in the midst of ethnic conflict and in a settler colonial context, is a deliberate process with intended consequences. It is the rupture and assault of culture in physical, emotional and ideological senses. Inspired by Cook et al. (2003: 18), cultural wounding is taken as the violation of persons and their cultural lives through insult and injury, motivated by the desire to destroy or significantly harm this culture and its bearers. Forms of wounding are achieved through attacks on kinship, with kinship configured as a vast suite of meaningful relationships that people might establish with relational others, including humans and non-humans, places, ancestral beings and otherly agents (see Table 7.1).[2] Pathways to wounding cultural esteem, group solidarity and physical endurance are often sought through actions that attack relationships of importance.

---

2. This is a deliberately open view of kinship, which articulates more accurately Indigenous perceptions of the relational world, as made up of more than human beings. For Indigenous Australians, kinship is pervasive as an ordering device in the world, and brings people into meaningful relationships with non-human animals and flora, places and ancestral beings as otherly agents that exist in the world. For a more expansive discussion of kinship in these terms, see Battiste & Henderson (2000), Cajete (2000), Rose (2000) and Kearney (2016).

This may be an assault on the lands and waters, which matter most to a group, the denial of ancestral narratives, which substantiate group existence, the theft of children or the killing of non-human animals that exist as both resources and important kin for a cultural group.

Cultural wounding, whilst inflicting injury upon people and their relational worlds, manifests in the human psyche as insult or anguish for the recipients of cultural and actual violence. It finds its pathways by attacking the biological connections that bond members of ethnic groups as well as through the deconstruction of networks that lead to social kinship and sites of shared meaning for the group. Strategies for cultural wounding in ethnic contact zones involve acts such as genocide, forced relocation and the taking of lands and resources (see Kearney 2014). In turn, acts such as these are capable of instating ideologies that support racism and stigmatisation (see Table 7.1). Cultural wounding of this kind erupts from structures of assumed and real power, embodied by moments in which the powerful act intently upon those positioned as marginal, vulnerable or undesirable.

Cultural wounding is one part of a broader set of outcomes, which may be triggered by 'overheating' as an experience of cultural contact gone wrong, or prefaced on methods of violent expansion. Thus in the context of this chapter, overheating is understood as a climactic moment in which things substantially change, as illustrated by colonial expansion into Indigenous territories across Australia. Never benign, colonialism and colonial expansion are overheating events (both rapid and enduring) that bring elements together on terms that involve the threat of and actual change. In most cases, and as history attests, one element will struggle to prevail amid the conditions of rapid change (the Indigenous presence), whilst the powerful incoming agent, which sets the terms for change, begins to flourish (the invading colonial presence).

Across Australia, the overheating effects of cultural wounding have not been the same for all Indigenous groups. While for some the loss has been profound, as entire populations and families were killed, for others there has been a slow and gradual decline of language and cultural expressions followed by revitalisation in recent years (Roberts 2005; Babidge 2010; Hobson et al. 2010).[3] In order to localise this discussion

---

3. There are a vast number of sources that detail the experiences of cultural wounding across Indigenous language groups and communities in Australia. These three have been selected as illustrative of the diverse experiences concerning wounding and healing, as they recount the effects of colonisation on kinship, family life, language and culture. They convey the atrocities of genocide, linguicide, violence and state paternalism, yet also vividly recall Indigenous language and cultural revivals, the power and pervasiveness of kinship and the importance of social memory for Indigenous groups in Australia today.

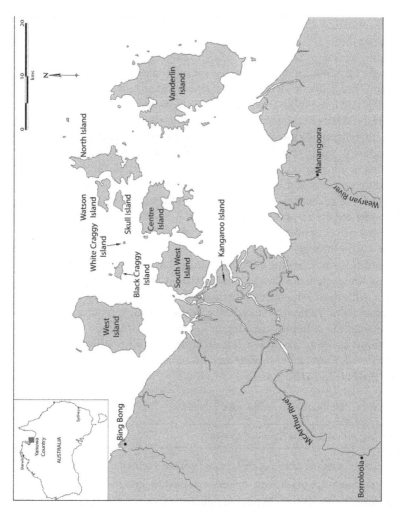

*Figure 7.1*  Yanyuwa homelands, northern Australia. Source: Brady (2014).

I turn to Borroloola, in northern Australia, and the experiences of Yanyuwa families (see Figure 7.1). Yanyuwa are li-Anthawirriyarra – saltwater people of the south-west Gulf of Carpentaria. They have survived historical and recent episodes of cultural wounding, and carry significant social memories of violence. So too, they have for generations identified actions to bring about healing within their community.

Dominating the Yanyuwa healing agenda have been actions that operate through a 'in-order-to' logic (Schütz 1976). Inspired by Schütz's writing on action (Schütz 1970, 1982), healing is approached as purposive conduct grounded in the interpretive consciousness of the individual and group. This action has its horizons of relevance and relatedness to a social reality, and it has motivation. Part of this motivation is faith in what will be realised after the action is undertaken, namely a projected outcome of health, burgeoning esteem for young generations or secured rights and equality. But part of it is also linked to the retention of memory from events or experiences past. These distinctions orient the healing action in different ways and highlight two kinds of motivation: 'because' and 'in order to' (Schütz 1976: 11). 'Because' motives refer to past or already-experienced events as the cause of action. A 'because' motive for healing is what drives demands for national apologies, the restitution of lands and waters through legislative process, and truth commissions. Viewed deterministically, healing undertaken in light of a 'because' motive places those who seek to heal in a particular relationship with their past and, in turn, with those who have perpetrated violence and cultural wounding against them. Actions prefaced by a 'because' motive require stepping back into the cultural wounding experience, and therefore reinstating relations between the often politically strong and the politically weak or oppressed. Examples of healing actions motivated by a 'because' motive are presented in Table 7.2.

Table 7.2   Healing based on 'because' motives.

| Healing Action Based in 'Because' Motives |
| --- |
| Resistance, warfare, rebellion, civil disobedience and activism |
| Seeking restitution of land and sea territories through legislative processes |
| Requesting national apologies and recognition of wrongs and suffering |
| Establishing national days of mourning |
| Seeking justice through truth commissions and inquiries |
| Establishing reconciliation councils and forums for policy consultation |
| Contesting historical narratives, revisionist histories and nationalist dogma |

'In-order-to' motives, on the other hand, are aligned with anticipated outcomes and are underscored by a desire to move onward rather than enact stasis that relies on the past. In other words, cultural wounding is recognised and acknowledged as a vital step in coping with or living with accelerated change without negating the fact that such change has occurred. It is through reflexivity that one imagines a project as completed, and this projection is configured as survival and states of healing. The 'in-order-to' motive of projection separates the wounded from the attacker, thus creating a space in which self-determination is not dependent on what the powerful might do or say. These identities disrupt the centrality of wounding, so too they often disrupt normative views on how things should be and take back control of the healing project (see Table 7.3). Yanyuwa approaches to healing have heavily aligned with 'in-order-to' motives, in particular those actions that invigorate identity through acceptance of change, esteem building among young people and diminished reliance on measures of 'ethnic purity'.

*Table 7.3*    Healing based on 'in-order-to' motives.

| Healing Action Based on 'In-Order-To' Motives |
| --- |
| Fostering organisational affiliations, social kinship and establishing new terms for ethnic loyalty |
| Invigorating identity through acceptance of change; accepting a new habitus as part of ongoing cultural production |
| Diminishing reliance on 'tradition', 'aesthetic' or linguistic measures of ethnic 'purity' |
| Harnessing creative and performing arts forums for identity assertion |
| Launching independent broadcasting platforms for autonomy of voice |
| Creating youth mentoring and youth excellence programmes and leadership institutes |
| Self-determining through sovereignty or self-governance |

Illustrative of this mode of healing have been several projects that have sought to control the terms by which people heal. Such commitments are expressed through youth mentoring and leadership programmes, creative arts and digital animation projects aimed at recording and presenting ancestral knowledge to young people in new ways, and via interactive forums (see Bradley et al. 2011; Kearney et al. 2012). Healing motivated by a future outcome of strength underscores these, and also a diminished reliance on tradition or linguistic measures of Yanyuwaness. This has come about largely in response to the reintegration of kin who were forcibly removed by government agents (as Stolen Generations; see Commonwealth of Australia 1997, Moses 2004, Read 1999), institutionalised or educated away from their homelands. So too, it has proved essential for building esteem among those younger generations who have been raised in a largely English-speaking social world and educational context. Independent radio broadcasting, music, film-making and an Indigenous sea ranger programme have also become avenues for shaping and expressing a Yanyuwa identity in the present and into the future. Many of these healing actions are directed at the well being of young people, and awareness of generational habitus is strong in this community and expressed through the design and objectives of several healing initiatives.

## BEING YANYUWA IN A CHANGING WORLD

There is no simple or correct way of being Indigenous or being in a relationship with kin and country,[4] yet the experiences born of settler colonialism and cultural wounding have left many Indigenous Australians deemed to be paradoxically situated somewhere between the 'traditional' (authentic) and the 'divergent' (inauthentic) (Povinelli 2002). These registers, most often implemented by the ethnic majority and those who wound, distil to allegations of being either inside or outside of culture. Change as a vital part of Indigenous cultures has been under-appreciated and undervalued.[5] Appreciating that change occurs in contexts of cultural wounding and healing is central to this discussion (Kearney 2014). Yet it is change as much more than decline and loss that stands as a vivid reminder of ongoing and deliberate cultural production.

Since the earliest periods of colonisation (around 1886), the conditions for transmitting and safeguarding Yanyuwa ways of life and law have been challenged. This has led to a shift in the way different generations express their identity. Colonisation induced cultural wounding and impacted significantly on Yanyuwa lives, leaving its mark on each generation in some way or another. Settler colonialism causes particular forms of overheating that manifest as wounding, and in the context of Yanyuwa country this has been achieved through land, sea and resource theft, forced removal and alienation from home territories, child removal, stigmatisation of cultural practices and languages, imposition of non-Indigenous governance structures, educational and social disadvantage

---

4. Being 'in a relationship with country' conveys a sense of emplacement whereby a person is not only in a relationship with their ancestral territories but also the social, political and economic elements these contain.

5. For exceptions, see Russell (2006), Andrews & Buggey (2008) and Cowlishaw (2010, 2011, 2012).

and poverty through powerlessness (ibid.). From these experiences people have had to heal and through deliberate action protect their kin and capacity to prevail as a cultural group. This has generated within the community a powerful need to protect self and group against imposed change by striving to slow down the rapidity of its impact. Attempts are routinely made to slow down the pace and nature of such change by committing to efforts of ancestral knowledge transfer, securing land rights to ensure economic and cultural practices can prevail and adapting the broader sense of what it means to be li-Anthawirriyarra in an ever-changing world.

Healing efforts are expressed vividly through the grounded and deliberate action that is the broader habitus within this community. Healing as a habitual practice that marks survival and most importantly endurance 'is an action that resists hopelessness and helplessness' (ibid.: 8). 'Understood as a process marked by acts that increase the effectiveness of recovery, healing from cultural wounding requires resilience to absorb and expand with the ever changing terms of daily life, and resistance to hopelessness in the aftermath of wounding' (ibid.: 72). In the aftermath or in the midst of cultural wounding, healing works to regenerate and proliferate the benefits of 'being an ethnic constituent'. Hope, born of recovery, is a fundamental aspect of this vision of healing (Staub et al. 2005: 305). It requires kinship to establish the social relations and parameters by which identities can be understood and taken into periods of recuperation. Through kinship, the terms of healing are established, with a sense of what the group can legitimately become and what it desires to be (see Kearney 2014).

Let me turn now to a discussion of Yanyuwa generational wounding and healing experiences, beginning with the words of a Yanyuwa elder, Old Pyro Dirdiyalma:

> Yes, I am telling you these things, the Aboriginal people who belong to this place Borroloola, we are now low down, the speakers of Yanyuwa, we are a long way down. The other people such as the Wilangarra and the Binbingka, they no longer exist, they are all dead. The white people, they are high above us, the language and their ways of acting have climbed up above us and they have smothered our languages and our culture completely. This is the way it now is.

In 2013, Yanyuwa elder Roddy Harvey Bayuma-Birribalanja narrated her position in the world as *Rrinkyunya-nganji, ruthu ngarna, a-karing-uthundanga waliwaliyanguyu*: 'I am another kind of person, a woman from the north, from the islands'. For Yanyuwa, kinship is everything, for it locates an individual within a world of meaning and ensures the possibility of maintaining a sense of being Yanyuwa into the future. Roddy's declaration reflects the Yanyuwa practice of declaring ethnic consciousness. Central to this identity is the distinction that they are li-Anthawirriyarra, people of the sea. When asked what it means to be Yanyuwa today, Roddy stated, 'It's law, *kujika* (songlines), language and country, without that you've got nothing'. It is a fear of 'nothing' remaining that preoccupies the concerns of many elders in the community today. In particular, they worry that young people will end up with no real sense of what it means to be Yanyuwa, a threat posed most heavily by dominant white educational experiences and town-based lifestyles and influences.

For elders, relationships to their homelands are defined by ancestral law and governing systems of knowledge, conveyed through language, ceremony and kinship (Bradley et al. 2005; Bradley 2010; Yanyuwa Families and Bradley 2016). Indigenous testimony and ethnography have shown that for the present generation of elders the depth of this knowledge is considerable, and reflects their apprehension of the law for country and ancestral connections. Elders speak of hearing country and longing for it.[6] A frequently cited concern is that 'country is lonely' and empty of kin, a reality traced to the forced removal of people and relocation to Borroloola Township after 1901. Present-day elders hold social memories of life before the overbearing presence of state paternalism that defines Yanyuwa experiences today and can recall the violence of frontier encounters. It is tracing this history of cultural wounding that leads them to lament the passing of a time when country was full up with people, resonating with the sounds of children and laughter, fighting, ceremony, song and language.[7] Country in this form is often referred to as 'lifted up' (Rose 1996).[8] The lack of such presences in the aftermath of frontier violence and pervading deep colonising[9] is a source of sadness and a catalyst for remarks that convey a sense of country being 'low down' – meaning without potency and strength, and 'closed up' – meaning apprehensive of people who enter and are potentially distant to those kin who do (ibid.).[10] In the generationally specific encounter of life, the overriding theme for elders is one of realising kinship with country and apprehending the law it contains. This law informs language, place names, ancestral narratives and songlines as

---

6. John Bradley (personal communication, 2014).

7. John Bradley (personal communication, 2014).

8. The point was also made to me by John Bradley (personal communication, 2014).

9. For a discussion of 'deep colonising' in Australia, see Bradley & Seton (2005).

10. This point was also made to me by John Bradley (personal communication, 2014).

well as aspects of the ecology that concerns bush medicine, food sources and a capacity to read and interpret natural phenomena (Povinelli 1993; Kearney & Bradley 2014). Being more closely attuned to this law ensures that elders are capable of finding pathways that fully immerse them in country and align them with the ancestors.

For middle-generation Yanyuwa, their social memories of cultural wounding are less intimately tied to periods of a pre-colonial way of life, nor direct colonial expansion and frontier violence. Instead, they are linked to everyday struggles, which involve fighting a different presence. This presence takes the form of state paternalism, along with the social dysfunction and depression that has become embedded with diagnoses of social ills and the hopelessness often assumed symptomatic of Indigenous community life (Kearney 2014). What these generations heal from are assumptions of terminal suffering, which, in the eyes of the Australian state, are evidenced by 'cultural loss and decline'. Depicted as an 'Indigenous problem', the struggles of daily life are treated by the state and many of the white majority as divorced from the cultural wounding that settler colonialism brought about. For those in their middle years, relationships to country and law are often embroiled in an experience of hardship, distance and uncertainty, born of habits formed through town life and significant lifestyle changes supported by welfare dependency, alienation from homelands and resulting poverty.

Many Yanyuwa aged between 30 and 50 have moved through non-Indigenous education programmes yet not at the expense of time spent learning from their elders. Most have spent periods of time working away from their community, but have also had experiences of country that involved extended visits during school holidays, and more recently travel across sea territories for the giving of evidence in land claims.[11] Structures that remain pervasive in the lives of those in their middle age pivot around kinship, ever-growing knowledge of ancestral narratives and a sense of responsibility in guiding younger generations in their becoming Yanyuwa. With age often comes the desire to learn more and be in possession of more expansive knowledge as shared by elders, as their Yanyuwa identity becomes a site of strength and empowerment. This has led to efforts aimed at reinstating relationships to country through the local Indigenous sea ranger programme, or the taking up of creative arts practices such as painting, singing and songwriting as a means of expressing knowledge of sea country and ancestral narratives.

11. Yanyuwa were heavily engaged in land claims, under the Aboriginal Land Rights Act (Northern Territory) 1976, during the mid and late 1990s. Much of this continued into the early 2000s. In 2006 they were granted exclusive title and land rights over an extensive portion of their island and coastal sea territories.

Re-engaging with country and law, through the lens of their own life experiences and out of choice is illustrative of their emerging into a stronger sense of being Yanyuwa. Those in their middle age have an archive of experience relative to daily life, apprehend the legacy of cultural wounding and ongoing cultural shift and a vision of an aspirational future in which the younger generations will ultimately come to look at them as elders.

For Yanyuwa youth, their ethnicity is not simply about recovering or mimicking traditions from the past, nor is it as heavily dependent on negotiating two worlds (Indigenous and non-Indigenous), as has been the case for middle generations. Most young people's lives have been heavily shaped by outside influences, whether through education, television, music or online contexts. A vital question for young people in Borroloola is: Why be Yanyuwa? In essence, ancestry matters only if it is useful for young people. This utility may be traced to how it helps people feel good about themselves, how it helps to explain a set of experiences, how it might help develop a sense of one's political identity or generate benefits and self-worth. For many young Yanyuwa,[12] relationships to their homelands and ancestors are characterised by a sense of inherentness, distance and curiosity. They are inherently linked to both, in that all young people are capable of being placed in a clan-based relationship with their sea territories and law by virtue of birthright and kinship. Beyond this they interact with such rights in distinctively young and emerging ways, in that discussions of law are reluctantly had and often inflected with a sense of uncertainty and shyness. Aware of this emerging apprehension, it is often the case that young people only begin to confidently interact with or express their knowledge of ancestry, law and country when free from the context of town. When travelling across country with extended kin groups, an enlivened sense of confidence commonly emerges, curiosity increases and children learn at a faster pace. This is due, in part, to the experiential nature of the learning encounter during these moments. In contrast, the mainstream school classroom and pressures of town life often inhibit free articulation of growing knowledge and confidence among young people.

---

12. By 'younger Yanyuwa' I am referring to those under the age of 30. There are of course significant lifestyle differences for those in their infancy, teens and twenties, yet what links these age groups resoundingly are the conditions of everyday life in Borroloola that have been in place since around the mid 1980s. Since this time, mainstream white education has dominated, almost no employment opportunities have emerged, contemporary youth and popular culture influences have fully entered the vernacular and aesthetics of everyday life, and use of Yanyuwa language has all but declined, with only five full-time speakers remaining.

Today, life is heavily town-based, which leads to a degree of distance in a physical sense and sometimes difficulty in attaching personal and experiential meaning to country (Kearney & Bradley 2014). This can lead to young people feeling unsure and to a degree distant in their accommodation of country and law for purposes of identity affirmation. Actual visits to country do occur, although rarely and most often in conjunction with shorter family trips on weekends, or during community festivals and events (ibid.). Young people are thus primarily building knowledge in new ways and via new forums for information sharing, including digital media and animation, story books, films and contemporary music. When obtained via such media, knowledge is acquired in less predictable ways and relies heavily on elders and parents not only to share information but make it relevant to the lives and world-views of young people today. Young people learn in new ways, which not only reflect but reinforce a distinct cultural habit that conveys generational personhood.

For young people, the motivation to be strong and healthy in their ethnic identity is about having this new habitus accepted as a legitimate way of being Yanyuwa. That this is recognised by elders and middle generation Yanyuwa as well as the wider Borroloola community is central to the development of esteem in young people. The same can be said for Indigenous people across Australia who have, through forces of cultural wounding, found new ways to enact their Indigeneity. This includes members of the Stolen Generations and others who have been raised far from their homelands and without networks of kin to support their enculturation.[13] Recognising multiplicities in what it means to be Indigenous in Australia today is a pressing demand made of the Australian state, including its populace and political leaders (Keen 1988; Beckett 1998; Cowlishaw 2010, 2011, 2012; Heiss 2012). While the young have some understanding of historical wounding as it has been distilled as social memory over time, in many respects it is remote from their present lives. Whether this is repressive erasure, structural amnesia or forgetting in order to constitute a new identity (see Connerton 2008), what ethnography reveals is that younger Yanyuwa strive to find the space to constitute their ethnic identity. They do not disavow their Yanyuwaness, yet recognise that their way of being Yanyuwa requires flexibility in the definitional limits of what this identity might be and how it might be

---

13. The Stolen Generations refers to generations of Indigenous Australian children, young boys and girls, who were forcibly taken away from their families from the late 1800s up to the 1970s by colonial administrators, the church and government agencies. Children were forcibly removed and placed in institutionalised care (see CoA 1997; Read 1999; Moses 2004). The Stolen Generations are also made up of the children of children who were forcibly removed, and who were never able to track their ancestry and locate their communities of kin (Read 1999: xi).

expressed through cultural habit. By spending some time with the idea of changing habitus I now reflect, in finer detail, on how wounding as a catalyst for overheating may be slowed or interrupted by way of healing actions that invigorate identity through the acceptance of change.

## APPRECIATING CHANGE IN RELATIONSHIPS TO COUNTRY AND HABITUAL PRACTICE

Habitus can change as part of a self-conscious effort and also as part of a wider response to events and experiences. As Navarro comments, habitus 'is created through a social, rather than individual process leading to patterns that are enduring and transferable from one context to another, but that also shift in relation to specific contexts and over time'; furthermore, it 'is not fixed or permanent, and can be changed under unexpected situations or over a long historical period' (Navarro 2006: 16). As profound experiences of 'change under unexpected circumstance', cultural wounding and healing trigger changes in habitus. Induced by the dramatic loss of kin and destruction of one's social matrix, an experience of deep wounding and trauma increases the likelihood of a cultural habit having to respond and potentially shift, both in its constitutive parts of physical behaviour, cognitive perception and understanding as well as axiological and spiritual encounters. Reflective not of decline, or habitual shift out of desperate necessity, this is better understood as a redirection or the finding of new pathways in the making and sustaining of self and group through cultural habit.

Earlier models of relatedness between the self, ancestry, law and country may no longer apply for younger generations as they encounter a different cultural universe that grants them less access to certain forms of knowledge and law but greater access to others (for example, the knowledge conveyed by a series of digital animations, contemporary music, or images of country via Google Earth). In which case, habitual relations with ancestry and country may come to be experienced through less intimate ways of knowing which may lead to feelings of uncertainty, fear or nervousness when interacting with law and country. A relationship still undeniably exists yet it does not exhibit the deep immersion and confidence that elders may have in their relationships to law and country. This is not uncommon for some middle generation Yanyuwa, but it is far more common for younger generations. Whilst elders may feel at home in country, having travelled it extensively over the life course and being in possession of insider knowledge that assists in the reading of country and understanding its law, middle and younger generations in particular do not yet, or may not ever, have access to such information. A realisation of this may lead to feelings of shame

– an insidious effect of cultural wounding – or it may also lead to the construction of new knowledge or acceptance of new elements in the people, law and country relationship. Constructions of new knowledge are necessitated by a Yanyuwa emphasis on 'being in a relationship with country', yet the way this relationship may be instated depends on the cultural habit of each generation.

Middle and younger generations may experience an outsider-like status and sense of distance when travelling across their homelands. These feelings can lead to a sense of incongruity between insider status as inherently Yanyuwa and outsider feelings as one without a particular set of cultural understandings (see Relph 1976; Seamon 1996). In contexts where persons are left reeling from the violence of cultural wounding, both insider and outsider experiences such as these may be encountered by an individual in the same moment. Traced to the often rapid decline of populations or sudden cessation of cultural practices and interruption of means for knowledge transmission, cultural wounding is such that people might find themselves fully aware of who they are but incapable of enacting the cultural habitus that has always reinforced and maintained this identity. Healing actions may work to minimise the experience of outsideness, but this takes time and the right conditions in which to find connections between person and country, or person and knowledge and law. If conditions of wounding change the pace at which one can access insider knowledge of the ethnic group or in fact cause such knowledge to decline, then it is likely that intermediate states of uncertainty and possibly fear will be experienced, and from this new cultural habits emerge.

States of fear and uncertainty are strong indications of a relational encounter between self, law and country. Whilst fear and uncertainty convey something of the difficulty in proceeding towards an insider status, they express a desire to comprehend and therefore an emerging sense of becoming an insider. Fear is as much a part of relating as is love and abiding respect. For some, fear is triggered by the paradox of return – not fear of the 'known' or 'unknown' but something else, namely having to establish the terms of relatedness when not familiar with the mechanisms to do so. In the context of ethnography, I have seen fear expressed on many occasions.[14] When approaching homelands in the

---

14. I argue that this is a particular type of fear, namely propositional fear. This is a relational fear that 'need not be occurrent, and may have no physiological effect', yet it is directed at 'something'. It has attitudinal and cognitive components and thus lends itself to inscription through habitus; entails aversion and uncertainty, not a lack of understanding or knowledge; and can only be overcome with certainty acquired through gaining knowledge or changing the rules of relating (Davis 1987: 288–90).

Gulf of Carpentaria, young people and at times middle-generation Yanyuwa can find themselves engulfed by an unfamiliar perceptional scene. Drawing on their cultural habit, people attempt to make sense of what lies before them. At times the response may be one in which the possibility of danger and threat seem very real. People may refrain from entering a place, remarking on the possibility of danger and the presence of ever-watching ancestors. This should not be translated as country being dangerous of threatening; rather, that in the absence of full knowledge of law and how to engage with country, dangerous or threatening circumstances may arise. Mindfulness of this can trigger the emotion fear, in this case born of uncertainty and apprehension of distance. In such moments people may refrain from continuing further, or will nervously continue, sticking close to their elders, or attempt as best they can to orient their presence and 'sing out' to the old people, assuring them of their kinship and good intentions (Rose 1996; Bradley 2001). Very few young people will venture off alone in country, and for middle generations this caution is often expressed through statements such as: 'don't go there, it's not real safe', 'those old people might be watching', or the more indeterminate, yet telling expression, 'there might be something' (Povinelli 1993). Even in the aftermath of calamitous community events or unusual weather occurrences – a car accident, a powerful storm, a waterspout at sea or even a bad dream – people may attribute blame to careless behaviour on country or the discontent of the 'old people' (ancestors). The desire to translate meaning in country is pervasive across generations and reveals a deeply relational encounter that all Yanyuwa are capable of instating, irrespective of their capacity to fully translate meaning of what they may be witnessing or experiencing. The prevailing condition of wanting to relate and seeking pathways to know and be 'in country' is what ensures Yanyuwa of all ages are capable of constraining detriment, slowing down the impact of change and knowledge reconfiguration.

In each of these instances, fear motivates a type of connection, and even transition of the self from a fearful state to a knowing state through repeated exposure, changed behaviour or realisation of non-threat. Apprehension as uncertainty may be superseded when fear is countered by a degree of certainty in the relationship to one's ancestors, country and law. Certainty may come about through the acquisition of new knowledge or even changing the terms of relating, thus ensuring that the habitus one possesses makes more sense in place and time. Negotiating fear is part of healing as motivated action, but it is not done in isolation, and it often requires kin and members of the wider community to offer support and share knowledge and insight, as well accommodate themselves to new ways of being. The desire to connect with country and ancestors is evident, but the pathways to do this must be sought. Younger Yanyuwa locate these pathways through some of the healing actions present within the community and will, into the future, continue to seek additional pathways to achieve this. These may involve working with the li-Anthawirriyarra sea ranger unit, practising at the art or language centre, working to record songlines with elders for a commercial music venture, joining the local Australian-rules football, soccer or softball team, or organising events for law and culture festivals that occur nationally. If firmly held by kin and family networks, younger generation Yanyuwa are positioned to receive knowledge of law if they feel the need for it and if it fits with their habitus for being Yanyuwa. What they do with this knowledge and how they come to fill gaps in their cultural universe, however, is largely in their own hands and an effort shared among their contemporaries and peer groups. When in the company of their peers they find currency in their cultural habit, which assures them of who they are and increases the scope for what it means to be Yanyuwa in a changing, sometimes simmering, sometimes overheating world.

OVERVIEW

In this chapter I have sought to engage with the importance of change, even fear and uncertainty, as necessary dispositions in the making of a cultural and ethnic identity. Often complexities of this kind are denied those emerging from episodes of cultural wounding, thus rendering healed states as mere survivals plagued by fracture and deviation from a 'pure state of being'. Gaps in cultural knowledge or practice that may come to exist in light of cultural wounding are often interpreted as fissures through which people fall into a loss of identity. This discussion, therefore, responds, if only in brief, to needling questions: What happens when the wounded survive? And what happens when cultures undergo change? I suspect that things are more complicated than overheating as an acceleration of change taking people further away from what they once were. As agents capable of responding to cultural wounding, Indigenous Australians, and in particular Yanyuwa families, have at times controlled the pace of change and harnessed change in ways that ensure the resulting way of life has relevancy within the context of law and country. There is no doubt that cultural wounding can generate an overheating of significant proportions and strikes down hard upon people and their sense of esteem. Yet what cannot be denied are the capacities to survive and the motivation to once again thrive.

More than merely coping, Yanyuwa have maintained a strong commitment to healing, ensuring that community and family-based healing actions accommodate generational shifts in habitus. Healing takes place with the knowledge that things may never be as they once were. This is not defeated resignation, but rather the echoes of a reflexive awareness within the community that strength is not always found in holding onto cultural remnants and hoping for the best. Whilst elders protest to the pervasive power of law, ancestry, country and song, motivated action has ensured that this community is capable of recognising the distinct nature of generational habitus. This is partly a response to imposed change, and the realisation that Yanyuwa and the world in which they live is different today. Yet it is also an inherent quality that was always befitting of this community. There are epistemological and ontological structures in place which articulate a reality in which young people must move into their Yanyuwa identity over time, as they acquire knowledge and as they advance towards the ancestors which stand ahead of them, instructing them in their qualities as a saltwater person.

Whilst it might be easy to read this recognition of generational habitus as some form of sad realisation that mid generations and young people do not possess a strong grasp on being Yanyuwa, or that people are increasingly accommodating mainstream Australian societal and cultural practices and values, this is certainly not the case. What would be a more accurate reading of how generational distinctions come to exist and then come to be held by this community is a two-fold understanding. On the one hand, this is an entirely natural disposition which has always existed and is expressed epistemologically and ontologically through Yanyuwa law and culture; on the other, it is the effect of overheating, but not an effect so pervasive that Yanyuwa cannot accommodate it and negotiate change in somewhat controlled and modulated ways.

Accommodating new expressions, and understanding dispositions of fear, and even uncertainty in young people's enactments of their ethnic belonging, reveals the sophisticated ways in which this community has potentially always negotiated itself, and in more recent decades the effects of wounding and need for healing. There is much purchase in the power of an aspirational future in which esteem is high and Yanyuwa are capable of identifying the 'something' that offsets their fear of 'nothing' remaining. Determining the healing actions and agreeing to a set of ever-emerging terms by which a sense of Yanyuwaness is defined illustrates the vitality of this community, as well as the prevailing nature of culture as an ongoing production.

## ACKNOWLEDGEMENTS

I wish to acknowledge the contributions of the following people to this work: John Bradley, Gloria Friday, Graham Friday Mudaji, Dinah

Norman Marrngawi, Pyro Dirdiyalma, Annie Karrakayn, Jemima Miller Wuwarlu, Rosie Noble Wundirrimara, Amy Friday Bajamalanya, Roddy Harvey Bayuma-Birribalanja, Roddy Friday Mayalkarri, Nancy McDinny a-Yukuwalmara, Leanne Norman Wulamara, Joanne Miller a-Yuluma and Rex Norman Wungunya.

## REFERENCES

Andrews, T., and S. Buggey. 2008. Authenticity in Aboriginal Cultural Landscapes. *Association for Preservation Technology International* 39(2/3): 63–71.

Babidge, S. 2010. *Aboriginal Family and the State*. Farnham: Ashgate.

Battiste, M., and J.Y. Henderson. 2000. *Protecting Indigenous Knowledge and Heritage: A Global Challenge*. Saskatoon: Purich Publishing.

Beckett, J. (ed.). 1998 [1988]. *Past and Present: Constructing a National Aboriginality*. Canberra: Aboriginal Studies Press.

Bradley, J. 2001. Landscapes of the Mind, Landscapes of the Spirit: Negotiating a Sentient Landscape. In R. Baker, J. Davies and E. Young (eds), *Working on Country*. Melbourne: Oxford University Press, pp.295–304.

—— 2010. *Singing Saltwater Country: Journey to the Songlines of Carpentaria*. Crows Nest, NSW: Allen and Unwin.

Bradley, J., G. Friday, A. Kearney and L. Norman. 2011. 'These Are the Choices We Make': Animating Saltwater Country. *Screening the Past* 31. Available at: www.screeningthe-past.com/?p=1030 (accessed 11 June 2016).

Bradley, J., M. Holms, D. Norman, A. Isaac, J. Miller and I. Ninganga. 2005. *Yumbulyum-bulmantha ki-awarawu (All Kinds of Things from Country): Yanyuwa Ethnobiological Classification, Ngulaig*. St Lucia: University of Queensland.

Bradley, J., and K. Seton. 2005. Self-Determination or 'Deep Colonising': Land Claims, Colonial Authority and Indigenous Representation. In B. Hocking (ed.), *Unfinished Constitutional Business? Rethinking Indigenous Self-Determination*. Canberra: Aboriginal Studies Press, pp.32–46.

Cajete, G. 2000. *Native Science: Natural Laws of Interdependence*. Santa Fe, NM: Clear Light Publishers.

CoA (Commonwealth of Australia). 1997. Bringing Them Home: National Inquiry into the Separation of Aboriginal and Torres Strait Islander Children from Their Families. Report of the Human Rights and Equal Opportunity Commission, Commonwealth of Australia. Available at: www.humanrights.gov.au/publications/bringing-them-home-stolen-children-report-1997 (accessed 11 June 2016).

Connerton, P. 2008. Seven Types of Forgetting. *Memory Studies* 1: 59–71.

Cook, B., K. Withy and L. Tarallo-Jensen. 2003. Cultural Trauma, Hawaiian Spirituality and Contemporary Health Status. *California Journal of Health* 1: 10–24.

Cowlishaw, G. 2010. Mythologising Culture, Part 1: Desiring Aboriginality in the Suburbs. *Australian Journal of Anthropology* 21(2): 208–27.

—— 2011. Mythologising Culture, Part 2: Disturbing Aboriginality in the Suburbs. *Australian Journal of Anthropology* 22(2): 170–88.

—— 2012. Culture and the Absurd: The Means and Meanings of Aboriginal Identity in the Time of Cultural Revivalism. *Journal of the Royal Anthropological Institute* 18(2): 397–417.

Davis, W. 1987. The Varieties of Fear. *Philosophical Studies* 51: 287–310.

Heiss, A. 2012. *Am I Black Enough For You?* Sydney: Random House.

Hobson, J., K. Lowe, S. Poetsch and M. Walsh. 2010. *Re-awakening Languages: Theory and Practice in the Revitalisation of Australia's Indigenous Languages*. Sydney: Sydney University Press.

Kearney, A. 2014. *Cultural Wounding, Healing and Emerging Ethnicities*. New York: Palgrave MacMillan.

—— 2016. *Violence in Place: Cultural and Environmental Wounding*. Abingdon: Routledge.

Kearney, A., and J. Bradley. 2014. When a Long Way in a Bark Canoe Becomes a Quick Trip in a Boat: Changing Relationships to Sea Country and Yanyuwa Watercraft Technology. *Quaternary International Online* 385: 166–76.

Kearney, A., J. Bradley, B. McKee and T. Chandler. 2012. Representing Indigenous Cultural Expressions through Animation: The Yanyuwa Animation Project. *Animation Journal* 20: 4–29.

Keen, I. 1988. *Being Black: Aboriginal Cultures in Settled Australia*. Canberra: Aboriginal Studies Press.

McConvell, P., and N. Thieberger. 2001. State of Indigenous Languages in Australia – 2001. Second Technical Paper Series No. 2, Natural and Cultural Heritage. Canberra: Environment Australia. Available at: http: //155.187.2.69/soe/2001/publications/technical/pubs/indigenous-languages.pdf (accessed 11 June 2016).

Moses, D. (ed.). 2004. *Genocide in Settler Society: Frontier Violence and Stolen Indigenous Children in Australian History*. New York: Berghahn Books.

Navarro, Z. 2006. In Search of a Cultural Interpretation of Power: The Contribution of Pierre Bourdieu. *Institute for Development Studies Bulletin* 37(6): 11–22.

Povinelli, E., 1993. 'Might Be Something': The Language of Indeterminacy in Australian Aboriginal Land. *Man* 28(4): 679–704.

—— 2002. *The Cunning of Recognition: Indigenous Alterities and the Making of Australian Multiculturalism*. Durham, NC: Duke University Press.

Read, P. 1999. *A Rape of the Soul So Profound: The Return of the Stolen Generation*. Sydney: Allen and Unwin.

Relph, E. 1976. *Place and Placelessness*. London: Pion.

Roberts, T. 2005. *Frontier Justice: A History of the Gulf Country to 1900*. St Lucia: University of Queensland Press.

Rose, D. 1996. *Nourishing Terrains: Australian Aboriginal Views of Landscape and Wilderness*. Canberra: Australian Heritage Commission.

Rose, D.B. 2000. *Dingo Makes Us Human: Life and Land in Australian Aboriginal Culture*, 2nd edn. Cambridge: Cambridge University Press.

—— 2014. Arts of Flow: Poetics of 'Fit' in Aboriginal Australia. *Dialectical Anthropology* 38(4): 431–45.

Russell, L. (ed.) 2006. *Boundary Writing: An Exploration of Race, Culture, and Gender Binaries in Contemporary Australia*. Honolulu: University of Hawaii Press.

Schutz, A. 1970. *On Phenomenology and Social Relations: Selected Writings*. Chicago: University of Chicago Press.

—— 1976 [1964]. *Collected Papers, Vol. 2: Studies in Social Theory*. The Hague: Martinus Nijhoff.

—— 1982. *Life Forms and Meaning Structure*. London: Routledge and Kegan Paul.

Seamon, D. 1996. A Singular Impact: Edward Relph's 'Place and Placelessness'. *Environmental and Architectural Phenomenology Newsletter* 7(3): 5–8.

Staub, E., L. Pearlman, A. Gubin and A. Hagengimana A. 2005. Healing, Reconciliation, Forgiving and the Prevention of Violence after Genocide or Mass Killing. *Journal of Social and Clinical Psychology* 24(3): 297–334.

Yanyuwa Families and J. Bradley. 2016. *Wuka nya-nganunga li-Yanyuwa li-Anthawir-riyarra: Language for Us, the Yanyuwa Saltwater People: A Yanyuwa Encyclopedic Dictionary*. Melbourne: Australian Scholarly Publishing.

# 8. Indigenous Endurance amidst Accelerated Change?

## The US Military, South Korean Investors and the Aeta of Subic Bay, the Philippines

*Elisabeth Schober*

### FROM NAVAL BASE TO SHIPBUILDING HUB

'*Anyeonghaseyo*', Arnold, one of the tribal leaders of San Martin, said to us, pronouncing the Korean word to near perfection.[1] He had just been introduced to my Korean husband, and had learned that I, too, had lived in Seoul for a number of years. Arnold, a member of the Aeta people, had never been to South Korea himself, or any other place outside of the Philippines. The seeming remoteness of his indigenous community, however, did not mean that he had not been exposed to a number of foreigners, including quite a few Koreans, over the course of his life. San Martin, located a half-hour drive from the next urban centre of Subic town, is home to about 100 Aeta families. There is a core settlement of approximately 50 households who live relatively close to each other at the end of a long, winding dirt road, families who also engage in farming alongside their foraging activities in the mountains that the Aeta, an upland people, are known for. Another 50 families that belong to San Martin live scattered in the mountains that make up the Redondo Peninsula, in which they roam, collecting what they need for their daily needs.

The close-knit settlement at the foot of the mountain has been around for approximately two generations, a rather long lifespan for an Aeta village, considering that some Aeta are still semi-nomadic. While it became an official resettlement area after the cataclysmic eruption of Mount Pinatubo in 1991, about a dozen Aeta families lived in San Martin beforehand (cf. Seitz 2004: 190–1).[2] This means that there was an Aeta burial site there before the volcanic eruption that displaced much of the

---

1. *Anyeonghaseyo* is a Korean greeting. All names of informants have been changed in accordance with social anthropological ethical practices.

2. For more on the resettlement centres, see Seitz (2004: 177).

existing Aeta population in the larger region – a site which has gained in importance as a piece of evidence in their legal case to have the area recognised as their ancestral domain.[3] The case has been in the courts for ten years now, and it does not look as if it will be resolved in favour of the San Martin Aeta anytime soon as there are competing parties trying to acquire the land they occupy. Land in the area has recently become very much sought after, with approximately 1,000 squatter families living a few kilometres away, having been repeatedly expelled from the parcels they occupied because various powerful actors hope to make a profit from expected future large-scale investments in the Subic area (see Schober 2016).

The dramatic changes in the value of land in the area that the San Martin Aeta inhabit is tied to a number of political and economic transformations that have been acting upon the larger region that goes by the name of Subic Bay.[4] Until 1991, the bay adjacent to the Redondo Peninsula was dominated by the US Armed Forces, as it was home to the largest US naval installation overseas. The Americans at that time were a source of income to many, including Arnold and his friends; while they were teenagers, they used to walk many hours along the bay to Olongapo, the city next to the naval base where military personnel used to hang out in their free time. Bribing the bouncers at the clubs and bars catering to the sailors there, they were usually allowed entry and could sell defanged baby pythons that they had caught in the mountains to the US sailors for US$20 a piece, who would play with the snakes on the bar counter to impress the local girls they were with.

The disparate livelihood opportunities that the US base provided for the Aeta living in the vicinity of the base was a key topic that people like Arnold, but also representatives of other Aeta villages in the Subic area, repeatedly brought up with me. From selling trinkets to sailors to scavenging on the landfills of the Americans, to working various odd jobs that were related to the base – people would, in an often decidedly nostalgic fashion, describe the opportunities that could be found in the shadow of the naval installation. To be sure, in this selective appraisal of the past, the Aeta I spoke to did not differ much from other residents of the Subic Bay region, amongst whom I could make out a veritable 'navy

---

3. On the complex issue of 'ancestral domains', the term used by the Philippines government to refer to the land traditionally used by indigenous populations, see Malayang (2001).

4. Subic Bay is a colloquial term, and does not correspond to an exact administrative unit. The actual bay encompasses two urban areas – Olongapo City and Subic town – which, while being adjacent to each other and nominally both part of the province of Zambales, fall under different jurisdictions, as Olongapo is governed independently.

nostalgia' that needs to be viewed in light of recent accelerated changes affecting the area (see Schober forthcoming).

After the closure of the base in the early 1990s (the details of which will be discussed in the next section), the large stretches of empty land left behind by the Americans would be turned into a Freeport Zone that has in the meantime attracted many foreign direct investors (FDIs) to the area. Replacing US sailors with FDIs, however, has been an uneven experience for many of Subic Bay's residents, the Aeta included. As part of these new economic endeavours, a giant US$2 billion Korean shipyard was built some 10 kilometres from San Martin in 2006. 'When I first heard about the shipyard', Arnold told us, 'I thought it was a gift sent from God!' Many more jobs would be made available for people in his community, he believed. As a consequence of the arrival of the Koreans, some of the dirt roads were paved in the area, and there were more motorcycle-taxis available to take villagers to Subic town. This has made life easier for San Martin's Aeta, he explained, as they could now get to Subic town or Olongapo with greater ease, and there they could sell their produce in the market or peddle souvenirs to tourists on the beaches nearby.

Initially, there was an increase in availability of work as a result of the shipyard, as Arnold had hoped: Arnold and ten other men from his community managed to get jobs in the shipyard in the 2000s. But the work was so hard that it nearly destroyed Arnold's health, eventually forcing him to quit his job. Like Arnold, all of the other workers from the community lost their jobs with the Koreans, or have quit of their own accord, as they found the work too strenuous or dangerous.[5] The Aeta villagers have now returned to small-scale economic endeavours like farming their tiny plots, selling handicrafts to tourists or collecting straw bundles in the mountains to be used for thatched roofs.

Arnold himself found another calling after quitting his job at the shipyard, becoming a pastor in a Pentecostal church that was founded in his community many years ago by an American missionary. Later during our visit, Arnold took us to the old pastor's house. Living out his retirement in a forlorn-looking building a few kilometres from the Aeta settlement, we met an old white man in his early nineties, who would speak to us slowly but decidedly of the mercy of God, standing in the midst of a compound filled with mango trees and roaming dogs. He had come to Subic in the 1980s while he was still with the US Navy, he explained

---

5. Elsewhere, I have explored labour management practices at the shipyard, which have arguably revealed contradictions between Korean and Filipino understandings of work, and led to a large number of work-related accidents (Schober 2017).

to us, and returned to the area after having left the military to become a missionary. He bought this piece of land for the very reason that it was located next to the Aeta settlement – and so he and his Filipina wife went about their work of converting the villagers. Once he retired from his mission, a younger Filipino pastor took over, who, as Arnold hinted, is nowadays much better connected with the many Korean church people present in the area than with the remaining American ones.

Since the arrival of the shipbuilders and their subcontractors in the mid 2000s, a number of other Korean actors have made their way to the Subic Bay area. Korean restaurant owners, hoteliers, shopkeepers, travel agents, pastors and tourists can be spotted easily in Subic nowadays. Consequently, in much the same way that the presence of the American base affected local lives and livelihoods a generation ago, since the erection of the Korean shipyard some distinct undercurrents of Korean language and culture have made their way into the most unlikely places, such as the indigenous village of San Martin. The morning I spent in San Martin was certainly not the only time I had found myself surprised by the presence of Korean influences amongst the groups of Aeta that are today scattered about the area. In February 2014, for instance, I spent some time with a group of Aeta at the Pamulaklakin Trail, a tourist attraction run by Aeta from Pastolan village. Our tour guide, Liza, insisted on singing the Korean pop song 'Gangnam Style' once she heard about our connections to South Korea, explaining that a group of Korean tourists had recently taught her the lyrics by repeatedly playing the song on their smartphones. And in March 2014, I attended a holy mass at a Pentecostal church in the community of Mampweng on the outskirts of Olongapo City that was conducted by a young South Korean pastor who had been brought in for the occasion.

Pastolan, Mampweng and San Martin are three Aeta villages in the Subic Bay area that, in the imagination of non-indigenous 'lowlanders' of Subic town and Olongapo have one thing in common: they are considered to be so culturally distinct and geographically so far removed from the urban areas of the region as to be uninfluenced by the many economic changes and foreign influences introduced since 1991. This kind of understanding of the Aeta as mostly untouched by exogenous change is, of course, to a large degree a myth that has to do with the specific role that this indigenous people have played in the imagination of local lowlanders, the US Navy and foreign ethnographers alike.

While anthropologists have often 'promoted strong concepts of community, indigeneity, race, or cultural difference, especially when these appeared to have strategic value in advancing an agenda they support' (Li 2010: 399), the usefulness of the category of indigeneity has over recent years come under much scrutiny. Anthropologists dedicated to paying attention to political economy in particular have argued that the concept often diverts us from looking at pertinent issues of livelihood, land-tenure systems and class (see e.g. Steur 2015). Adam Kuper, for instance, claims that:

> whatever the political inspiration, the conventional lines of argument currently used to justify 'indigenous' land claims rely on obsolete anthropological notions and on a romantic and false ethnographic vision. Fostering essentialist ideologies of culture and identity, they maybe have dangerous political consequences. (Kuper 2003: 395)

Less combatively, Tania Li has argued for an understanding of indigeneity as 'a mobile term that has been articulated in relation to a range of positions and struggles', with a crucial feature of the term having been 'the permanent attachment of a group of people to a fixed area of land in a way that marks them as culturally distinct' (Li 2010: 385). Seeking to untangle the seemingly self-evident connection between indigeneity and land, she urges us to focus on how the link between rural populations and the concept of indigeneity has actually been forged in specific historical contexts, and how our 'visions of cultural alterity and harmonious collectivity' has often blinded us to the very real processes of dispossession affecting these groups (ibid.: 385).

While not quite taking up Kuper's radical standpoint, with its demand that we discard the concept, I believe that critical perspectives on the matter at hand do need to be taken seriously. Arguably, no group that we or others label as 'indigenous' can reasonably be made sense of without at the same time also exploring how exogenous change, transformation and mixing have also shaped these people. By designating indigenous peoples as timeless, ethnic majorities and foreign explorers condemn them to a frozen existence outside world history, and contribute to their problems of engaging constructively with contemporary problems caused by accelerated change. This chapter will thus endorse an understanding of indigeneity as a category that needs to include space for both the exploration of social reproduction *and* of social identity. To be sure, the Aeta of the Subic Bay area are a group of people that has been dramatically affected by a number of large-scale externally driven projects, while at the same time retaining a unique way of life that sets them apart from other residents of the area.

To make sense of these developments, I outline how the US Armed Forces came to utilise the Aeta for their own purposes, a kind of militarisation of the Aeta which some residents of the Pastolan community close to the old naval base seem to still remember in a rather nostalgic fashion. Following a discussion of these issues I further delve into how today's understandings of the Aeta are built on the widespread distinction between corrupted lowlanders and pristine highland life, a binary that was first introduced during the US colonial period as a tool of governance. In the final section, I turn to a day I spent in an Aeta village near Mampweng, where I encountered the notion of 'endurance' – a phrase that I believe captures the Aeta experience in Subic Bay rather well. Endurance – the power to withstand the greatest pressures without breaking – seems to me to be an important aspect of these rural residents' engagement with outside forces, given that they have been exposed to such a wide variety of (neo)colonial, military, religious and economic projects over the centuries.

## THE MILITARISATION OF AN INDIGENOUS PEOPLE

The Aeta, understood to be part of the Philippines' aboriginal population, are one of over a hundred indigenous groups in the archipelago. Amidst an estimated eight to ten million indigenous people in the country, they make up an estimated 50,000 people (Gaillard 2006: 11). Their distinct appearance – 'characterized by curly hair, dark complexion and small stature and by their lifestyle with its strong focus on foraging strategies' (Seitz 2004: 1–2) – is much commented upon. They are usually categorised as former hunter-gatherers who inhabit the lower altitude tropical mountains of the Zambales region, of which Subic is part. Considered to be amongst the oldest groups to inhabit the Philippine archipelago, their ancestors are said to have first come to this region some 10,000 to 20,000 years ago, during a time when there still was a land strait connecting Borneo and the Philippines. Malays, in comparison, who are the forerunners of the Tagalog-speaking majority population of today, arrived as recently as 2,300 years ago.

The later arrivals were largely farmers and herders, and with their advanced technology they gradually pushed the Aeta into the more mountainous regions, from where the Aeta would then develop extensive economic exchanges with the lowlanders (with similar processes occurring in a number of locations across the archipelago and involving many different indigenous groups). Spanish colonisers, who arrived in the sixteenth century, further marginalised the Aeta, who proved largely resistant to attempts at Christian conversion. They called the Aeta 'Negrito', 'Little Blacks', a name with racist undertones that to some degree sticks with them today. In response to the kind of civilisation on offer by the Spanish and their *mestizo* elites, the Aeta, quite similar to the highland groups of mainland South-East Asia described by James Scott

(2009), opted with their feet and further moved into the mountains to be able to restrict interactions with lowland neighbours and maintain their unique cultural ways – a policy which, as we shall see in the next section, also turned them into a subject of interest to a number of anthropologists and other foreign actors over the years.

Once the Americans drove out the Spanish and colonised the Philippines in 1898, the new colonial authorities created the distinct legal category of 'tribe', thereby dividing the population of the Philippines into peasants and tribes (Li 2010: 392, 395), which allowed for easier governance of potentially unruly subjects. Early on during the period of US colonialism, the exceptionally sheltered deepwater anchorage provided by Subic Bay meant it became one of the largest of the US Navy's overseas bases. Gradually occupying much of the remote jungle terrain that was traditionally used by the Aeta, the US Navy became centrally involved in the fate of the indigenous group with whom they found themselves residing side by side. In the 1920s, for instance, the Americans established a reservation on Mount Pinatubo for the Aeta that was directly modelled on ones that had been erected for Native Americans in the USA. Subsequently, the Aeta and their exceptional skills were utilised by the US Armed Forces during the Second World War, when the Americans organised them into a guerrilla force that fought against the Japanese, who were hopelessly lost in the jungle terrain that was the Aeta's home.[6]

After the war, the Aeta's skills were further utilised for the training of US military personnel. The Jungle Environment Survival Training (JEST) camp was founded in the late 1960s during the Vietnam War – a unique training facility, where Aeta who hailed mostly from what is today the Pastolan community[7] were used as instructors to teach military recruits everything they needed to know in order to survive in the jungles of South-East Asia.[8] Those Aeta who were not recruited by the military as

---

6. See: Pension Elusive for Aeta Guerillas, *Philippine Daily Inquirer*, 2 March 2016 (available at: http://newsinfo.inquirer.net/769917/pension-elusive-for-aeta-guerrillas, accessed 18 June 2016).

7. The Aeta who had lived inside the territory that the base eventually covered were first relocated to nearby New Cabalan, a hilly area largely uninhabited at that time, but which is nowadays a rather populous suburb of Olongapo. With the spread of the city, the Aeta opted to relocate once more and came to settle in what is now Pastolan, a forested terrain that is already part of the province Bataan, but within walking distance of the Subic Bay Freeport Zone.

8. The JEST camp still survives, albeit as a tourist destination where foreign and Filipino tourists can go on jungle survival tours with Aeta guides, during which they are shown how to make fire with nothing but a bamboo stick and a machete, how to locate water and hunt with the most limited resources available.

trainers, or who could not find other jobs at the base, found other ways to make do with what their new foreign neighbours brought to the area.

A further significant livelihood opportunity to emerge among the Aeta was that of scavenging among the base's rubbish dumps. 'In 1960 the American base authorities', writes Roland Simbulan, 'in exchange for occupying the traditional lands where Negrito lived as hunters and food gatherers, agreed to grant them the exclusive right to scavenge the Subic dumpsite and sell stateside scraps themselves' (Simbulan 1985: 263). This deal, however, was broken in 1964, when local authorities stepped in as intermediaries and direct negotiations between the Americans and the Aeta ceased. From being able to sell what they had scavenged without go-betweens, they were soon reduced to being contract workers: 'Their … job was to sort out the garbage and metal scraps from the dumpsite' (ibid.: 264), which entailed a reduction of their wages from 100 pesos to about 30 pesos a day. The scavenging 'privileges' they obtained also meant that Aeta came into unsupervised contact with certain undefined substances dumped by the Americans, a fact which some argue has led to quite a few premature deaths in Pastolan.[9]

The year 1991, which brought so many political and economic upheavals to other parts of the world, also triggered some transformations in the Philippines, with the Aeta particularly affected. Over the course of just half a year, a catastrophic volcanic eruption and an unexpected political victory would come to act upon and dramatically alter the location of Subic Bay in the Philippines. While the eruption of nearby Mount Pinatubo on 15 June 1991 covered the US naval base in half a metre of ash, in December of the same year the Philippine Senate voted against extending the lease of the US base under which the naval facility was operating. As a consequence, 1991 brought an end to more than a century of US tutelage for the Philippines. Subic Bay, an area that had been economically, politically and socially dependent on the patronage of the US Navy, soon became a site of neoliberal economic globalisation in the Philippines. As mentioned earlier, amongst the FDIs now active in Subic is a South Korean shipyard, which today employs 34,000 Filipino workers.

During fieldwork in Subic Bay in 2013/14, I heard of an explanation for the eruption of Mount Pinatubo that seemed rather surreal at first: geothermal drilling had caused the dormant volcano to come to life again. What was more, the Aeta, who thought of Pinatubo as their holy

9. See: Decades Later, US Military Pollution in Philippines Linked to Deaths, *Stars and Stripes*, 2 February 2010 (available at: www.stripes.com/news/decades-later-u-s-military-pollution-in-philippines-linked-to-deaths-1.98570, accessed 18 June 2016).

mountain, had been warning of an imminent eruption in the months prior to the catastrophe, a story I later found repeated in newspapers at that time: 'Edward Santos, one of about 30,000 Aeta aboriginal tribesmen evacuated from the slopes of Mt. Pinatubo, says geothermal drilling on the mountain angered Apo Namalyari, the Aeta god of the volcano', reads one *LA Times* article. 'Worse, the government geologists refused to sacrifice a young goat to appease the volcano god. Hence, the sky fell in'.[10]

Whatever the reasons behind the eruption of Pinatubo, it certainly led to the collision of two major forces in the region: the Aeta's ancestral domain of Pinatubo on the one hand, and the US military on the other. When the volcano erupted, it not only drove the Americans out of the nearby Clark airbase, a facility that was completely destroyed and eventually abandoned, but it also had a huge impact on a number of Aeta communities settled close to the volcano. After the eruption, which many Aeta still claim has been caused by too much 'development', tens of thousands of Aeta were forced to abandon their old lands in the forested highlands and head for government resettlement centres near urban areas such as Subic. Many of the Aeta who survived the explosion found their native lands so destroyed that returning to their homes seemed impossible, so the resettlement centres seemed attractive. However, what was meant to be a temporary solution has for many become a permanent home, with the knock-on effect that many have shifted from being upland foragers to urbanised 'wage hunter and gatherers' (Breman 1994).

## 'NAVY NOSTALGIA' IN PASTOLAN

Taking a taxi from one of the gates of the Freeport, we drove past the shopping malls and gas stations, the McDonald's and 7-Elevens until the wealthy, quasi-urban structures of the part of the Subic Bay Freeport Zone that is nearest Olongapo City gave way to nothing but rainforest. The last sign of the vast riches of this Special Economic Zone was the extensive golf course under South Korean management, and then came another ten minutes of driving along a deserted jungle road until our taxi finally came to a halt. At the beginning of the mountain trail, we were greeted by a large number of people who were hanging around in the middle of the forest. The Pamulaklakin Trail has some 30 people working at any given hour during the day, all from Pastolan, the Aeta community that is situated on a mountain plateau nearby, and who hike downhill for an hour to the trail, where they wait for tourists to show up

10. Under the Volcano, *Los Angeles Times*, 11 August 1991 (available at: http://articles. latimes.com/1991-08-11/magazine/tm-798_1_pinatubo-ash, accessed 18 June 2016).

and request their services. Unlike some other corporate-driven tourist destinations that focus on jungle exploration within the Freeport Zone, the Aeta manage their trail independently, so whatever revenue they gain from tourists is entirely theirs to keep. This also means that all the risk is theirs, too – and during the rainy season, when no customers show up, the trail still needs to be maintained, so they put in plenty of time out of season to keep it up to scratch. Liza, our tour guide for the day, did not get paid in September and October – two months without an income, during which she made her way down the mountain and up again every single day to offer her services.

Liza, a feisty woman in her 50s who zoomed in on my husband and me the moment we arrived, quickly agreed to take us on her 'ecological tour', a two-hour-long hike through the jungle up to Pastolan village. Liza, walking swiftly ahead of us, got our small party of three started – across a bridge over the Pamulaklakin River, past a scenic little clearance and then steeply up into the mountain, following a very lightly trodden path into the depths of the rainforest. There was fallen bamboo along the path, an endless number of plants we had to shove out of our faces and sticky leaves and clingy plant tentacles to be kept away from our arms and legs. A large knocking sound echoing off the trees somewhere nearby – a big lizard, Liza explained, and every once in a while there was the rustling noise of a snake making a hasty retreat from the ruckus we created. Liza pointed at a scar on her foot:

> Here, that's where a snake once bit me. My husband was shaking so much when he saw it, and I laughed and asked, 'Was it you who got bitten or me?' I went to the hospital and told the doctor that I was bitten by a large snake, and they said they first wanted 2,000 pesos down-payment for taking me in. I just laughed, 2,000 pesos? No, goodbye then, I will just go home and die!

But miraculously the snake bite did very little damage to her health. Another doctor once told her, half jokingly, 'Please don't ever bite anyone, my dear, you will probably poison them instantly with all that snake venom in your blood!' Liza seemed to like that idea a lot: 'If I ever get in trouble with someone', she said, 'I will bite and kill them, just like that!'

While trying to keep pace with Liza, listening to her talk while making our way up the mountain along the little trail, the heat and humidity quickly became unbearable, so we were deeply grateful for any break our swift guide gave us. Occasionally she grabbed a leaf, rubbed it between her palms or the tips of her fingers and listed all the medical qualities of this plant or that – good for asthma, treats diarrhoea, helps you with erectile problems, strengthens the bones of a baby so it will learn to walk faster, gets rid of an unwanted pregnancy. She learned all about these plants from her mother, she said – not having access to health care for their family, they would treat any kind of injury with what they could find in the forest instead. 'My mother, she must have learned it from her own grandparents, and so on, and so forth. And me, now I teach my own kids', she said. The Aeta, she added, usually do not have much formal education, but this kind of herbal knowledge they certainly possess – and lots of people come here to learn from them nowadays through the tours they offer. Doctors from Manila, eco-tourists from Europe, the daughter of a famous politician who promised her that they would write a book on herbal remedies together ('I'm still waiting for her to return', she added after a moment of hesitation).

Liza learned English when the US Navy base was open, she said – Aeta tend to speak English much better than the lowlanders, she insisted, because of their daily encounters with the Americans who occupied their ancestral lands. She herself worked for the Americans when she was young, before the base was closed down; they paid her well and she remembers her time with the Americans very fondly. The Aeta had it good back then, she said – for instance, due to connections made amongst navy personnel she delivered three of her four children at the fancy American hospital without having to pay a single peso. One child was born by Caesarean section, too, she said, so she was very lucky that she could go to the American hospital and have the doctor there take good care of her.

The Aeta nowadays all try to get jobs at the Freeport Zone, which has become the main source of employment since the US Navy left, Liza says. No one from Pastolan has been able to get a job at the Korean shipyard, she says, as they ask for too many educational certificates, which people are unable to provide. She herself worked as a security guard for eight years in the Freeport Zone. She earned 330 pesos (about €6.30) per night shift, midnight to 8 AM, wearing a guard's uniform and carrying a loaded weapon and a walkie-talkie while making her rounds. She eventually lost her job because the security company that she worked for went into bankruptcy, and since then she has had trouble making ends meet. After running a little *sari-sari* (convenience) store in her village for a while, she started working at the Pamulaklakin Trail, and at the time of our visit she took tourists on jungle tours. On a good day she earns 150 pesos (roughly €2.90), but there have been a lot of bad days lately.

'Life was so much better when the Navy was still around', she says, adding force to her words by shaking her head at her life these days. When we arrived in her village, located in a beautiful spot on top of the mountain, I had asked her how things had changed since the Americans left. She was in the middle of giving us a little tour through the village, and we were now standing in the midst of the well-kept little primary school. 'Here', she pointed to an old building located at the edge of the school courtyard. 'This was donated by the Navy. They were the first to build up this courtyard, too. They helped us when no one else did'.

## LOWLAND CORRUPTION AND HIGHLAND INDIGENEITY IN ANTHROPOLOGICAL DISCOURSE

Anthropologists who have engaged themselves with the Philippines have often headed for the mountains to look for secluded indigenous groups, and arguably they did so because they understood these areas and groups as culturally distinct from the lowlanders inhabiting the Philippines, who are often perceived as too mixed up with and contaminated by the outside forces of colonialism, imperialism and, nowadays, globalisation. The Aeta, most certainly, have sparked interest among foreign researchers for that particular reason too. German anthropologist Stefan Seitz, for instance, notes:

> I had decided to visit the Aeta mainly because I was then interested to see how their situation compared to that of central African hunter-gatherers, who had previously been the focus of my research. Once in Zambales, I concentrated on the Aeta occupying the hinterlands of Botolan, who had been as '*exposed*' to the scrutiny of anthropologists, as had their counterparts residing in the San Marcelino uplands. Although the Aeta in Zambales had for centuries maintained contacts with their agricultural neighbors in the lowlands, they had managed to preserve their traditions, which ... still retained numerous basic elements of a hunter-gatherer society. (Seitz 2004: iii, emphasis added)[11]

Only in the highlands, it seems, is one able to experience remnants of the ancient Philippines that has seemingly been thoroughly destroyed in low-lying areas. Following this logic of purity and contamination, the Subic Bay area with its exposure to the US military can be classified amongst the most mixed regions in the Philippines, and it has often been described in such terms: 'The existence of the bases has inflicted much harm on the Filipino people', Roland Simbulan writes.

---

11. For other twentieth-century anthropological work on the Aeta, see e.g. Shimizu (2001) and Tima (2005).

These military installations have been the breeding grounds of 'sin cities', where prostitution, gambling, smuggling of tax-free goods, blackmarketing, extortion and drug trafficking flourish, eroding the moral fabric of Philippine society. Prostitution and drug-dealing in fact, are among the most thriving 'industries' created by the bases. (Simbulan 1985: 251)

The deconstruction of the dichotomy between uncultured, impure lowlands and the pure, cultured highlands in the Philippines has been a central theme in the work of anthropologist Fenella Cannell (1999). In her work, Cannell foregrounds the idea of corruption, understood in the wider sense as a category with connotations of contamination and moral decline, which has repeatedly been utilised in descriptions of life in the lowlands of the Philippines by foreign commentators, including anthropologists. Corruption is a deceptively potent metaphor for everyday life in Subic Bay – not only do foreigners talk about the rampant amount of corruption, but it was also a central term used by nearly every Philippine national I encountered in Olongapo and Subic town: no matter who one spoke to, what their social background was, they would soon comment negatively on the political, moral, cultural and sexual corruption of the area they lived in. When asking my informants whether there were any exceptions to be found to this, they would usually tell me to head for the mountains or remote rural areas instead, where they believed I would be able to find a more authentic version of the Philippines than that of urbanised Subic Bay.

The dichotomy between corrupt lowlanders and pure highlanders, Cannell argues, as compelling as it may seem to our informants, actually has a particular conceptual history built into it – namely, the fact that early American ethnographers introduced this binary when they came to the Philippines at the turn of the twentieth century. Ethnographers at that time were usually affiliated with the Bureau of Non-Christian Tribes, a colonial state agency that first collected data on indigenous people in the Philippines. Amongst these American commentators, she writes:

Highland groups were seen as the bearers of a certain form of authenticity evidenced by their adherence to their own forms of social rules, and reluctance to alter them ... Stereotypically, they were seen as honest; as ruthless enemies, therefore, but *true friends once won over to the American side*; lowlanders were characterised as slippery, evasive, and lacking in individuality, autonomy, and vitality. (Cannell 2005: 164, emphasis added)

A good example of an ethnographer working during the US colonial period is William Allan Reed. To my knowledge he was the first anthropologist to work on the Aeta in the Zambales region, and he published a short monograph on them in 1904 based on a three-month field trip (Reed 1904). Reed's book is replete with the usual examples of the questionable kind of scholarship anthropologists at that time produced, including detailed bodily measurements of 77 Aeta individuals, whose heads, arms, noses and ears Reed had examined. To be sure, William Allan Reed only had access to this particular area because he must have collaborated intimately with the colonial government and the American military present in the area; US colonial forces, after all, had only taken over the Subic Bay naval base – a facility originally built by Spanish forces in 1885 – five years earlier, in 1899.

## ENDURANCE AMIDST CHANGE?

Since the abandonment of the military base and the establishment of a Freeport Zone in Subic Bay, which manages the old US facilities, a rapid and ferocious scramble for land has occurred. In the post-Pinatubo era, the Aeta of Subic Bay, some of whom have left the resettlement centre and moved to land nearby, find themselves further squeezed by 'development'. The social reproduction of their lives is ever more put into question – an issue I came face to face with during my second visit to Mampweng. Located at the foot of a mountain on the rural outskirts of Olongapo, Mampweng is a village primarily inhabited by indigenous Aeta. Olongapo is today a sprawling city of 200,000 inhabitants, and Mampweng is a thirty-minute ride away from the packed streets of the city. It can only be reached by taking a rusty pickup truck into the increasingly empty wilderness that the city gradually gives way to if you keep driving away from the sea towards the mountain ridge behind the city. I had already visited Mampweng once, before I came to hike through it again a few months later when I attended a mass baptism conducted by a South Korean pastor in February 2014. Incidentally, most of the children that were baptised that day were from a small breakaway Aeta village called Limuran, which I visited in the company of a number of Filipino NGO workers in mid-April 2014.

The families of Limuran – existing without electricity and running water on a plateau near the top of the mountain behind Mampweng – had broken away from Mampweng in the mid 1990s because in their view Mampweng had become too influenced by lowlanders nearby. Around that time, the Iram Resettlement Area was established on a plot within walking distance of Mampweng, where many Aeta refugees who had been displaced by the Mount Pinatubo eruption had found a temporary home. Both the communities of Mampweng and Iram attracted a number of poor Tagalog-speaking 'invaders', which led to a rapid increase in intermarriages in the area. In the midst of this, the families that formed Limuran packed up their belongings and with the permission of the local authorities moved away from Mampweng and further into the mountains in the belief that no lowlanders would come after them into this difficult terrain.

During our journey to Limuran, we halted in front of Mampweng's church, where I had earlier attended the baptism. This time around, the church was deserted, but I saw a large banner tagged to the front of the building, advertising the festivities that would mark the twenty-eighth anniversary of the ministry. I was struck by the motto and the picture chosen for the celebrations: 'Endurance', it said in large letters, together with a photograph depicting several Aeta from Limuran, who were in the middle of the toughest stretch of their journey down the mountain. At least once a week, a group of Aeta from Limuran would head down to Mampweng on foot, where they paid to go by pickup truck to Olongapo's public market. There, they would spend a day or two, selling charcoal, fruit and the birds they catch in the forest so that they can buy rice and other goods.

On the four-hour hike from Mampweng up to Limuran, I got a glimpse into why not many lowlanders voluntarily make their way up to this area. First, some sections of the Zambales mountains are rather infamous, as they still shelter a number of armed Maoist rebel groups, and every person going into the mountains is strongly advised to register with the police for reasons of safety. Beyond these political dangers, the rough terrain is not very inviting either. Our way led us along a river (and across it on a dozen occasions), one which is largely impassable during the rainy season. Nearly every rainy season, several Aeta drown in this river while attempting to cross it. Making our way on a small trail that often ran at perilous heights above the river, we were quickly overtaken by a sense of fear as to whether or not we would all make it up and down the mountain safely. Our Aeta companions heightened this tense atmosphere by constantly frowning and shaking their heads at the poor motor skills we displayed throughout the journey.

The tense atmosphere reached its height when we came to a small pool. Our party took a short rest, and the Aeta began to talk about how the pool was jinxed. An Aeta couple had drowned here a while ago, they said, when they followed a big fish with golden earrings into the water; a white woman could occasionally be seen in this area too, sitting on a large stone, trying to convince young men to join her in her world. 'My brother disappeared for several days after he met her here', an Aeta leader explained, 'and he was out of his mind for months to follow. I once saw her myself when I was hiking here alone, and quickly hid from her in the bushes over there'. 'Terrible things happen on days like these when the weather changes so fast', another Aeta woman present interrupted him. 'Look, first the sun was out, and then it's been disappearing quickly behind these clouds that we didn't see coming. That's the kind of weather during which the worst accidents happen'.

Surprisingly, no calamity struck us. We made it safely up to Limuran, and spent the next few hours playing games and drawing with the children, preparing and eating a meal with the villagers and delivering the goods we had brought with us. In contrast to the tense atmosphere on our way up, the hike back down the mountain was a quite joyous affair. Our Aeta guides, who had earlier frowned and sighed whenever one of us slipped over a stone, now shared smiles and laughs with us. It dawned on me how much of a burden we had been to them in the morning; they had probably feared the trouble that would come to them if any of us injured ourselves on our way up to Limuran. My presence, in particular, was a cause for concern, I assumed: a double intruder, a lowlander and a foreigner, coming to their place. A white woman showing up in the mountain is clearly a sign of trouble for the Aeta – matter out of place, possibly bringing danger and disturbances to them. But then outsiders, in a way, are the kind of necessary evil that needs to be endured. And the encroachments faced by intruders seem to be a fact of life to be reckoned with in Limuran, too, as land up here, despite the fact that it is rather far removed from lowland life, will perhaps too become a scarce resource. On our way to the village, examples of the growing number of new fences that had recently been erected by outsiders were pointed out to us with great concern.

To be sure, despite the remoteness of places like Limuran, agents of exogenous change have acted upon Aeta groups in the area. Simultaneously kept at bay and brought closer every once in a while, foreigners have proved to be a volatile force that Aeta have to reckon with. What arguably gives the Aeta a sense of community and identity is not the purity of their culture or a lack of engagement with modernity, but their small-scale, egalitarian social organisation and political autonomy. Their indigeneity, it is important to note, is a social phenomenon, not a cultural one. Through the scramble for land and the privatisation of land rights, their relative autonomy, which is linked to their particular usage of the landscapes they inhabit, is what is threatened. Losing their land would mean losing their economic flexibility and ultimately the little bit of self-determination they have managed to retain, leading to their dispossession in both a literal and figurative sense.

## ACKNOWLEDGEMENTS

This chapter is based on data collected during seven months of ethnographic field research in the Subic Bay area between September 2013 and April 2014. Funded by the European Research Council as part of the project 'Overheating: The Three Crises of Globalisation', I studied the social, economic and environmental changes that the arrival of Korean foreign direct investors has triggered. It is important to note that Aeta informants were initially not sought out by me in order to gain a deeper understanding into issues of indigeneity, but rather as one group of actors amongst many in Subic Bay who had been affected by the economic and political transformations in the area since 1991.

## REFERENCES

Breman, J. 1994. *Wage Hunters and Gatherers: Search for Work in the Urban and Rural Economy of Southern Gujarat.* Delhi: Oxford University Press.

Cannell, F. 1999. *Power and Intimacy in the Christian Philippines.* Cambridge: Cambridge University Press.

—— 2005. Immaterial Culture: 'Idolatry' in the Lowland Philippines. In A.C. Willford and K.M. George (eds), *Spirited Politics: Religion and Public Life in Contemporary Southeast Asia.* Ithaca, NY: Cornell Southeast Asia Program Publications, pp.159–84.

Gaillard, J.-C. 2006. Traditional Societies in the Face of Natural Hazards: The 1991 Mt Pinatubo Eruption and the Aetas of the Philippines. *International Journal of Mass Emergencies and Disasters.* 24(1): 5–43.

Kuper, A. The Return of the Native. *Current Anthropology* 44(3): 389–95.

Li, T. 2010. Indigeneity, Capitalism, and the Management of Dispossession. *Current Anthropology* 51(3): 385–414.

Malayang, B.S. 2001. Tenure Rights and Ancestral Domains in the Philippines: A Study of the Roots of Conflict. *Bijdragen tot de Taal-, Land- en Volkenkunde* 157(3): 661–76.

Reed, W.A. 1904. *Negritos of Zambales.* Manila: Bureau of Public Printing.

Schober, E. 2016. Between a Rock and a Hard Place: Land and Labour in the Philippines. *Ethnos* (special issue), in press.

—— 2017. The (Un-)Making of Labour: Capitalist Accelerations and their Human Toll at a South Korean Shipyard in the Philippines. In C. Hann and J. Parry (eds), *Regular and Precarious Labour in Modern Industrial Settings.* Oxford: Berghahn Books.

—— Forthcoming. Building a City: Korean Capitalists and Navy Nostalgia in the Subic Bay Area. *History and Anthropology.*

Scott, J.C. 2009. *The Art of Not Being Governed: An Anarchist History of Upland Southeast Asia.* New Haven: Yale University Press.

Seitz, S. 2004. *The Aeta of the Mt Pinatubo, Philippines: A Minority Group Coping with Disaster.* Quezon City: New Daily Publishers.

Shimizu, H. 2001. *The Orphans of Pinatubo: The Ayta Struggle for Existence*. Manila: Solidaridad Publishing House.

Simbulan, R.G. 1985. *The Bases of Our Insecurity*. Manila: Balai Fellowship.

Steur, L. 2015. Class Trajectories and Indigenism among Agricultural Workers in Kerala. In J.G. Carrier and D. Kalb (eds), *Anthropologies of Class: Power, Practice and Inequality*. Cambridge: Cambridge University Press, pp.118–30.

Tima, R.G. 2005. *Leaves on the Water: The Struggle for Survival of Pinatubo Aetas*. Olongapo: Olongapo City Printing Press.

# 9. The Politics of Localness
## Claiming Gains in Rural Sierra Leone

*Robert J. Pijpers*

Ideas of 'localness' have become increasingly important during the recent expansion and contraction of the iron ore mining industry in Marampa chiefdom, Sierra Leone. The upsurge of notions such as local-local, local, national and expat, notions based on people's ethnic background and belonging and used in discussions regarding opportunities brought about by the mining operation pinpoints the increasingly heated nature of identity politics in Marampa.

After going through a decades-long period of economic decline, conflict and poverty, inhabitants of Marampa perceived the re-opening of the iron ore mines by London Mining in 2006 as an opportunity to realise the change they had been longing for; to many, it essentially represented an opportunity to secure a better life.[1] However, over the past few years it has become apparent that the imagined and expected benefits of the re-opened mines are limited, and not enough to guarantee everyone their desired share. In particular, regarding employment opportunities, people are disappointed: there are fewer jobs available than expected and, according to local inhabitants of the chiefdom, too many of the jobs are given away to outsiders or strangers (Sierra Leoneans from different ethnic backgrounds and/or expats). Besides employment, the mining operation offers other opportunities for financial gains, such as financial compensation for the loss of crops and the leasing of land, which is especially relevant for those people within the area of the mining concession. Yet this is paid to the owners of the land or crops, excluding a considerable amount of people who live inside the concession area but do not own land. As a result of the limited resources that are available, combined with the many people that desire to access them, competition over these resources – that is, employment and compensation – has

---

1. This chapter is based on field research conducted between September 2013 and June 2014, prior to the Ebola outbreak in West Africa. Since then concerns have shifted to the consequences of the outbreak, and London Mining went into administration in October 2014. Although Timis Corporation has taken over the Marampa mines, the future of the operation is uncertain.

intensified. Ideas of identity and belonging, or more precisely of 'being local', as these ideas are rooted in ethnic background and social standing (being a landowner/first-comer or stranger), become increasingly instrumental in these struggles.

Naturally, identity is not restricted to serving as 'just' an instrumental tool, and the variety of ideas about identity are rooted in social structures – such as kinship, ethnicity and autochthony – that go beyond its instrumentalisation at a specific point in time. Yet, in situations marked by both economic despair and hope for a better future, certain identities serve well to create social boundaries between groups, govern resource flows and maximise (individual) benefits (see e.g. Bourdieu 1991; Harrison 1999; Eriksen 2005). In Marampa, this is reflected in the increased usage of social categories such as local-local, local, national and expat, whereby local-local identifies the closest relationship to the actual place and expat signifies the most distant.

As Eriksen and Schober argue in the introduction to this volume, this book aims to bring identity, delineated as both social belonging and self-consciousness, into conversation with social reproduction and change. In my particular case, this focus leads me to ask: What kinds of identities are staged, under what circumstances and by whom? And, to which kinds of social reproduction, and what changes, does this politics of localness contribute?

In addressing these questions, this chapter discusses how imaginations of identity, framed by ideas and degrees of being local, are employed and contested in Marampa in order to claim rights to benefits and resources linked to the iron ore mines. Local inhabitants increasingly push for an acknowledgement of their localness and argue that this should be reflected in prioritised access to the opportunities that the mining operation might bring. The increasing emphasis on being local, on being an 'autochthon' (see Ceuppens & Geschiere 2005; Geschiere 2009) is mainly due to the rising and fading opportunities associated with the global mining industry. Consequently, although discussions focus on ideas of the local, they are used to gain access to the opportunities, imagined wealth and power of the global (Ceuppens & Geschiere 2005; Mbembe 2001).

In what follows, I analyse several ethnographic vignettes from Marampa that focus on finding employment with, and receiving financial compensation for the lease of land and the loss of crops from, the mining company. First, however, I turn to Marampa chiefdom's recent history and contemporary developments to touch briefly upon the role of identity and belonging in economic competition.

## MARAMPA CHIEFDOM: HIGH EXPECTATIONS IN A HOT-SPOT

The discovery of iron ore in the 1930s and its subsequent extraction by the Sierra Leone Development Company (Delco) turned Marampa into one of the most prosperous chiefdoms of Sierra Leone (Jarrett 1956; Gamble 1963). Lunsar, the main town of Marampa chiefdom, was transformed into a focal point of the wider surroundings, as Jarrett observed some sixty years ago: 'From a tiny village of about half a dozen huts in the 1920s the town has increased steadily in population since 1930, until today its population is estimated at about 15,000' (Jarrett 1956: 153). The majority of the people in the chiefdom are Temne, one of the major ethnic groups in Sierra Leone, but the iron ore industry that emerged under Delco 'opened up' the chiefdom and triggered an influx of people from different ethnic backgrounds. The growing importance of mining brought new challenges to the chiefdom. For example, there were concerns that the town of Lunsar was underdeveloped compared to the mining compounds, and that social tensions would rise due to the mixture and gradual juxtaposition of too many ethnic groups (ibid.). Moreover, the pressure on land increased to such an extent that it was 'no longer possible for an inhabitant to secure land to farm unless he is a native of the area, and preferably a Temne' (ibid.: 157). Yet, the Delco period is also vividly remembered as a positive one: Delco brought jobs, money and a good life. As Marampa's paramount chief, Bai KobloQueen II, explained to me: 'Just imagine, we had a good living with the Delco, the Austromineral. We can interact, we can see development, we can see life, we can see a lot of accessibility in terms of infrastructural development'. The chief's statement reflects a widespread sentiment in the chiefdom. Although, as I argue elsewhere (Pijpers 2017), such memories should be seen as part of a micro-politics that unfolds in the context of, and allows people to make claims towards, the current mining operation, it can be argued that the Delco period represented a brighter part of Sierra Leone's recent history. After the mines closed in 1975 – and briefly, but unsuccessfully, reopened under the management of the Australian company Austromineral in the early 1980s – a dwindling economy and a ten-year-long civil war that lasted from 1991 to 2002 turned the area into one of the poorest of Sierra Leone.

After the civil war, the chiefdom slowly recovered but remained a place characterised by small-scale agriculture and hand-to-mouth survival strategies. Yet, the re-opening of the mines in 2006 injected a common feeling of excitement and announced a period in which a promising future could be imagined. 'People are happy. In every house there are workers. When they cook, the rice will be shared and maybe they give some money to the children for school', an inhabitant of one of the villages around Lunsar told me. Moreover, during this period, electricity and public water pumps were made available, restaurants and bars opened, motorbikes could be seen transporting people, small eateries appeared on street corners and more and more cars were to be seen driving around. In early 2014, workers even started digging trenches for fibre-optic cable, a visible sign of the promise of wireless internet for the whole country.

Marampa is rapidly changing and is in some ways exemplary of Sierra Leone as a whole. It is often stated that, prior to the Ebola outbreak in 2014, Sierra Leone had one of the highest growth rates in the world, a claim that the government eagerly shared with its citizens at public events.[2] As a small number of large-scale (foreign) direct investments make up for most of the national growth rate, it is not surprising that the areas surrounding these investments, such as the iron ore mines in Marampa, develop into national focal points, sometimes dubbed 'growth poles' (Kayonde et al. 2013). However, not only economic and demographic, but also social, political and physical landscapes are impacted by investments, and people respond to, influence and act with(in) these changes in different ways. The term 'growth pole' might therefore lead our attention away from the micro-politics, the numerous contestations and negotiations that take place within these investment arenas. Sikor and Lund (2009), for example, show that land claims – like other large-scale investments, I would argue – generate spaces that are subsequently open to negotiation between different forms of power and authority. Large-scale investments, in that sense, create fields of friction (Tsing 2005), or what I have elsewhere called hot-spots: 'contested spaces characterized by accelerated change and an increased density of activity and claims, where power is deployed in various forms' (Pijpers 2014: 35). Marampa has developed into such a hot-spot, where change indeed seems to be accelerating.

Part of the accelerated change unfolding in this hot-spot has to do with the creation of expectations: expectations of employment, being able to buy a phone, a television or even a car, having more to eat or enough money available to be able to construct a concrete rather than a mud-block house – all those material improvements that symbolise progress and development in this particular locale. For quite a few, their

---

2. On Sierra Leone's growth rate, see 'Top Growers', *Economist*, 18 November 2013 (available at: www.economist.com/node/21589184, accessed 22 January 2015) and the country report of the African Economic Outlook (available at: www.africaneconomicoutlook. org/fileadmin/uploads/aeo/2014/PDF/CN_Long_EN/Sierra_Leone_EN.pdf, accessed 22 January 2015).

expectations are met, but for many others these expectations remain promises that are indefinitely put off for the future. Many people have a job, but many more do not. Many people experience change, but for many the changes are not occurring (fast enough). Many people see new opportunities, but how to grasp and hold onto to them? How to join in the new possibilities and fulfil the promise of a better life, how to secure a (fair?) share of the potential gains? Identity, rooted in ideas of ethnic background and autochthony, has increasingly become a popular and instrumental tool that people use to claim a share of the benefits that have arrived together with the mining industry.

## IDENTITY, BELONGING AND ECONOMIC COMPETITION

Eriksen (2005: 359) has argued that ethnic identities and boundaries are social constructions that change through time and have variable relevance. He also shows how ethnic identities, relations and boundaries have important economic dimensions, especially when ethnic organisation turns out to serve the economic interests of the members or leaders of ethnic groups (ibid.: 353). Not surprisingly, (ethnic) identities may gain importance in rapidly changing situations when an influx of jobseekers contributes to fierce competition over new economic possibilities. Eriksen's discussion of the case of the Zambian Copperbelt, based on the work of Epstein (1992) and Mitchell (1956), exemplifies this situation. In the Copperbelt, 'far from making tribal identities irrelevant [due to increased ethnic mobility and integration], wage labour and integration into the mining industry led to a re-emergence of ethnicity (labelled re-tribalisation at the time), whereby job allocation, leisure habits and residential arrangements were regulated by ethnic identity' (Eriksen 2005: 358).

Similar processes can be seen in Marampa and its major town Lunsar, which, due to the growing nationwide importance of the iron ore mines, has developed into a melting pot of different ethnic groups from different parts of Sierra Leone. This is not a new phenomenon. Although there have been marked ethnic divisions in Sierra Leone for quite a long time, in the past mining has proved to be an incentive for ethnic relocation and has contributed to increased ethnic diversity by establishing attractive economic centres (Conteh-Morgan & Dixon-Fyle 1999: 48). Lunsar, during the Delco period (from 1930 to 1975), was such a centre, developed around its mining industry. The senior district officer of Port Loko district (of which Lunsar is part), for example, explained to me that during the colonial period, movement between the protectorate and the colony was restricted, but that the Marampa iron ore operations in Lunsar triggered migration from Freetown and brought about 'inter-tribal movement' within the country, thereby encouraging ethnic relocation and diversity. Although many people left Lunsar after the closure of the mines, many stayed as they had settled, married, had children, built a house and created social ties. Yet, while the area may have become an ethnic melting pot, control over land and positions in decision-making structures have remained in the hands of so-called first-comers, landowners or stakeholders. Similarly, ethnic migration in Lunsar today is not leading to a decreased importance in ethnicity or autochthony, but rather to its increased importance, especially in the context of claiming rights to opportunities offered by foreign direct investments, and mining companies in particular.

The abundant number of claims made towards a limited resource – such as jobs in the mining industry – and the increased importance of identity in Marampa, resonates well with Harrison's discussion of identity as a 'scarce resource', in which he clearly shows that there are situations in which the 'preservation of a distinct ethnic identity, or of the rights (such as land rights) that are associated with this identity, depends on the ability to prevent one's practices from being reproduced or appropriated by outsiders' (Harrison 1999: 248–9). In other words, at times, one's ability to successfully claim rights that are associated with one's identity is connected to denying someone else access to the rights this identity brings. As a consequence of this dynamic, social boundaries increasingly become accentuated and enforced.

The role that ethnic identities play in spaces of competition in Sierra Leone has already been highlighted (e.g. Kilson 1966; Horowitz 1985; Kandeh 1992). Discussing the political position of Creoles in Sierra Leone, Jimmy Kandeh argues:

> political ethnicity is primarily an instrumental phenomenon, its primordial underpinnings notwithstanding. As an instrumental construct, political ethnicity tends to collapse the distinction between ethnic identity, on the one hand, and political choices, affiliations and loyalties, on the other. It can express as well as distort common descent, expand as well as contract ethnic boundaries, benefit as well as neglect the mass of ethnically defined political groupings. In other words, ethnopoliticisation can be a strategy for social and political emancipation or it can serve as an instrument of political and class domination. (Kandeh 1992: 81)

As we will see below, this also applies to the increased focus on localness in Marampa. Incorporating localness in popular and official discourse, not only emancipates and protects certain local groups, it also gives rise to the marginalisation and exclusion of others. It invokes a 'politics of belonging: fierce debates on who belongs where, [the] violent exclusion of "strangers" ... and a general affirmation of roots and origins as the basic criteria of citizenship and belonging' (Geschiere & Nyamnjoh 2000: 423); or, to stay closer to my ethnographic terminology, a 'politics of localness': a struggle through which localness becomes an instrument for accessing and claiming (rights to) opportunities brought about by the mining operation.

## THE RIGHT TO EMPLOYMENT

The process of change in Lunsar was clearly spelled out one day by Papa Kamara, a town councillor, who told me: 'People are moving well ... There is rapid development in the community: solar lights, streets, water in the township. It's better than before, life is improving. And every day Lunsar is becoming more populated, every day people are coming for jobs'. The main expectation that people had when the mines re-opened was that there would be an abundance of new jobs; people longed for employment. However, every day people arrive in Lunsar and this high influx of newcomers increases pressure on the local population, who are also vying for the available jobs. Moreover, many jobs require skills that, according to employers, are not easily found in Marampa. Outsiders – that is, nationals who received their education in Freetown and expats – are regularly recruited, to the frustration of local inhabitants. As Santigie Kamara, an elder from one of the villages just outside the London Mining concession explained: 'look at the youth passing-by now, none of them belong to any job. It is a lot that they expected to see, but they are very disappointed ... They don't know why they are not employed, they are now sitting here.'

In response to increased pressure on jobs and people's frustrations with the alleged preference given to outsiders, a discourse has emerged that claims that Temne, the 'born and bred' indigenes of Marampa chiefdom, should be privileged when it concerns employment. These claims draw upon local power structures based on ideas of authochthony and landownership. Moreover, this discourse is not restricted to street talk but is promoted in various ways by different stakeholders such as the local member of parliament, the paramount chief and the Land Owners Association, but also by national politicians seeking support from citizens. During the opening of the first international bank in Lunsar in November 2013, several important local and national politicians, including the president, were invited. Nearly all the speakers took the opportunity to push investors to do more locally: to hire more locals and not source labour and materials from elsewhere.

Due to grumbling in the street and the accompanying political push, combined with contemporary approaches to corporate social responsibility that emphasise the importance of local content,[3] as well as companies' need to ensure a 'social license to operate' (Bridge 2009; Baba & Raufflet 2014), being local has become an advantage in application procedures. The assistant to the local member of parliament, for example, told me in February 2014 that the MP and the paramount chief were trying to become more involved in the recruitment process of London Mining, especially in evaluating the 'localness' of applicants.[4] Furthermore, several distinctions between local and local-local have begun to emerge, and although the criteria are yet to be further negotiated and written down on paper, it has become public knowledge that being a local inhabitant, which implies being a Temne from Marampa, is important when applying for jobs.

Since it has become advantageous to be able to claim a relationship to Marampa, people try to establish such links in various ways. 'Localising' CVs was one of the ways of doing this, as I experienced when helping out the night-time security guard at the compound where I lived. Since there was still construction going on in our compound, the landlord had hired a security guard to prevent building materials falling into the hands of so-called 'night carpenters'. The guard had accepted the job, but aimed to find employment in the mining industry, which was the main reason he had come to Lunsar from Freetown. Since he only had a handwritten CV, I offered to help him out and type it up. He gave me two CVs, his own and someone else's. The two resembled each other quite a bit and I immediately noticed that he copied some information from the other CV. His own mentioned that he was born in Marampa, went to school in Lunsar and had held several jobs here. I knew, however, that he was from Freetown and had received his schooling there. After a while it transpired that he had inserted these things because the mining companies prefer

---

3. Local-content policies are often promoted by national governments and civil society groups, and focus on the use of local products, resources and workers by extraction firms. Also in Sierra Leone there is a debate about how to increase the level of local content in businesses.

4. The involvement of local authorities in sourcing labour has a long history in the establishment of capitalist projects in Africa. Geschiere and Nyamnjoh, for example, argue that 'capitalist agencies tried to make "traditional authorities" play a role in the recruitment and control of labourers' (Geschiere & Nyamnjoh 2000: 447). Interestingly, in the case of Marampa's labour politics, 'traditional' or local authorities push for involvement themselves.

people that come from the Marampa area. An interview would not be a problem, he argued; he was able to speak the local language and would talk his way out of any potential trouble.

As the discussion above suggests, 'local' is not a neatly fixed and defined category; there are various forms of localness and some people claim and/or are seen to be more local than others. A statement by one of the executive members of the Land Owners Association[5] further highlights this division: 'The most important thing', Mohamed said, 'the company has to employ the landowners. You cannot take someone's land and then not employ them'. Statements such as this are not uncommon in the area. During a meeting between an agricultural investor and people from the village where the investor's operation was located, landowners claimed that the company had done nothing for them, and that they are not even employed. When it was pointed out that there were actually several people from the community employed, the response of PaKamara, one of the main community speakers, was:

> Do you want to say Samba [one of the employees] is representing Makomp? Makomp has four families who own the land. Sometimes Samba recruits [people], but sometimes he doesn't know the people from Makomp. Someone from the four families should be in the management.

The community elder quoted above clearly argued that even though people were employed, these people were not deemed to be community members as they did not belong to landowning families. Furthermore, these people – Samba serves as the example in this case – do not exclusively recruit labourers from landowning families. As I have been following this particular investment closely since 2008, I knew how to interpret this comment. Not only had several members of landowning families been employed, the people that were not considered full community members were those that had been living in the village for long periods, sometimes several generations. Such claims based on landownership thus seem to divide villages, and to both empower and marginalise different groups. Naturally, these claims are not uncontested.

The senior district officer of Port Loko district, Mr Kargbo, who is involved in Marampa as an official government representative and regularly attends meetings between London Mining and community

5. The Land Owners Association claims to represent local landowners. The legitimacy of the association was contested and many people doubted whether the chairman was a landowner at all. However, its members were influential in local politics related to investments (such as mining) based on their claim to being landowners.

stakeholders, commented as follows when I asked him for his opinion regarding such statements: 'On the side of the people, the landowners, they think that their lands have been taken away from them, for mining activities, and the expectation is that they should be rich at all cost'. Land-ownership is a highly important feature of local politics in rural Sierra Leone since landowners, to put it simply, constitute the local ruling elite; they provide both paramount and village chiefs, they control and govern the land and they have high positions in the secret societies.[6] Landowner-ship is organised along ethnic lines and usually draws upon ideas of being a first-comer to the region; it is thus based on autochthony. Subsequently, villages usually consist of several landowning families (in the case used below there are two), with male family heads being most powerful, and a much larger number of families who are considered strangers. The landowners, as I show below, can 'give out' land to strangers to use for farming or building houses. It goes beyond the scope of this chapter to critically delve into the landownership system, but for our purposes here it will be sufficient to make clear that in Marampa, landowners can (and often do) use the power of their position as first-comers and landowners in order to claim certain rights (such as rights to employment). This is part and parcel of the 'localness' discourse that currently operates in Marampa's investment landscape.

Although emphasis on localness and local content are often seen by governments and (international) NGOs as positive vantage points through which to stimulate local economies, we have to be aware that these forms of local identity politics may result in the inclusion of certain people, but also in the exclusion of others.[7] Thus, whereas popular discourse surrounding the issue of 'being local' might emphasise how identity is used as a strategy for social emancipation and development, it also illustrates how identity and social position simultaneously serve as instruments of social domination and exclusion. The following case of the Delco-brought people in the village of Chaindatha makes this process more explicit.

---

6. Secret societies, for both men and women, are very important in decision-making and (land) governance processes. Meetings and initiations usually take place at sacred sites in the bush where outsiders are not allowed. For further discussions of secret societies, see e.g. Little (1965, 1966), Ferme (2001), Fanthorpe (2007) and Jackson (2007).

7. For example, Ceuppens and Geschiere (2005: 390) argue that the shift in development approaches from state towards civil society triggered debates regarding belonging by raising issues about who can participate in projects. This case shows that similar things happen in investment discourses, which also witnessed increasing pressure to ensure local beneficiation, for example in the form of sourcing labour and materials at the local level as much as possible.

## THE 'DELCO-BROUGHT PEOPLE'

Osman explained that when the consultants did the land survey in Chaindatha, PaDauda Kabia told him that the Kabias really wanted to be resettled within their own land. The reason being that in this way, they would maintain their position as landowners leaving the others as they are now: subjects, second-class citizens, Delco-brought people. If they would be resettled in a place that was completely new, this would imply that nobody could claim to be a firstcomer, an indigene or landowner.

—Fieldnotes, 26 May 2014

Chaindatha is a village in Marampa chiefdom, located in the London Mining concession. The name Chaindatha, meaning 'under the hill' in the local Temne language, refers to its first location. When iron ore was discovered in the 1930s and extraction started, Chaindatha soon appeared to be too close to Delco's mining operation, and the village had to be relocated. Yet, its second location interfered with mining operations as well, and Chaindatha was moved once more. Despite these relocations, a village elder emphasised how good their life had been during those days.[8] Moreover, people were employed, Delco constructed good roads and they provided water. The third location seems to have offered a good new place for the villagers to settle down in.

With the arrival of London Mining and the re-opening of the mines, Chaindatha found itself once more located inside a mining concession. Being on the fringes of the concession, the village was relatively far away from mining activities to begin with, but with the expansion of mining, the company's infrastructure came closer and closer, which made another resettlement necessary. In order to facilitate the resettlement process and to appropriately compensate the owners of land, crops and houses, a land and household survey proved essential. This survey was conducted by an international consultancy group, Borealis, and supported by local consultants (from Freetown and Marampa). The registration of both external and internal land boundaries, interestingly enough, came to highlight and sharpen existing village hierarchies and power positions based on identity.

Before the land survey began, several meetings between the company, the consultants and the community were held. It was a few days after

---

8. As I mentioned earlier, these positive references to the Delco period are part of a micro-politics that allows making claims concerning the current mining operation.

one of those meetings that the term Delco-brought people was first mentioned to me. Abdul, a youth leader, grumbled and explained that:

> He [one of the landowners] is only here when he hears of something beneficial. They take their shares when anything from London Mining comes around. That is the biggest problem we are encountering with these people. They only own three houses, the rest of the houses are owned by the Delco-brought people, but after Delco [left], we stayed here.

A subsequent meeting between Chaindatha and the consultants illustrated what Abdul meant. Before the meeting got started, a small group of landowners left and gathered for a so-called 'pocket meeting' – a closed meeting of a certain faction within and during a larger meeting. In response, a much larger group consisting of the Delco-brought people also held their own 'pocket meeting'. The actual meeting place was left half empty, with only some old people, children and visitors sticking around. The boundaries between the landowners and strangers could not have been made clearer than through these spatially segregated meetings.

The deep segregation of these groups, who independently prepared for a meeting in which they would negotiate as a single community with London Mining and the consultants, is a clear indication of social

*Figure 9.1*   The 'pocket meeting' of the landowners.

*Figure 9.2*　The 'pocket meeting' of the Delco-brought people.

*Figure 9.3*　The half-empty meeting ground.

divisions within the village based on unequal power relations resulting from landownership. This came to light explicitly in such instances, when the distribution of benefits to be gained from the mining company was negotiated.

During the actual land survey these divisions became even clearer. The survey began by establishing the external boundaries of the village. Mostly, the Kamara and Kabia families, the two landowning families in the village, joined the survey, all of them men. According to oral history, they were the first to settle the area and are therefore the legitimate owners of the land. (There is, however, some disagreement over this version of history, as the Kabias argue that they are the true first-comers.) Over time, other families have settled as well. But, whereas land given to someone to build a house on belongs to the house-owner, farmland is often 'given' to people in exchange for a token, and thus based on a system of use rights. Often, these use rights are silently, or at least unproblem-atically, extended over time. In some cases, second generation incomers have taken over use rights over land from their parents, sometimes without knowing that the land did not actually belong to their parents. As one can imagine, a system in which use rights and lease payments or tokens are not registered in writing, the interpretation of people's rights can be flexible. With financial compensation coming up, use rights have become contested. Moreover, the two landowning families argued extensively among themselves about the exact location of the boundaries between their lands.

After two weeks, the external boundary survey was concluded and the internal boundaries had to be established. This, too, triggered various discussions, and the display of power by landowning families became very evident. Every family was involved in the discussions, as the survey concerned farm land, but based on their powerful position as a landowning family, the Kabias, in particular, turned out to be successful in claiming or re-enforcing ownership of a large amount of land. What I witnessed was framed as follows by someone involved in the survey:

Now PaDauda Kabia is trying to intervene in all the surveys that take place in Chaindatha, not only on his own land, but also on other people's land, saying that, 'This tree is mine, this tree is mine'. So, he is interfering, when money is around ... Before, when people needed land, the landowners would just point with their hands: 'From this place to this place, from that tree to this tree, that is your land, just go and plant a stick there'. But when these companies came, also the use of surveyors came into being. Then land became demarcated in plots of 90 by 90 feet, called a town lot. But soon people realised that the land is getting more value and it was changed to 90 by 70 feet. Now people in Chaindatha are saying that PaDauda is limiting everybody's land, bringing everything down to town lots.

Thus, the landowners used their power, based on their identity and their social standing as first-comers, or autochthons, to enforce a system that was not in place when initial land agreements were made. For the strangers, the Delco-brought people, there was little they could do, as the same person explained:

Ninety per cent of the people in Chaindatha don't have a voice, only the big people like the town-lots-Kabias. For the majority it's a pity. The Delco-brought people are very much less powerful. When it comes to votes, they will say, 'Ooh, David, you are a citizen. Come and vote'. But when I need land, they will say, 'No, you are a stranger'. When they need something from me, I am a citizen; when I need something from them, I'm a stranger, even though I am [sic] born here. I don't know where my father came from, all I know is Lunsar.

Indeed, this impression could be drawn from the survey period. During meetings people were heard and listened to, everybody could speak. Yet, in the end, the landowners govern the land and are able to demarcate plots. Bringing people's land down to smaller plots of course implies that more land, and therefore more compensation money, would be generated for the landowning families.

The frustration of the Delco-brought people accumulated over time, and it was during village meetings that anger was expressed most explicitly. The focus-group discussion between the consultants and the Chaindatha women was such a meeting. When the women were asked where they would like to live, they mentioned that they wanted to live along the road.[9] The discussion continued and the majority of the women reasoned that if the consultants and London Mining built a new village, the villagers should not all live together. Instead, they suggested that the landowners should live somewhere else, and some even began talking about three future villages. One woman, Memusu Kalokoh, then turned to me and furiously said that she did not want the landowners to put their hands in her pocket: 'We are going to divide this village into three: the Kamaras, the Kabias and we, the strangers. My father has bought

9.  The village was located not far from the main road that connects the area to the major cities of the country. Moving to a settlement located along this road is considered an advantage, especially for trading purposes.

land in the village and now I even have to pay the landowners again to get the land. I am going to leave now', she concluded, and stood up and left.

The case of the Delco-brought people, of the 'strangers', shows clearly how village hierarchies are intensely reinforced when the expectation of benefits comes into play. Similar to the issue of job applications, in this instance, too, talk of identity and autochthony, rooted in ideas of first-comers and strangers, provides a highly important and instrumental argument. In the wake of expected compensation for land by the mining company, the landowners re-established their rights as landowners, re-accentuated their power and accompanying social boundaries, which left 'strangers' (even though those may have been born in the village) with very few assets. The land compensation scheme, consequently, allowed the elite to socially and materially empower themselves, while socially and materially dominating and marginalising the strangers.

## MINING AND THE POLITICS OF LOCALNESS

In this chapter I have discussed how identity is used in order to claim certain rights and benefits from a mining company operating in Marampa chiefdom, Sierra Leone. Identity, in this context, draws heavily on ethnic background and social belonging, thus on autochthony, which has increasingly become an important concept for defining identity in the African context (Ceuppens & Geschiere 2005; Geschiere 2009). The identities that are put forward come into being in notions such as the local-local and the national, and are thus expressed and hierarchised in degrees of 'localness'. The more local one is, the more rights or benefits can be claimed. Identity becomes an instrumental concept that, through processes of inclusion and exclusion, empowers and marginalises. In this chapter I have scrutinised this 'politics of localness' through the negotiations that took place in Marampa regarding rights to employment and the mining company's financial compensation scheme involving the lease of land and lost crops.

Naturally, taking identity as my main focus narrows the analysis at the expense of other important elements in the micro-politics of employment in, and compensation from, mining in Marampa. For example, I have not addressed the role of personal relationships or bribery. I have also not paid much attention to how essential it is for many people to get a job, as it represents a way of securing a livelihood, nor have I addressed the challenges that come with the (un)availability of skills. In the discussion of land, I did not delve into the system of land ownership or scrutinise the commoditization of land. I intend to address these and other topics elsewhere; for now, my aim has been to show how identity is played out between and within groups in the community around the mining operation in times of accelerated change and competition over economic opportunities.

In the case of Marampa, we see that the increased availability of resources – in this instance employment and financial compensation – and the desire of an increasing number of people to lay claim to these resources, generates an intensified form of identity politics, which reifies existing social identities and turn them into instrumental tools. Localness takes centre stage, either in the form of being a local Temne or, even more so, a local Temne landowner. Depending on the scale at which negotiations take place, different in and out groups are created. At one scale, all of Marampa's Temne are claimed to have advantages, especially when the group they find themselves in competition with consists of nationals and expats. Yet, when scaling down, local Marampa Temne are also divided between landowners and strangers, between first-comers and Delco-brought people in the case of Chaindatha. Yet, whatever the scale of analysis chosen, identity is used in all instances as a way of optimising both group and individual benefits, thereby marginalising other people's chances and thus facilitating a continuous process of inclusion and exclusion at different levels. The politics of localness that unfold in Marampa's landscape of extraction thus enables both social reproduction as well as a contestation of existing social hierarchies, boundaries and inequalities based on kinship, ethnic origin and claims to localness.

## ACKNOWLEDGEMENTS

I wish to thank both of the editors of this volume for their insightful comments and suggestions. Great appreciation also goes to those who shared their views, and engaged and talked with me during my fieldwork in 2013/14. This research was conducted as part of the University of Oslo project 'Overheating: The Three Crises of Globalisation', funded by the European Research Council.

## REFERENCES

Baba, S., and E. Raufflet. 2014. Managing Relational Legacies: Lessons from British Columbia, Canada. *Administrative Sciences* 4(1): 15–34.

Bourdieu, P. 1991. *Language and Symbolic Power*, trans. G. Raymond and M. Adamson. Cambridge: Polity Press.

Bridge, G. 2009. The Hole World: Spaces and Scales of Extraction. *New Geographies* 2: 43–8.

Ceuppens, B., and P. Geschiere. 2005. Autochthony: Local or Global? New Modes in the Struggle over Citizenship and Belonging in Africa and Europe. *Annual Review of Anthropology* 34: 385–408.

Conteh-Morgan, E., and M. Dixon-Fyle. 1999. *Sierra Leone at the End of the Twentieth Century.* New York: Peter Lang.

Epstein, A.L. 1992. *Scenes from African Urban Life: Collected Copperbelt Essays.* Edinburgh: Edinburgh University Press.

Eriksen 2005. Economies of Ethnicities. In J.G. Carrier (ed.), *A Handbook of Economic Anthropology.* Cheltenham: Edward Elgar Publishing, pp.353–69.

Fanthorpe, R. 2007. Sierra Leone: The Influence of the Secret Societies, with Special Reference to Female Genital Mutilation. Writenet Report for the Status Determination and Protection Information Section, United Nations High Commissioner for Refugees. Available at: www.refworld.org/docid/46cee3152.html (accessed 10 June 2016).

Ferme, M. 2001. *The Underneath of Things: Violence, History, and the Everyday in Sierra Leone.* Berkeley: University of California Press.

Gamble, D.P. 1963. The Temne Family in a Modern Town (Lunsar) in Sierra Leone. *Africa* 33(3): 209–26.

Geschiere, P. 2009. *The Perils of Belonging: Autochthony, Citizenship, and Exclusion in Africa and Europe.* Chicago: University of Chicago Press.

Geschiere, P., & F. Nyamnjoh. 2000. Capitalism and Autochthony: The Seesaw of Mobility and Belonging. *Public Culture* 12(2): 423–52.

Harrison, S. 1999. Identity as a Scarce Resource. *Social Anthropology* 7(3): 239–51.

Horowitz, D.L. 1985. *Ethnic Groups in Conflict.* Berkeley: University of California Press.

Jackson, P. 2007. Reshuffling an Old Deck of Cards? The Politics of Local Government Reform in Sierra Leone. *African Affairs* 106(422): 95–111.

Jarrett, H.R. 1956. Lunsar: A Study of an Iron Ore Mining Center in Sierra Leone. *Economic Geography* 32(2): 153–61.

Kandeh, J.D. 1992. Politicization of Ethnic Identities in Sierra Leone. *African Studies Review* 35(1): 81–99.

Kayonde, S., L.H. Alexandre and J.F. Speakman. 2013. Sierra Leone – Growth Pole Diagnostic: First Phase of the Growth Poles Program. Report. Washington: World Bank.

Kilson, M. 1966. *Political Change in a West African State: A Study of the Modernization Process in Sierra Leone.* Cambridge, MA: Harvard University Press.

Little, K. 1965. The Political Function of the Poro, Part 1. *Africa* 35(4): 349–65.

Little, K. 1966. The Political Function of the Poro, Part 2. *Africa* 36(1): 62–72.

Mbembe, A. 2001. Ways of Seeing: Beyond the New Nativism. *African Studies Review* 44: 1–14.

Mitchell, J.C. 1956. *The Kalela Dance.* Manchester: Manchester University Press.

Pijpers, R.J. 2014. Crops and Carats: Exploring the Interconnectedness of Mining and Agriculture in Sub-Saharan Africa. *Futures* 62 (A): 32–39.

Pijpers, R.J. In press. Lost Glory or Poor Legacy? Mining Pasts, Future Projects in Rural Sierra Leone. In S. Luning, J.B. Gewald and J. Jansen (eds), *From Corporate Paternalism to Corporate Social Responsibility (CSR): Mining, History and Heritage.* London: Routledge.

Sikor, T., and L. Lund. 2009. Access and Property: A Question of Power and Authority. *Development and Change* 40(1): 1–22.

Tsing, A.L. 2005. *Friction: An Ethnography of Global Connection.* Princeton: Princeton University Press.

# 10. Too Many Khans?

## Old and New Elites in Afghanistan

*Torunn Wimpelmann*

Since the beginning of the wars that have troubled the country since 1978, the influx of resources – cash, weapons and employment – have opened up new avenues for leadership and accumulation in Afghanistan. Two generations ago, local influence or 'being a leader' was mainly based on landownership and relations to rulers in the capital, with khans and maliks acting as intermediaries between the government and their dependents. Centring on the accounts of members of one extended family, this chapter explores how new opportunities have challenged the position of traditional elites, and how this group strategises about and reflects upon their diminished position as self-evident community leaders. I suggest that elections in many ways might have transformed relations between leaders and followers into a monetary, short-term transaction, replacing more constant and intimate reciprocal obligations. Whereas being a leader previously meant everyday attendance to the needs of followers, slowly consolidating one's position, contemporary aspirants to leadership can turn fast cash into equally fast access to influence. At the same time, tensions between ideals of equality and realities of hierarchy (Abu-Lughod 1986) that existed within the 'old' model of leadership are evident in the dismissal of new elites as lacking established family names. Moreover, an ambivalent relationship exists between the new elites and the central government. Members of the new elite often speak disparagingly about the alleged dysfunctional nature of the government, while simultaneously depending on it as a source of their own power.

## LEADERS IN AFGHANISTAN: FEUDAL RULERS OR HUMBLE PUBLIC SERVANTS?

A central feature of both academic and political debates around elites in Afghanistan, and political life more generally, has been the relationship between leaders and their 'people'. Echoing the discussions generated by Fredrik Barth's work on the Swat Pathans, scholars have debated whether

Afghan leaders, personified in the traditional khan, have derived their position from more enduring hierarchies related to landownership and lineage, or whether their role as leaders is mostly earned through personal initiative, capability and long-standing service to people (Barth 1959; Edwards 1998). In the view of Jon Anderson, the khan was historically little more than a 'civil servant' (Anderson 1978). The khan's position is tenuous and constantly needs shoring up through the performance of services for the people of his community. The majority of his surplus is, or at least was, until the monetisation of the rural economy in the 1970s, reinvested in the local community in the form of hospitality and social services. A khan was expected to maintain a guesthouse where followers could be fed and housed, and to support them in unexpected expenses for such things as medical treatment and dealings with the government. Leadership being based on repeated performance means that it is personal abilities that give rise to and sustain power. A leader should be eloquent, charismatic, generous and able to command both loyalty and respect. He should be brave and able to enforce the decisions made within his sphere of influence.

Others emphasise the differentiated status that these interactions confer on leaders and followers. In a system where autonomy is highly valued, those who profess their dependence on others insert themselves at the lower level of the social hierarchy, even if such inequality is masked by investing 'independence with responsibility and a set of obligations, and dependency with the dignity of choice' (Abu-Lughod 1986: 78). For instance, the celebrated ability of khans to 'solve conflicts' often entails an act of admission of weakness by 'followers'. In a murder or elopement cases for instance, those unable to obtain revenge or restoration on their own would transfer the responsibility to restore honour or reputation to a leader in a manner that signified dependency.

It is also pointed out that the khans increasingly acted as intermediaries of the government, in ways that are ultimately exploitative. Having been conferred land rights by the government by virtue of being a valuable ally, the khan and his close allies derived additional power by acting as a broker for peasants and the poorer segments of the population in their dealings with the state, 'adding to their armament of dispensable favours' (Anderson 1975: 598). Giustozzi (2013) emphasises that with the advent of a centralising state during the 1880s, local leaders also became dependent in some ways, as the government selectively attempted to marginalise, co-opt or eliminate local men of prominence in order to create more reliable and pliant allies. In some areas, including the province under study in this chapter, certain population groups (mainly but not exclusively Pashtuns) were enlisted as partners in government campaigns of pacification.

When civil war broke out in the late 1970s, it brought with it new sources of accumulation that would transform the basis of leadership in Afghanistan, and with it the debate about the exact nature of the relationship between conventional khans and their followers. In the early 1970s, the gradual monetisation of the rural economy had led to declarations that 'there are no khans anymore'. The arrival of the market economy meant that khans would divert wealth to other sectors than their home areas, putting money into business in the capital instead of reinvesting in the social currency of patronage (ibid.). Poorer groups went from being sharecroppers to short-term wage labourers, as new agricultural inputs such as tractors led to increased rural stratification. All of this had the effect of potentially de-socialising rural social relations in the sense of transactions becoming more monetised.

Yet it was the wars of the 1980s that drastically changed the political economy and the sources of social power in Afghanistan. After the Soviet Union invaded to prop up a faltering socialist government in 1979, the country became a key geopolitical site, prompting an enormous flow of aid and weapons from the USA and Saudi Arabia in particular. Peaking at around US$1.5 billion annually (Rubin 2002), this aid amounted to almost half the country's economy prior to the war. At the same time, the war played havoc on livestock and land, reducing the relative importance of rural production. The external funds were channelled through a host of often competing mujahidin parties, a deliberate divide-and-rule strategy by the Pakistani intelligence services (Dorronsoro 2005). As a result, a new class of leaders emerged: commanders whose military skills or political entrepreneurship enabled them to set up 'fronts' with supplies from Pakistan. Even if traditional rural leaders from established families were willing participants in the jihad, they did not come to dominate it; instead, prominent jihadi commanders tended to come from more modest backgrounds, often with religious credentials (Roy 1994). This meant that the older khans lost their position as the chief gatekeepers between rural society and the 'outside' world. However, the personalised, clientelistic logic through which older leaders had operated was often emulated by jihadi leaders. For instance, Giustozzi suggests that the newer leaders often took up the practices of the old khans: distributing largesse to their followers and indulging in competition over women and personal feuds (Giustozzi 2009: 34).

The new order ushered in following the 2001 US-led invasion marked another dramatic change in the political economy of Afghanistan and to routes towards leadership. The new ruling constellation in Kabul was an often uneasy mix of old jihadis, being rehabilitated to power after a period of displacement during the Taliban government, and technocrats returning from exile. The post-US invasion resources flowing into the country dwarfed those of the 1980s; at the peak of the international intervention around 2010, US expenditure alone was estimated at four times the size of the Afghan economy (Cordesman 2013).

In addition, the new order prescribed elected representatives at all levels, from the president to the parliament to the provincial councils. Yet to many, the introduction of all these elections had the effect of decreasing the accountability of leaders in Afghanistan. People were merely courted at the time of voting, through small sums of cash, replacing the more constant and intimate reciprocal obligations of the past and transforming relations between leaders and followers into a monetary, short-term transaction. Fraud appeared to be routine, leading Coburn and Larson (2014) to conclude that elections were not about representation but a tool through which elite bargains were made, over which ordinary people had limited, if any influence. Instead, results were often bought directly from those tasked with overseeing or counting the votes, dispensing with the need for ordinary people's support altogether. In other words, compared to older models of leadership, accountability – whereby those most responsive to community concerns were deemed the best to represent it – declined (ibid.). Yet such claims must be treated with caution because the moral critiques launched against new leaders are laden with a measure of nostalgia that carries certain class dimensions. This becomes clearer if we examine tensions in narratives of the older leaders as they reflect upon their fall from positions of influence at the hands of new elites.

## THE HEROIC FEATS OF MOHAMMAD ASHRAF KHAN

In a central province of Afghanistan, one of the three leading families prior to the outbreak of conflict in the late 1970s is generally considered to be the Arsala family.[1] In this family, a figure of pride is Mohammad Ashraf Khan. He is recalled as a heroic man who earned the name the family still enjoys today. His colourful life was recounted to me as follows:

In the 1920s, Mohammad Ashraf regained previously confiscated land from the government with the help of his mother's connections to an influential Sufi leader in Kabul. He then eliminated his nephew, his main rival regarding the land. For this act he was forced into nine years of exile in the western city of Herat, where he developed a reputation for bravery.

---

1. All names used in this chapter are pseudonyms.

Amongst his exploits was the capture and killing of a notorious bandit, for which he received a government reward, and aiding the government against its war efforts in the north against the refugees displaced by the Soviet campaigns in Central Asia. Having thus received from the government 'nine-hundred guns and many golden coins', Mohammad Ashraf had become quite a rich man, and he continued to cultivate his relationship with one of the most influential Sufi leaders, who had already helped him retrieve his land some 15 years back. Back in his home province he bought more land, and started challenging the other established leaders of the area by taking the side of the poor against the oppression (*zulm*) meted out by the khans.

As his influence and reputation grew, Mohammad Ashraf was also expected to manage conflict in the local area, although this was fraught with peril. In one case, he was asked for help by the head of the local madrasa to end the embarrassing visits of a widow who would come to grieve on the grave of her deceased lover, a young student who had perished from a fever. Mohammad Ashraf brought her to see him, but the widow refused to cease visiting the graveyard, instead hurling great insults at him. In response, he had her beaten, leading to a conflict with the woman's part of the village. As they confronted him, Mohammad Ashraf, superior both in marksmanship and firepower, killed six men. Bracing himself for another prolonged period of exile, he was convinced by older family members to surrender to the government instead, and rather than being imprisoned he was placed under house arrest at the residence of a government technocrat. Back in his village, his adversaries demanded six girls to be given in marriage as compensation for the murders. In a show of loyalty still remembered and treasured to this day, six poorer families offered their girls in place of Mohammad Ashraf's daughters and nieces.

Meanwhile, Mohammad Ashraf's achievements continued. According to family legend, having alerted the government to a coup plot, he went on to negotiate the release of a hundred captured women whom the government, now at war, had taken from a neighbouring tribe ('sending them back home each cloaked in a new *chador*'), greatly improving relations between the two tribes. Now quite influential, the government occasionally sought to contain Mohammad Ashraf, for instance by taking his sons as virtual hostages under the pretext of offering them education in Kabul. But it was family rivalries that would lead to Mohammad Ashraf's downfall.

His eldest son, today generally spoken of as a 'thief, madman and idiot', was a drifter who spent most of his time with local nomadic bandits. When, in the 1970s, a demand for half of his father's inheritance was refused, he appropriated parts of the wheat harvest and, in the ensuing confrontation between father and son, Mohammad Ashraf was shot and died. In turn, the eldest son was killed by his younger brother to avenge the death of Mohammad Ashraf, and the dead son's widow opted to marry her husband's killer, who was already her brother-in-law.

## CRUMBLING INFLUENCE: THE RISE OF THE JIHADI PARTIES

It was Mohammad Jan, the eldest son of Mohammad Ashraf's third wife, who emerged as the next leader. His ascendancy came during the 1980s jihad against the Soviet-backed government, when the family faced a different challenge, that of young men from poorer families who joined the most radical of the jihadi parties, Hizb-e Islami. One of these poor young men was Isaq, who is recalled in the Arsala family with resentment and disappointment. Son of the family retainer, Isaq was part of a group of Hizbi soldiers who imprisoned Mohammad Jan during a petty conflict over irrigation channels, a great affront to a member of a leading family. Mohammad Jan was eventually released through the mediation of others, and Isaq was later killed in an ambush, but the imprisonment is still remembered as an unsettling incident that foretold of the diminishing position of the family in the decades to come.

A local intellectual from a more modest background explained why Hizb-e Islami became so powerful amongst poor and middle-class men in the area. He argued that the party recruited from the first generation of young men who had received education as part of a universal schooling policy in the 1950s and 1960s. These men, many of them school teachers, were attracted to Hizb's more assertive stance against elites, such as the argument that Islam gave poor people certain rights such as *zakat*, which meant that they should not consider themselves to be the recipients of the goodwill and charity of leaders. Mohammad Jan and other members of the provincial elite had detected in Hizb a blanket hostility to their kind, and instead opted to join the more moderate jihadi party led by Pir Gailani, an establishment figure whose relative had assisted Mohammad Jan's father in retrieving his land a generation before. However, this choice was later to be the source of some regret. Gailani's party proved weak, both in terms of political influence within Afghanistan and in its ability to attract foreign patronage. Mohammad Jan found himself increasingly unable to exercise influence in the province and moved most of his family and supporters to exile in Pakistan. A distant relative with more foresight had switched to an Islamist party, and was the recipient of considerable foreign support. He became the dominant commander in his area, and a venerated figure amongst Western mujahidin supporters, before eventually going into exile as the tide of the war changed with the withdrawal of the Soviets.

Hizb-e Islami lost some of its position after the jihadi parties self-destructed in a vicious civil war after the collapse of the communist government, and during the Taliban years the Arsala family fared somewhat better. In one of many local deals cut in order to rule the country, the Taliban stated that they trusted the 'white beards' (elders) of the area to govern community affairs and were happy to devolve power to the Arsala family at the local level. At the same time, the family was unable to make inroads with the central authorities, which were dominated by the clergy, and mainly kept a low profile in the local area. Doing otherwise would have risked inviting Taliban retaliation, and suffering a public beating from a low level Talib mullah would have been an irreparable blow to the family's reputation. Many Afghans of similar background recall as their greatest fear during the Taliban period this possibility of humiliation in the view of others. Travelling by car and bus, for instance, one was at risk of encountering Talibs who would not hesitate to mete out physical punishments for religious non-adherence – such as beards of insufficient length. Rather than the beating itself, what they dreaded was the enormous loss of face that such an incident would entail for people who were still able to preserve some of the status they had held in the past.

## COMPETING WITH THE SONS OF UNKNOWNS

Today, fifteen years after the US overthrow of the Taliban government, Mohammad Jan still maintains aspirations to be a khan, but acknowledges that he is a mere shadow of his father. Instead, a handful of other actors have emerged as leading figures in the province. One, a long-time minister in the Karzai government, rose to prominence through his background in Hizb-e Islami and his work with international aid organisations. During the years of the anti-Soviet resistance, Western-funded aid organisations found much of their cadre amongst actors of the political jihadi parties such as Hizb-e Islami, which tended to attract educated technocrats from poorer and middle-class backgrounds. The long-time minister's path to influence was in many ways typical: a self-made man who never speaks of his family background, he obtained a scholarship through Hizb-e Islami, and then rose through the ranks of various aid organisations who recruited much of their staff from groups headquartered in the Pakistani city of Peshawar. By the time the new political order fell into place under President Karzai, the minister had both the technical qualifications (including skills in English and aid administration) and political connections to enable him to land a ministerial appointment. According to some of the older elites, the minister is engaged in ruthless racketeering and worse, but they grudgingly admit that a certain level of political clout and consistent cultivation of a client base in his home district might ensure continued influence beyond the lifetime of his ministerial post.

Less sophisticated, and unworthy as serious rivals in their eyes, are the local MP and his brother, who, while possessing 'not even a Toyota Corolla' prior to 2001, are now often seen as the most important actors in the province after securing lucrative construction and logistics contracts with the US military. Their newly built house in a prestigious area of Kabul – a large, white construction resembling a modernist Gulf palace, complete with external chandeliers and under 24-hour armed guard – is testimony to their wealth and aspirations. Finally, there is the senior intelligence officer who has somewhat inexplicably gained influence, when 'nobody even knows his father's name'.

The minister, the MP and his brother, the intelligence officer – according to the Arsala family, these people are not leaders in any proper sense. A real tribal leader should first and foremost be at the constant service of his people. As Mohammad Jan stated:

> Why was my father so famous and amongst the three most important khans in the province? He was always there to protect the poor. He allowed no oppression. All his hours, day and night he devoted to the service of the tribe (*qawmi*). He spent his money on them, he solved their difficulties with the government and their private problems, he was generous, merciful, gracious and not afraid to stand up to the authorities. One time he even beat the district governor after he had tortured the local people.

Mohammad Jan tries to live up to these ideals today, but he is struggling:

> I would be more influential and effective if I had money. If my brother had enough money … I could have been a tribal leader full time, but instead I had to take a job with the government. Many days, when I come home at 4 o'clock, somebody is there in my house, needing my help … I will take off my uniform immediately and go with him, coming back late. Sometimes I cannot go to work at all, because there is a *shura* [an informal council] or because I have to go with someone to another government office. I have problems with managing everything … I often have to ask my colleagues at work to cover my responsibilities. So busy am I that I sometimes don't even know what

day it is, if it is a Friday [a holiday for Muslims] or a workday ... But if I can serve the tribe, I am happy, this is all that I want to do.

Mohammad Jan went on to recount an incident where, out of nowhere, a man appeared on his path and threw his turban at Mohammad Jan's feet, thanking him for his help in securing him government papers for this land. At times like this, Mohammad Jan said, it felt like it was all worth it; even if you suffer, having to go to offices, asking for personal favours (*wasita*) – when it works out, you feel so inspired.

The new leaders that have sprung up in recent years are seen to shirk such responsibilities. Instead, they are said to buy people's votes at election time, or they simply bribe election officials in order to fabricate the results. They use their influence with the government to dispense positions, but they are not, according to the older elites, interested in serving the people. Thus a member of the old elite proudly recounted how a man from his province expressed amazement that a traditional leader had apologised for the simple dinner he had served when the man had come to his house for some help with a government document: 'For one week I tried, I could not even get a meeting with [the minister or the MP]. You have not just helped me, you have also served me dinner, even asking me whether I found it tasty'.

Moral critiques of unaccountable leaders are also framed in terms of their distance from the community, both physically and morally. Their use of armed guards is taken as another sign that the new leaders are not 'real'. 'If you are a true leader, you can live amongst the people, the tribe will protect you – there is no need for armed guards'. Moreover, the lifestyle of new leaders, and in particular their failure to uphold the gender norms of rural Afghanistan, are presented as evidence of their disregard for ordinary people, as a random conversation with a man from the province revealed:

T.W.: Abdul Khalique, does your wife work?
ABDUL KHALIQUE: Only women from poor families and civilised families work ... Some years ago I had to move in with my brother. His wife could not cook, clean and wash the clothes for all of us, it was too much for a single person so it was decided that I should get married. Although I am a researcher, an intellectual, my wife is illiterate. I would have liked to have married an educated woman, even for my children it would have been good, to have an educated mother. But in our province, it is not acceptable for women to go outside, to work outside. So I married a woman who was not working, who would not go out. She is illiterate. In order to satisfy the people in my local

community, to not upset them, I did this. You see, in my province, in my home area, I am well-respected. I can go anywhere in my province, people will look up to me, even if I work for an NGO. Some people from my province … well, they might have successful careers … but when they go to their home area, people do not respect them, because of the way they live, because they don't have any regard for the feelings of their own people. For instance, they will go for trips to Tajikistan without care about how others feel.

While Abdul Khalique is regretting the restrictions gender ideals have placed on his own life, at the same time he finds the selfishness of those who choose to disregard them abhorrent. For him, to refuse to live by such norms is a deeply anti-social act, a signal to one's local community that they and their sentiments do not matter. There is a more prudent concern with one's own status and ability to save face here as well, but this easily slips over into questions about morality and respect for one's community. Marrying women who 'go out', or openly going to Tajikistan, often considered a place where Afghans go solely for the purpose of pursuing illicit pleasures that are unavailable (legally) in Afghanistan – such as drinking and womanising – are not just transgressions of gender norms. These practices are taken as signs that the new leaders have exited the local moral community altogether (Martin 2010), and that they therefore cannot be counted on to pay any attention to the lives of ordinary people. Money is seen as the key factor that has caused relations of respect and obligations to degenerate. Because votes and elections can be bought, leadership positions are obtained through bribes – whether paying voters one-hundred dollars each, or giving several hundred thousand to election officials. Relations of trust and reciprocal obligations have been replaced by simple, one-off monetary transactions. The older elites, however, still harbour hopes that the newfound influence of their rivals will prove short-lived: 'When they lose those government jobs, people won't even know who they are', Mohammad Jan predicted. In contrast, he hoped that a family name and reputation for long-term service to the community would ensure him and his peers continued esteem: 'Those whose fathers and grandfathers were khans, they are still respected and people trust them. With wet soil, you need less water'.

## CONCLUSIONS: 'TRUE LEADERS ARE HIDDEN FROM VIEW'

Others have pointed out how much of social interaction in Afghanistan is structured around egalitarian ideals (Barth 1959; Anderson 1978) Yet, up to a point, the enactment of these ideals often serves to mask actual relations of inequality. The tendency of the older elites to dismiss those emerging today with statements of how nobody knows their grandfather, or even their father's name, contradicts the constant referencing of egalitarian notions of merit. Instead, it suggests that leadership is not merely about individual competence, but also about more durable properties, like a family name. Another paradox is the relationship between the older elites and the government: on the one hand, a source of much of the influence enjoyed by the family for generations, and on the other, the subject of many complaints. When looking at the rise of Mohammad Ashraf two generations ago, it is clear that much of his growing influence and prestige was entwined with the alliances he forged with the government, whether it was as an enforcer of the law or as what was effectively a government mercenary. The government conferred certain privileges on him, such as land in return for various services – for instance, marshalling expeditions against government enemies. However, in the Arsala family's accounts, it is, unsurprisingly, Mohammad Ashraf's individual accomplishments and outright heroism that constituted the key to his success.

At the same time, the government has become inaccessible to the dependents of the older leaders, and this very inaccessibility has provided a rationale for why the khan or the malik must 'help' the people and, at the same time, the very source of their power. As long as the government is dysfunctional and makes obtaining identity papers, permits and deeds an impossible undertaking without the right connections, the services of the khans are necessary. However, in the eyes of the old elites, this was not an exploitative relation, but instead, the provision of an all-consuming task which, if not carried out to the satisfaction of clients, would lead to the loss of position altogether. This stands in a sharp contrast to today's situation, where no such work is required – leaders at best take the time to buy people's votes, but more likely, they simply bribe election officials. To the older elites, this is unearned leadership, far removed from the dutiful service that they carried out in their time, and which they have to some extent have continued to do. The 'newly rich' people need to spend their time in Kabul, where instead of serving ordinary people they pass their time cultivating relations with the government and international forces in order to get the contracts necessary for their businesses. In any case, according to one individual, this is just as well, because the 'new rich' do not have the ability or stamina to work with the tribe. Even in the tribal *shura* (an informal council of influential people from the main tribe of the province), they claim, the MP and his brother resorted to buying support in order to displace Mohammad Jan as leader.

Yet interspersed with criticism of the new leaders were some dismissive comments about ordinary people. Some have become 'greedy' and short-sighted, thinking of monetary gains and 'forgetting about history, and about relations', unhindered by the shame that would stop people from displaying such fleeting loyalties in the past. 'This kind of competition', complained Mohammad Jan, was not something they had faced before. As a result, today those who want to remain khans in the proper sense do so at increasing cost to themselves. His near exhaustion from multi-tasking work duties and the demands placed on him as a tribal leader is a case in point.

Moreover, the old elite claims, in a situation where the faithful provision of brokerage is no longer an option, that the government has become completely unresponsive, and thus, in frustration with the predations of an unaccountable state, people have turned once again to the Taliban. Such statements are not necessarily an indictment of systems of patronage per se, since the Taliban to a large extent are implicated in relations of patronage with Pakistani and Arab backers, but rather a wish to see it restored to a state in which it is more predictable and ordered, with a single set of interlocutors. Such hopes might be further removed from realisation than ever. The province is now increasingly insecure, and neither old nor new elites can actually travel to their home areas, being restricted to Kabul, or at the most to provincial or district capitals. Under these conditions, according to the intellectual mentioned earlier, knowing who the real leaders are is becoming increasingly impossible. In a situation where 'men cannot even step out of their houses and talk freely to their community about matters of leadership', Kabul-based pretenders find ever more fertile ground.

## REFERENCES

Abu-Lughod, L. 1986. *Veiled Sentiments: Honor and Poetry in a Bedouin Society*. Berkeley: University of California Press.

Anderson, J.W. 1975. Tribe and Community among the Ghilzai Pashtuns. *Anthropos* 70: 575–601.

Anderson, J.W. 1978. There Are No Khans Anymore: Economic Development and Social Change in Tribal Afghanistan. *Middle East Journal* 32: 167–83.

Barth, F. 1959. *Political Leadership amongst Swat Pathans*. London: Athlone Press.

Coburn, N., and A. Larson. 2014. *Derailing Democracy in Afghanistan: Elections in an Unstable Landscape*. New York: Columbia University Press.

Cordesman, A. 2013. *The Afghan War in 2013: Meeting the Challenges of Transition*, Vol 2: *Afghan Economics and Outside Aid*. Lanham, MD: Rowman and Littlefield/Center for Strategic and International Studies.

Dorronsoro, G. 2005. *Revolution Unending: Afghanistan, 1979 to the Present*. London: Hurst.

Edwards, D.B. 1998. Learning from the Swat Pathans: Political Leadership in Afghanistan, 1978–1997. *American Ethnologist* 25: 712–28.

Giustozzi, A. 2009. *Empires of Mud: The Neo-Taliban Insurgency in Afghanistan, 2002–2007.* New York: Columbia University Press.

—— 2013. If Only There Were Leaders: The Problem of 'Fixing' the Pashtun Tribes. In B.D. Hopkins and M. Marsden (eds), *Beyond Swat: History, Society and Economy along the Afghanistan–Pakistan Frontier.* London: Hurst, pp.239–48.

Martin, K. 2010. The Death of the Big Men: Depreciation of Elites in New Guinea. *Ethnos* 75: 1–22.

Roy, O. 1994. The New Political Elite of Afghanistan. In M. Weiner and A. Banuazizi (eds), *The Politics of Social Transformation in Afghanistan, Iran and Pakistan.* Syracuse, NY: Syracuse University Press.

Rubin, B.R. 2002. *The Fragmentation of Afghanistan: State Formation and Collapse in the International System.* New Haven: Yale University Press.

# 11. Do Homosexuals Wear Moustaches?

## Controversies around the First Montenegrin Pride Parade

*Branko Banović*

The global era is characterised by local cultural divergences as much as it is by the process of unification, and every globalisation project is shaped by somewhat unpredictable interactions among specific cultural legacies (Eriksen 1995, 2003, 2007; Appadurai 1996, 2002; Tsing 2002; Hannerz 2003). Located in the central part of the Balkan Peninsula, Montenegro (a much neglected part of former Yugoslavia, and perhaps the part least studied by Western scholars) carries a legacy of extreme patriarchy and masculinity. In addition, it has been exposed to the influence of global processes and currently finds itself in the process of negotiating European Union membership. These factors mean that Montenegro offers itself as a uniquely interesting site for conducting research on struggles over masculinity, sexuality, belonging and heritage, which I examine in the light of the first Pride parade in Podgorica, Montenegro's capital.

On its path to EU membership, Montenegro has experienced shifts on gender issues and enacted legislation to prohibit discrimination based on sexual orientation (Pearce 2014: 2, 6). A key issue here is the moustache, which has clearly shown overheating effects resulting from accelerated change in national gender policies. As homosexuals are perceived as a novelty in Montenegrin culture, a European import, predominantly connected with the process of EU integration, the moustache as the logo of the first Pride parade in Podgorica has exposed a lot of tension between 'old' and 'new' gender ideals. The fast, sudden and unexpected shift in the semantic area traditionally covering the moustache (honour, pride, morality, heroism, bravery and so on) into the context of contemporary struggles for sexual minority rights has brought to the fore the clash between the traditional patriarchal Montenegrin identity and a new, 'European' man. Thus, focusing on controversies over the moustache, I want to show how the struggle over sexuality, masculinity and heritage has played out in the Montenegrin public arena and in everyday life.

Pride parades are a global phenomenon that overheated and destabilised Montenegrin society for the first time in 2013. They are events held annually throughout the world to commemorate the Stonewall rebellion, a spontaneous and violent reaction by gay men and lesbians against a police raid that took place in New York City on 28 June 1969. Since the Stonewall riots, expressing sexual identity has been closely associated with political activism, so that these riots mark the most important shift in the politics of homosexual rights, as well as the beginning of the modern fight for sexual minority rights (Johnston 2005; Fejes 2008; Enguix 2009). Along with smaller marches in Chicago, San Francisco and Los Angeles, the June 1970 march in New York was the first of what would become annual commemorations of the Stonewall riots. While they are often fantastic spectacles that have a festive character in countries with a long tradition of LGBT(IQ) movements (Johnston 2005: 1),[1] Pride parades usually take the form of political activism with a focus on demonstrating against discrimination in countries that lack this tradition.[2] The EU has recognised Pride marches as an important marker of democratisation and human rights promotion. By showing its commitment to human rights, in order to bolster its application for EU membership (Kelley 2004; Kahlina 2013), Montenegro has organised three Pride parades and has witnessed a shift in the acceptance of sexual minorities over the last three years.[3] Aside from claiming a physical presence in city spaces traditionally taken to be heterosexual, these events have helped Montenegro's LGBTIQ community increase its visibility.

---

1. The struggle for sexual minority rights in Montenegro has been influenced by the global LGBTIQ movement, and thus encompasses gay, lesbian, bisexual, transgender, intersex and questioning minority groups. By contrast, in private discourses those minority groups are almost always subsumed under the term homosexuals, gays or sometimes under the term LGBT. In anti-gay discourses, they are often labelled with various pejorative terms.

2. Prejudice against homosexuals, including discrimination and charges of immorality, are widespread, especially in Eastern Europe. Thus, while in most Western cities, Pride marches transform city centres into sites celebrating LGBT culture and pride, in many cities in Eastern Europe, aggressive and militant anti-gay protesters are commonly encountered (Zick et al. 2011; Pearce 2014: 7).

3. While militant and especially aggressive counter-protesters were an integral part of the first parade in Podgorica in October 2013, the second parade (in November 2014) was held in a peaceful atmosphere without incident. However, should the third parade be successfully and peacefully held, this should not be taken as indicating the widespread acceptance of homosexuality in Montenegro. Some representatives of the LGBTIQ community think that they are still very vulnerable in everyday life, and that the peacefulness of the second parade mainly depended on a heavy police presence.

The Pride March is premised upon the right of assembly in the liberal democratic societies and it usually consists of a short march through the city centre finishing with political speeches and a short entertaining program. In addition to the impact of the EU accession, Pride Marches in the post-Yugoslav states have also been influenced by the global LGBTIQ movement ... With the development of communication technologies and the fresh influx of capital coming from the Western donors, the global LGBTIQ movement became an important source of influence for the emerging politics of visibility and transformations of sexual citizenship in the post-Yugoslav space. (Kahlina 2013: 16)

Accelerated change in gender policies produces many overheating effects both in the Montenegrin public arena and in everyday life. Namely, the moustache as the logo of the first Pride parade in Podgorica was more than enough to trigger an interesting culture war which highlighted central aspects of Montenegrin masculinity and collective identity.[4] In combination with various meta-discursive practices, this traditional symbol mediated between Montenegrin tradition, current struggles for sexual minority rights and the imagined future of Montenegro. In this respect, controversies over the moustache have proved to be especially relevant in obtaining information on how the struggle over sexuality, masculinity, belonging and heritage has occurred in the everyday life of Montenegro. Additionally, the research showed that the Pride parade is seen as a mere demonstration of sexuality (rather than a political protest against discrimination). Thus, based on studies on masculinity (e.g. Mead 1963; Clatterbaugh 1994; Connell 1995; Gutmann 1997; Carrigan et al. 2004; Kimmel 2004a, 2004b, 2005), and starting from the premise that concepts of masculinity vary from culture to culture, within each culture, within each individual over time, and in various individuals within a single group, I will establish those characteristics assigned to homosexuality that are perceived to be the most threatening for Montenegrin masculinity. What is revealed in determining their meanings and functions is the social state from which they emerge, in which they are reproduced and extinguished, something that emphasises the social importance of this study. The study is based on ethnographic research conducted in 2014/15 in Podgorica, the capital of Montenegro, and Pljevlja, a religiously, ethnically and nationally mixed

---

4.   In fact, it was the second Montenegrin Pride march. Officially, the first Pride parade was held in the coastal town of Budva in July 2013. However, this was a small-scale event in comparison to the march in Podgorica in the following October.

town in northern Montenegro. As many public figures participated in the struggle over the moustache, I have also drawn on material from newspapers and the internet from 2013/14.

## THE MOUSTACHE AS A MARK
## OF TRADITIONAL MASCULINITY

An understanding of the construction of traditional Montenegrin masculinity is essential in considering the historical development of the moustache as a symbol of manliness in Montenegro. The social-constructivist doctrine is most strongly linked precisely with questions of gender, and some of the earliest constructivist premises have their roots in anthropology (Mead 1963). In accordance with the premises of social construction, masculinities refer to social roles, behaviours and meanings assigned to men in a given society at a given time (Kimmel 2004b: 503).

The roots of the dominant cultural model of traditional Montenegrin masculinity should be sought in the tribal structure of traditional Montenegrin society between the sixteenth and nineteenth centuries.[5] A particularly significant role in the creation of the dominant model was played by the semi-nomadic shepherding economy and system of collective property among the tribes. The extensive shepherding economy awarded collective property an important role, and communal life with the flock meant constant battle readiness, as well as frequent clashes over the control of economic resources. This, in turn, drove the culture towards an extreme form of patriarchy, greatly privileging the male gender. Thus, ensuring basic necessities in traditional Montenegrin society was specifically male work, and the dominance of the shepherding, warrior, plunderer economy precipitated an extremely masculine, patriarchal culture. In addition to the economic context, frequent fighting with the Ottomans also played a significant role in the 'making' of the model of traditional Montenegrin masculinity. Historical, ethnological and

---

5.  On the one hand, gender roles contain certain standards, expectations or norms to which the individual ought to aspire, even if only a very small number of individuals can possibly reach the standards and norms set by society for their gender roles. On the other hand, the literature on traditional Montenegrin patriarchal-warrior society details cultural norms regarding gender roles, and not particular individuals who may or may not fulfil socially prescribed gender roles. This means that if we start by researching traditional Montenegrin masculinity from the standpoint of narratives about the past, the result of our research will necessarily be a model – and not only a model, but most often the highest representation of the model, to boot (Banović 2016: 23–55). Regarding the problem of (not) distinguishing real and imagined order in ethnographic literature, see Rihtman-Augustin (1988).

fictional narratives about Montenegro's past suggest a constant state of siege throughout the period of Ottoman rule over Montenegro. Since wars necessarily greatly influence the structure of gender relations and the creation of masculinity (Klein 1999; Solomon 2007), and given that the popular and popular-science narrative about Montenegro's past is one of permanent war against the Ottoman Empire, we can say that the tradition of frequent fights against Ottomans, whether in reality or at the level of narrative, had a great impact on the structure of traditional Montenegrin gender roles (Banović 2016: 23–53).

The model of traditional Montenegrin masculinity is character-ised by especially high standards regarding two important norms of masculinity: the toughness norm (that a man ought never show emotional or physical pain, ought to perform physical violence and enjoy dangerous situations), and the anti-femininity norm (in which a man ought never conduct any activity traditionally associated with women). For example, let us look at how a man belonging to the 'ideal type' in Montenegrin traditional society would score on the toughness and anti-femininity norm of the male role norm scale (MRNS), a scale developed for studying contemporary masculinities (Thomspon & Pleck 1986).[6] I will cite only certain commonplace issues encountered in the literature dealing with traditional Montenegrin society (Gezeman 1968; Cvijić 1991; Pešić 1996).

History testifies to the virtues of Montenegrin warriors, who guarded their independence almost throughout the Ottoman reign. Warrior vainglory, pride and arrogance had no limits. What filled the life of each tribesman, what occupied his thoughts to the exclusion of everything else, was heroism. Only courage and action, not wealth, elicited respect and awe in traditional Montenegrin society. Naturally, what these Montenegrins talked about was what interested them most: in the first place, war with the Turks, heroism, who behaved how in battle. In a community that refers to men capable of carrying weapons as 'guns', in which love and familial tenderness (except between brother and sister) is withheld, in which the meaning of sex is marriage and maintaining the lineage and tribe, the most significant event in the family is the birth of a male child, the future tribesman. Should a parent not have any male children, they will be forced to fend for themselves, feel lost and alone. When a man and wife travel, the man rides the horse and the woman walks next to him, carrying a load on her back. If a woman encounters a

6. Thomspon and Pleck (1986) used the the male role norm scale to assess attitudes towards masculinity in three different areas: status/rationality norms, toughness norms and anti-femininity norms. On problems with measuring masculinity, see King (2000).

man on the road, she stands aside, letting him pass. The man goes ahead, and if the woman accidentally overtakes him, she will stop to let him pass.

The model of traditional Montenegrin masculinity is tightly interwoven with traditional *humanitas heroica* (*čojstvo i junaštvo*)[7] and with all the virtues connected with this system of Montenegrin patriarchal-warrior morality (such as honour, pride, morality, heroism and bravery). Since the faces of all prominent Montenegrin national heroes and rulers were decorated with moustaches, and since the face of the ideal model of traditional Montenegrin masculinity cannot be imagined without the moustache, the moustache has become one of the most important symbols of Montenegrin traditional manliness and the traditional system of morality (*humanitas heroica*).[8]

## THE MOUSTACHE AND THE STRUGGLE
## FOR SEXUAL MINORITY RIGHTS

As a symbol of manhood, moustaches have a symbolic significance in many cultures around the world (Bromberger 2008). In Montenegrin (hyper-masculine) culture, where there is a strong synecdochical relationship between traditional manliness and the moustache, my analysis of controversies over the moustache as the logo of the Pride parade will highlight struggles over masculinity, sexuality, heritage and belonging in an interesting way. Notably, due to the logo of the Pride

---

7. During the Ottoman period, a large proportion of Montenegro's mountains remained untouched by Ottoman culture, so that the old, patriarchal *humanitas heroica* (*čojstvo i junaštvo*) and customary law prevailed. Marko Miljanov, a famous and highly respected Montenegrin hero, noted nineteenth-century examples of Montenegrin *humanitas heroica* and offered moral guidance for behaviour in accordance with traditional Montenegrin values (Miljanov 1964). The Montenegrin *čojstvo*, 'humaneness of a hero' - or as Gerhard Gezeman has defined it, *humanitas heroica* (Gezeman 1968: 181–98) - means that in order to be heroic in the true sense of this concept, a hero needs more than mere hardihood or bravery; he must also place restraint upon these characteristics and thus become a human being. In this system of morality, where humaneness and heroism must be in a state of equilibrium, tolerance is directed towards all others, but never towards oneself. See also Arbatsky (1962).

8. Faces of famous representatives of the model of the traditional Montenegrin masculinity - such as national heroes, dukes and *serdar*s (Marko Miljanov, Jole Piletić, Miljan Vukov Vešović, Novica Cerović and many others), rulers (Danilo I, Sava II, Vasilije III, Petar I, Petar II, Prince Nikola) and saints (Saint Peter of Cetinje) - were decorated with moustaches. What Montenegrin 'great men' looked like, and how they were depicted, can be seen in the documentary *Glasoviti crnogorski junaci* ('Famous Montenegrin heroes'), made by Montenegrin national television and available in three parts on YouTube (available at: www.youtube.com/watch?v=3z8J-D6P-Do, www.youtube.com/watch?v=sblrcb82hrk, www.youtube.com/watch?v=5GPCnILdquI, accessed 5 October 2014).

march, the semantic area covered by the moustache was transferred to the context of the modern struggle for sexual minority rights. By 'claiming their right' to the Montenegrin moustache, organisers of the Pride parade wanted to send a message that sexual minorities share the same history and tradition as the rest of Montenegro and that they must be full and equal members of Montenegrin culture. My interlocutor, Danijel Kalezić, president of the managing board of Queer Montenegro, explains how and why the moustache was selected as the logo of the first Pride parade in Podgorica:

> Thinking about a logo for the Pride march, we started from the word 'pride'. As we talked about Montenegrin pride, we came to the moustache. On the one hand, the moustache is a symbol of Montenegrin pride, a symbol of Montenegrin bravery, a symbol of Montenegrin heroism. On the other hand, it is also a symbol of male dominance through heteronormativity. Then, we asked ourselves: 'Are we brave? Yes, we are. Are we proud of who we are? Yes, we are. Do we seek to be accepted for who we are? Yes, we do. Can we also be proud of the moustache? Yes, we can'. Thus, if we seek our rights, if we have always been a part of Montenegrin history and tradition, invisible but present, if we have the courage to enter the streets despite the fact that I don't know how many hooligans would be rushing to kill us – then, like all other people, we also have the right to the moustache.

By contrast, defending the moustache, different public figures stood up for Montenegrin tradition in the guise of historical, ethnological and fictional narratives, so that traditional Montenegrin manliness (with its focus on *humanitas heroica*) and homosexuals who intentionally attack it were the main discursive elements in various anti-gay discourses.[9] According to those discourses, LGBT people do not have a right to the moustache, and by selecting the moustache as the logo of the Pride

---

9. Supporters of Montenegrin tradition included Mitar Vuković, a member of the Socialist People's Party: 'I cannot believe that they dared to violate the historical core of humanity and morality. Our great men, Vuk Karadžić, Jole Piletic, Marko Miljanov and many others, used to wear moustaches' (quoted from: Brkovi isprovocirali Crnogorce, *Dan*, 19 October 2013; available at: www.dan.co.me/?nivo=3&rubrika=Povodi&datum=2013-10-20&clanak=402294, accessed 3 March 2014). The deputy leader of the Social Democratic Party, Džavid Šabović, who has a moustache, also commented on the logo of the Pride parade: 'If the moustache is a symbol of masculinity, I do not know what happens in their "wise" and "smart" heads. I have not seen any Miss Universe title holder with the moustache so far. I have always been and I will always be against that even if all NGOs attack me and prevent me from looking towards Europe … I think these people need medical help, not a parade' (quoted from: Oni treba da se liječe, *Dan*, 20 October 2013; available at: www.dan.co.me/?nivo=3&rubrika=Povodi&datum=2013-10-20&clanak=402294, accessed 3 March 2014).

march they desecrate and dishonour Montenegrin history and tradition. Coming from the outside – a consequence of Montenegro's advance towards EU membership – the Pride parade reflects accelerated change in Montenegrin society. In almost all anti-gay discourses, homosexuality is perceived as a European import and a novelty in Montenegrin culture. Some discourses emphasise that the EU is forcing the Pride parade upon Montenegro in order to impose a new identity and distorted standards of normalcy. These opinions are particularly common in the northern part of Montenegro, where Serbs are the majority in several districts. Notably, Montenegrin Serbs believe that, since independence (gained in 2006), ruling elites have been pushing a new Montenegrin identity and that the EU wholeheartedly supports the denial of the 'old' character of Montenegrin history and tradition.[10] According to their views, by selecting the moustache as the logo of the Pride parade, Montenegro's ruling elites and the EU have taken another step against 'old' Montenegrin identity and tradition. The loudest of these voices and a particularly influential one was Metropolitan Amfilohije of Montenegro and the Littoral,[11] who claimed in his interviews before and after the Pride

---

10.    At the turn of the twenty-first century, determining the national identity of older Montenegrins and their contemporary heirs is a perpetual conundrum in the public sphere, and the search for an answer is complicated. A significant portion of the ethnographic and travel literature points out that the Montenegrins who traditionally lived in Montenegro were Serbs. Further, it is not uncommon in nineteenth- and twentieth-century sources to find a description of influential Montenegrins as pro-Serbian. This helped create a dual narrative in Montenegro for the reproduction and perpetuation of a fluid identity that can be interpreted both as Montenegrin *and* Serbian. When it comes to the belief that the 'old' character of Montenegrin history is being denied, what Montenegrin Serbs claim is that ruling elites supported by the EU are deliberately reshaping history, avoiding all mention of anything to do with the Serbian character of Montenegrin history and tradition. On the dual and fluid nature of Montenegrin identity and other identity issues in Montenegro, see Banović (2016: 40–41, 85–104, 109–17).

11.    The canonical territory of the Serbian Orthodox Church covers Serbia, Montenegro, Macedonia, Croatia and Slovenia. There are also many parishes of the Serbian Orthodox Church in the diaspora. The territory of the Serbian Orthodox Church is divided into 35 eparchies (dioceses) and 4 metropolitanates (Australia and New Zealand, Dabar-Bosna, Montenegro and Littoral, Zagreb and Ljubljana). The eparchies are headed by episcopes (bishops) and metropolitanates are headed by metropolitans. Additionally, the Montenegrin Orthodox Church, created as an NGO movement in 1993 and registered later as an NGO at the Montenegrin Ministry of the Interior, also acts in Montenegro. The Montenegrin Orthodox Church is separate from the Serbian Orthodox Church and considers itself to be the sole legitimate representative of Orthodox Christianity in Montenegro. However, it remains canonically unrecognized by other Orthodox churches, and has significantly fewer adherents than the Serbian church in Montenegro. The Serbian and Montenegrin Orthodox churches had opposing views of Montenegro's first Pride parade. While Metropolitan Amfilohije spoke out aggressively against the event, the metropolitan of the Montenegrin Orthodox Church of Mihailo, in his public statements, promoted peace and tolerance.

parade that its organisers (which he called the 'parade of shame' and the 'parade of death') intentionally dishonoured Montenegrin moustaches by order of the EU:

> What happened today dishonours Montenegrin moustaches and the whole of Montenegro. I urge 'European gay paraders', who blackmail Montenegro, if they intend to help Montenegro, to consider their acts and stop the violation of human morality. They should not desecrate the Montenegrin moustache, which is the sanctity of Montenegro and which contains Montenegrin morality, the morality of St Peter of Cetinje and Basil of Ostrog.[12]

He also pointed out that 'there is a danger for heroism to turn into the adornment of the European Union, as well as for *humanitas heroica* to turn into gay-parading':

> Those unfortunates, the bearers of the sin of Sodom and Gomorra, have taken the moustache as their symbol. We know very well what moustaches mean to our men. People died for their moustaches. They are the symbol of our honesty and honour. The European gay lobby groups poison our soul.[13]

> Over the centuries, Montenegro has tried to be the bearer of the virtue of *humanitas heroica* … Gay-parading begins to replace the real *humanitas* and human dignity even here, in the land of Njegoš and Marko Miljanov.[14]

---

12. Quoted from: Amfilohije: Gej paraderi da prekinu nasilje nad moralom i savješću, *Portal Analitika*, 21 October 2013 (available at: www.portalanalitika.me/drustvo/vijesti/119982-amfilohije-gej-paraderi-da-prekinu-sa-nasiljem-nad-moralom-i-savjeu, accessed 5 April 2014). St Peter of Cetinje, or Petar I Petrović Njegoš (1748–1830), was both metropolitan and ruler of Montenegro. Known for pacifying warring clans and introducing the rule of law, he was canonized Saint Peter of Cetinje by his successor, Petar II Petrović Njegoš. Basil of Ostrog, meanwhile, is so named after the monastery of Ostrog, situated high on a rocky massif near Nikšić. Ostrog is the biggest religious sanctuary in Montenegro and the most important site for Orthodox Christians in the country.

13. Podgorica: Krvava parada ponosa, *Večernje Novosti*, 20 October 2013 (available at: www.novosti.rs/vesti/planeta.300.html:459733-Podgorica-Krvava-parada-ponosa, accessed 30 June 2014).

14. Quoted from: Amfilohije: Heroizam se pretvara u europoklonstvo, a čojstvo u gej paradiranje, *Portal Analitika*, 5 February 2013 (available at: www.portalanalitika.me/drustvo/vijesti/90702-amfilohije-junatvo-se-pretvara-u-europoklonstvo-a-ojstvo-u-gej-paraderstvo, accessed 5 April 2014). Petar II Petrović Njegoš (1813–1851), was a prince cum bishop of Montenegro, as well as the greatest Montenegrin poet. Owing to the fact that his poetry had a decisive impact on the creation of modern Montenegrin identity, Petar II is often called the father of modern Montenegro (see Banović 2016: 46–53). Marko

Highlanders from Durmitor, in northern Montenegro, were particularly insulted by the Pride parade's appropriation of the moustache:

> We, proud highlanders from Durmitor, whose faces are decorated with moustaches, bear this insulting decision with a great deal of indignation and revulsion ... They have already taken everything, so they want to strike at our honour, culture and tradition now, the only things that these impoverished, but proud peoples, have retained. We ask the government and its prime minister how they think to look Njegoš and other Montenegrin great men in the eyes: St Peter of Cetinje, Marko Miljanov, King Nikola, Janko Vukotic, Novica Cerović and many others whose faces were decorated with moustaches.[15]

One Montenegrin man gave an interview to the daily newspaper *Dan*, in which he explained in detail why he had shaved off his moustache. Even though it was very hard for him, he said, the Pride parade had 'forced' him to remove his moustache after fifty-seven years. The way he views male homosexual acts was one of the factors in his decision, prompted when 'some people decided that the moustache is the trademark of the backside':

> I was shocked when I heard that the moustache would be the logo of the Pride parade. The moustache is a mark of humanity, morality and every virtue. Montenegrin people are heroic, and talking about the moustache as the logo of the parade is shameful, because our greatest men wore moustaches ... While my moustache was being shaved, I cried, because it was very hard for me.[16]

The idea that homosexuality is a European import – or even part of a conspiracy led by the USA, NATO or Freemasons – which attacks Montenegrin identity and is completely inconsistent with Montenegrin culture and tradition was also explicit in various comments posted on the most popular Montenegrin websites.[17]

---

Miljanov (1833–1901) was a famous and highly respected Montenegrin hero. His writings on manliness and heroism (see Miljanov 1964) shaped the consciousness of patriarchal values characteristic of traditional Montenegrin society.

15. Zbog gej parade obrijao brkove nakon 57 godina, *Dan*, 20 October 2013 (available at: www.dan.co.me/?nivo=3&rubrika=Povodi&datum=2013-10-20&clanak=402294, accessed 3 March 2014).

16. Zbog gej parade obrijao brkove nakon 57 godina, *Dan*, 20 October 2013 (available at: www.dan.co.me/?nivo=3&rubrika=Povodi&datum=2013-10-20&clanak=402294, accessed 3 March 2014).

17. 'The moustache: there is your new modern European Montenegro! E Viva Montenegrin moustache!' 'I cannot stand looking at the moustache as the logo of someone's rear end'.

## THE VISIBILITY OF LGBT PEOPLE
## (WHEN EVERYBODY TALKS ABOUT THE MOUSTACHE)

As we can see, controversies triggered by the moustache overheated the Montenegrin public arena in a specific way, but if we analyse anti-gay arguments used in this culture war we can conclude that they do not differ a lot from the arguments used in controversies over other Pride marches. Although controversies over the moustache were specifically Montenegrin, they were structured according to a basic pattern, the main elements of which are well-documented: the centrality of the dichotomies normal/abnormal, natural/unnatural and moral/immoral; homosexuality regarded as an illness; religious institutions and officers that play an important role in public debate about homosexuality; LGBT people attack core national values; the battle between the police and right-wing groups (see Fejes 2008; Baer 2009; Mole 2010; O'Dwyer & Schwartz 2010; Zick et al. 2011; Alonso 2013; Slenders et al. 2014). The conceptual connection between homosexuality and the West or Europe is also well documented in other countries (Stychin 2004; Drezgić 2010; Jovanović 2013; Kahlina 2013; Pearce 2014).

Since open discussion about sexual minorities in Montenegro was principally motivated by the process of EU integration, 'homosexuality' and 'Europe' are closely connected (Brković 2013: 176; Kahlina 2013: 8–12). Homosexuality is perceived as a novelty in Montenegrin culture,

---

'You want to be a NATO member? Ok, but you first need to go to Afghanistan. You want to be a member of the EU? Ok, but you first need to organise the Pride Parade. You want to be a part of Western civilisation? Ok, but you first need to give up your identity'. 'Who donates money for it? I will tell you – Freemasons, the USA, Israel, they want to take our dignity, faith and honesty'. 'I do not need European values if I have to spit in my own face'. 'Heroic Montenegro has to act according to the orders of "superior Western civilisation"'. 'Let us see how many LGBT people live in Montenegro, but do not import foreigners … Surely, they will not be enough to fit in a van'. 'Who got the idea to take the moustache as the symbol of this morbid circus? Does no one remember Njegos's verses: "O scowling Vuk, lift your moustache for me and let me see the breastplates on your chest, that I may count the holes from rifle bullets, see how many of them broke up your plates!" What is going on with Montenegro nowadays?' Phrases quoted from: Parada ponosa u slikama (available at: www.cdm.me/drustvo/crna-gora/foto-parada-ponosa-u-slikama, accessed 30 March 2014), Amfilohije: Heroizam se pretvara u europoklonstvo, a čojstvo u gej paradiranje, *Portal Analitika*, 5 February 2013 (available at: www.portalanalitika.me/drustvo/vijesti/90702-amfilohije-junatvo-se-pretvara-u-europoklonstvo-a-ojstvo-u-gej-paraderstvo, accessed 5 April 2014), Amfilohije: Gej paraderi da prekinu nasilje nad moralom i savješću, *Portal Analitika*, 21 October 2013 (available at: www.portalanalitika.me/drustvo/vijesti/119982-amfilohije-gej-paraderi-da-prekinu-sa-nasiljem-nad-moralom-i-savjeu, accessed 5 April 2014) and Policija spremna, prijetnje ozbiljne, *Vijesti*, 20 October 2013 (available at: www.vijesti.me/vijesti/policija-spremna-prijetnje-ozbiljne-155813, accessed 29 October 2013).

predominantly connected with the process of EU integration and mainly seen as a European import. By contrast, the moustache commonly refers to Montenegro's heroic tradition and the model of traditional masculinity. I think that there is no need to explain why Montenegrin tradition is considered a purely heterosexual domain that excludes any presence of homosexuality,[18] and why the moustache and the Pride parade are perceived as incompatible entities in Montenegro. However, in this incompatibility lies the tremendous capacity of the moustache to improve the visibility of LGBT people in Montenegro. Talking about the moustache as the logo of the Pride march, Danijel Kalezić continues:

> We selected the moustache to provoke a discussion about LGBT people. We succeeded because the discussion took place in parts of Montenegro in which it had never taken place before. For the first time, people in every Montenegrin village talked about LGBT people.

While the moustache helps homosexuals increase their visibility in society, for some people they are acceptable only as 'invisible' – in other words, they are not acceptable at all.[19] Furthermore, choosing the moustache as the logo of the Pride march helps break prejudices about who is entitled to wear it, but many of my interlocutors (regardless of their religious, national or ethnic identity) consider this symbolism

---

18.  In fact, Montenegro is not traditionally exclusively heterosexual, but has also seen well-documented transgender cases, namely 'sworn virgins'. These were women who adopted a male gender identity and lived in the nineteenth and twentieth centuries in the patriarchal western Balkans, mainly Albania, Kosovo and Montenegro. A 'sworn virgin' would take a vow of chastity, swear to never get married, wear male clothing, adopt a male gender identity and continue to live as a man. Owing to the fact that families in Montenegro were patrilineal and patrilocal, a woman would mainly become a 'sworn virgin' if the family was left without male children (Barjaktarović 1948, 1966; Šarčević 2004). There are a few anecdotes about how the Montenegrin ruler Nikola Petrović (1860–1918) punished homosexuals. The core of the anecdotes lies in the following: he would put homosexuals in 'big barrels of faeces', so that they could realise 'where their "manliness" enters'. The concept of dirt, always defined by society's notion of disorder (Douglas 2002), is more than obvious in these anecdotes.

19.  These positions are reflected in the following statements: 'I am against violence, but I am also against the Pride parade'. 'I can't understand why homosexuals still want to parade if they only provoke people in that way'. 'I don't pay attention to gays, but I start hating them when they start talking about the parade'. 'Instead of being ashamed, they want to parade'. 'I would protect homosexuals, but I wouldn't let them parade in Montenegro'. 'Sexual orientation is an exclusively private matter. Why would I display my sexual orientation to anyone – they also shouldn't do that'. 'I would banish them from Montenegro'. 'I would beat faggots whenever I see them'. 'I support violence against homosexuals'. 'They don't deserve a normal life'. 'I would completely destroy all those sick people'.

inappropriate or aggressive. A well-educated teacher from Podgorica, drawing parallels between Montenegrin tradition and the modern fight for sexual minority rights, finds the logo of the first Montenegrin Pride parade humiliating and degrading:

> LGBT people want a modern, European Montenegro. I also want a modern European Montenegro. Countless symbols surround us, yet they chose the moustache. Why? By accident? The EU demanded a moustache on LGBT flags? I don't think so. They could have taken any other symbol, but they internationally want to attack our history, trample our national pride and provoke. It is aggressive and humiliating. The moustache is a symbol of traditional Montenegro and the last thing that should be the logo of the Gay parade. They want tradition, but putting homosexuals in big barrels of faeces, the way King Nikola punished them, is also a part of our tradition. If someone mentioned it, their NGOs would burn Montenegro. What about HIV vulnerability?

While running in a park in Pljevlja, I ended up talking to a group of secondary-school and college students who were doing push-ups and crunches, who gave a few interesting comments about homosexuality and the moustache. From those comments we can see that young people sometimes perceive a correlation between the Pride parade and the funding of NGOs fighting for sexual minority rights. Talking about the moustache, Marko said: 'If you open any history book about Montenegro, you will find Montenegrin heroes with moustaches. They should have more respect for our history'. His friend Elvis, a student of economics, found a correlation between the moustache and the question of funding:

> Oh, guys, why are you against faggots? They are paid for it. I have heard that parade participants were paid 500 euros each. They pretend that they are gays, and get money, cars, trips, conferences, all-inclusive hotels. I bet that Cimba [Cimbaljević], the guy who got asylum in Canada, currently lives with his chick. Are you so stupid? They chose the moustache because they knew that they will provoke negative and aggressive reactions. In that way, they can go to the institutions that fund them and say: 'We are European, West-oriented and liberal, but homophobes, traditionalists, nationalists and others endanger us. Please help us and support our fight for human rights and modern Montenegro'. Everything is a business nowadays.

One of my interlocutors was a young man who is a close relative of the man previously mentioned who shaved his moustache because of the Pride march. In his words, we can find an interesting clash of generations regarding the acceptance of the Pride parade in Montenegro:

> He is my grandfather, or precisely, my father's uncle. It was funny to me because I knew that he had been dared to shave his moustache a few years ago. His son had promised to pay him 500 euros only to see him without his moustache, but he didn't want to shave it. Now, he explains: 'If moustaches decorate faggots' asses, I don't want a moustache to decorate my face anymore'. His logic is clear [*he smiles*]. I can't understand that someone acts in this way, but he swears that he doesn't have anything against homosexuals. He just rejects that pride has anything to do with their parade. I also think that the organisers of the Pride parade could have avoided the moustache. However, in my opinion, Gay Pride is a phenomenon held all around Europe, and Montenegro also should have its Pride. If I was in power, I would arrest all those hooligans who attack LGBT people. They are the last people who can judge what is good or wrong.

It is worth mentioning that I noticed a discourse on Montenegrin tradition that condemns violence aimed at sexual minorities. A few young, well-educated and Western-oriented interlocutors think that it is not LGBT persons but the hooligans attacking them that are those who drastically break the basic principle of Montenegrin *humanitas heroica*: 'bravery is to defend yourself from another, and *humanitas heroica* (*čojstvo*) is to defend the other from yourself'. The core of their argument lies in the following: if hooligans acted according to Montenegrin tradition, they would never attack those weaker than themselves and they would protect sexual minorities from being attacked.

## HOW DO HOMOSEXUALS ENDANGER MONTENEGRIN MASCULINITY?

Anthropologists have played a prominent role in documenting the diversity of human sexuality as it is understood and expressed in different cultures around the world (Mead 1963; Sonenchein 1966; Davis & Whitten 1987; Lyons & Lyons 2004; Epprecht 2006; Boellstorff 2007). The research showed that the Pride parade is seen as a mere demonstration of sexuality (rather than a political protest against discrimination) that opens the door for new and distorted standards of normalcy and masculinity. While unalterable gender roles are the main component of the stereotype that represents normalcy, the stereotype that represents abnormality is marked mainly by homosexuality, and it is perceived to coincide with belonging to 'the Western world'. For example, Boban, a college-educated man in his thirties, thinks about the Pride parade as 'a demonstration of sickness':

> Please, were you able to imagine fifteen years ago that homosexuals would parade throughout Montenegro? Of course, no. Are you able to imagine that paedophiles could also parade after fifteen years? Gays nowadays, but who is next? Paedophiles, necrophiliacs, rapists, zoophiles? Where does it end?

While speaking, his friend Danilo interrupts him:

> I have heard of a bordello for zoophiles in Denmark. In my opinion, wealthy people are the source of all perversions. While we contemplate how to survive, they invent and enjoy various perversions and want to spread them as if they were normal.

Many scientists who have done research on the topic agree that the definition of masculinity relies more on what masculinity is not rather than what it is (Clatterbaugh 1994: 200; Carrigan et al. 2004: 151; Kimmel 2004a: 182–96).[20] While masculinity is traditionally defined (among other things) as that which is not feminine, under new conditions masculinity becomes also defined as that which is not homosexual. Bearing this in mind, I also wanted to determine those characteristics assigned to homosexuality that are perceived as the most threatening to Montenegrin masculinity.

The research showed that effeminacy is the main feature of homosexuality that endangers masculinity – according to such views, future generations of Montenegrins are especially in danger.[21] People (particularly middle-aged and elderly) perceive a direct link between

---

20. Gutmann points out that the fluidity of this concept 'pushes' anthropologists to define masculinity in four ways: as male identity – a concept of masculinity in which masculinity is by definition everything that men think or do; manhood – according to which masculinity is everything men think or do in order to be men; manliness – which makes some men more manly than others; and men's role – a view that emphasises the male–female relationship, such that man is that which woman is not (Gutmann 1997: 385–409). As different forms of masculinity coexist, the hegemony of any given form is constantly subject to challenge (Connell 2000: 54).

21. These positions are reflected in the following statements: 'I look at those secondary-school students, they look more like women than like men'. 'Each successive generation is more effeminate'. 'Kristijan was right – "they are not generation, but they are degeneration"'.

physical appearance and sexuality. Effeminacy is a feature of homosexuals that is mainly connected with leanness, high-pitched female voices, body piercing, hair colouring, depilation and other traditionally female characteristics (sometimes perceived as sickness). Homosexuals and heterosexuals are also perceived to have distinct personalities. While the former are mainly associated with traditionally feminine traits (they are sensitive, emotional, quiet, weak, soft and so on), the latter have traditionally masculine traits (they are strong, active, aggressive, courageous, engaged in sports). The fact that mainly effeminate men are victims of violence against LGBT people also indicates that effeminacy is the most hated feature of homosexuality. Apart from effeminacy, a higher risk of HIV transmission is also perceived as a very dangerous feature of homosexuality.

Young people in Montenegro often link the Pride parade to pro-homosexual propaganda and the entertainment industry centred on Hollywood. According to these views, the image of good looking and wealthy gay men who spend time working out and partying at gay nightclubs could be very attractive to future generations. In that respect, Emir, a young Muslim, currently a student of law, explains his attitude about the Pride parade as a phenomenon that gradually establishes new standards of masculinity:

> The gay lobby is very powerful in Hollywood. In every single American film, in every popular TV series, there is a character who is nice, good-looking, well-educated, rich, successful and, of course, gay. In that way, after some time, homosexuality will become the preferred standard of sexual behaviour and the Gay Parade will be a prestigious event.

We can also see that the term homosexual has an ever-changing collection of meanings, covering a broad and elastic semantic area. Not only sexuality, but also new norms, values, lifestyles and modes of dress (new elements can always be added to this list) can be considered 'less macho', 'feminine', 'wimpy', 'sissy' and so on (depending on various male role standards), and these can be enough for someone to be perceived as a homosexual.[22] For example, not long ago, if a man wore an earring, this

---

22.  In my opinion, an analysis of an old and popular joke from the standpoint of the anthropology of folklore (focused on the social and cultural determinants at play in producing humorous elements) would tell us a lot about this phenomenon: 'After spending some time studying abroad, a young Montenegrin visited his family. After waking up, he did push-ups, took a shower, shaved his beard, put on perfume, ate a healthy breakfast and went to the toilet. Surprised by these changes, his father took his rifle, stood in front of the

was taken as evidence of his 'homosexuality'. Nikola, an engineer from Podgorica, remembers:

> While I was a student in Belgrade during the mid nineties, I used to meet young men completely different from us. They didn't look like men, but more like women, with those high-pitched female voices. I especially hated their earrings, and I couldn't stand looking at them. A few students like that lived in the student dorm, and they were especially strange for us who came from Montenegro: they didn't enjoy male activities, didn't play football, basketball or any other sport, spent time only with girls ... We called them faggots and stayed far away from them.

By contrast, Montenegro has witnessed a shift in accepting males who wear earrings over the last few years. For Danijel Kalezić, such shifts indicate that there is room for change towards the acceptance of sexual minorities:

> Five or six years ago, TV Montenegro organised a talk show in which participants discussed if men should wear earrings. During the talk show most participants used various arguments to explain why it is wrong for men to wear earrings. Nowadays, nobody cares if men wear earrings. So, there is room for improvement.

## CONCLUSION

Owing to their multivocal and dynamic character, symbols carry multiple and sometimes contradictory meanings (Turner 1975). Power struggles often crystallise around a single 'thing' which comes to carry heavy and contested symbolic weight (Bennett 1994). In that way, the struggle over masculinity, sexuality, heritage and belonging provoked by the first Pride parade in Montenegro's capital crystallised around the moustache. Notably, after applying for EU membership (in 2008) and acquiring candidate status (in 2010), Montenegro opened accession negotiations with the European Union in 2012. As the EU has recognised Pride marches as an important marker of democratisation and human rights promotion, in order to show its commitment to human rights, Montenegro organised its first Pride march in 2013. Although

---

toilet and said: "If he squats (like a woman) while urinating, I am going to kill him'". As we can see, the student only practised some 'new' ('European') habits, which was enough to make him be perceived as a 'woman' (figurative: 'homosexual', 'less macho', 'wimp', 'faggot' and so on).

Montenegro has witnessed a shift in acceptance of sexual minorities in recent years, controversies over the moustache as the symbol of the first Montenegrin Pride parade clearly show that rapid change in national gender policies is accompanied by many overheating effects, as well as that different parts of Montenegrin society are moving toward the EU at different speeds. The attempt of the Montenegrin LGBTIQ community to transfer the semantic area traditionally covering the moustache (honour, pride, morality, heroism, bravery and so on) to the context of contemporary struggles for sexual minority rights, resulted in an interesting and a 'typically Montenegrin' culture war. By 'claiming their right' to the moustache, and by breaking prejudices about who is entitled to wear it, the Montenegrin LGBTIQ community also 'claimed their right' to Montenegrin history and tradition, pointing out that sexual minorities must be full and equal members of Montenegrin culture.

By contrast, people with opposing views consider the LGBTIQ community's appropriation of the moustache an attack on Montenegrin identity, tradition, history and national pride, and find this 'usurpation' aggressive and humiliating. Discourses in which the EU is claimed to be forcing the Pride parade upon Montenegro in order to impose a new identity are particularly common in the northern part of Montenegro, where Serbs are the majority in several districts. Montenegrin Serbs believe that, since independence (gained in 2006), ruling elites (supported by the EU) have been intent on imposing a new Montenegrin identity. By selecting the moustache as the logo of the Pride parade, Montenegro's ruling elites and the EU have taken another step against the Montenegrin identity and tradition of old. Although controversies over the moustache were specifically Montenegrin, anti-gay arguments used in this culture war were structured along the lines of a well-known pattern. This pattern includes the use of the dichotomies normal/abnormal, natural/unnatural and moral/immoral; the perception of homosexuality as an illness; pronouncements about homosexuality by religious institutions and officers that play an important role in public debate; and the arguments that LGBT people attack the very core of national values. Homosexuality and homosexuals are perceived as a novelty in Montenegrin culture, a European import, predominantly connected with the process of EU integration. The Pride parade is perceived as a mere demonstration of sexuality, and an instrument for imposing new standards of normalcy and masculinity on Montenegrin society. The semantic area covering the term 'homosexual' is broad and elastic, and effeminacy is the feature of homosexuality that is perceived as the most threatening to Montenegrin masculinity and culture (a higher risk of HIV transmission is also perceived as a very dangerous feature).

Be that as it may, it seems that the blow struck by the moustache was unexpected and unpredictable in 2013. The moustache still carries on its life in the struggle for sexual minority rights. The logo of the second Pride march in Podgorica in November 2014 was the stylised face of a Montenegrin woman, wearing both a rainbow coloured headscarf and a moustache. This logo refers to the image of the traditional Montenegrin woman (as suggested in the literature dealing with traditional Montenegrin society), also depicted in a well-known photo: a man rides a horse while a woman with a black headscarf walks next to him, carrying a load on her back. It is clear that the aim of this logo is to encourage not only sexual minorities but all those who remain oppressed by the well-established system of heteronormativity to fight for their rights.

The struggle over tradition is itself gradually becoming a tradition of the Montenegrin LGBTIQ movement. Apart from fighting for their rights and for equality, Montenegrin LGBTIQ activists are also fighting for their space in Montenegrin tradition and history. The result of this struggle is a hybrid and doubly fast change, in which the moustache mediates between extremely patriarchal Montenegrin tradition and the current struggle for sexual minority rights. Having this dual struggle in mind, it is open to question whether the contrast between Montenegrin heteronormative tradition and 'effeminate Europe' would be so sharp and visible if Montenegrin LGBTIQ activists had not tried to find their space among moustache-wearing Montenegrin warriors.[23] It seems that the past-oriented part of the dual struggle has intensified and accelerated the clash of cultural values. Thus, in making shifts in gender policies on its path towards EU accession, Montenegro has experienced a hybrid and dual accelerated change, offering a typically Montenegrin contribution to global re-traditionalisation (Milenković 2008) and world-wide overheating.

## REFERENCES

Alonso, M. 2013. *Best Inclusion Practices: LGBT Diversity*. New York: Palgrave Macmillan.

Appadurai, A. 1996. *Modernity at Large: Cultural Dimensions of Globalization*. Minneapolis: University of Minnesota Press.

—— 2002. Disjuncture and Difference in the Global Cultural Economy. In J.X. Inda and R. Rosaldo (eds), *The Anthropology of Globalization*. Oxford: Blackwell, pp.46–65.

Arbatsky, G.Y. 1962. Traits of Humanitas Heroica in the Extreme North of the USSR. *Slavic and East-European Studies* 7(1/2): 93–7.

Baer, B. 2009. *Other Russias*. New York: Palgrave Macmillan.

Banović, B. 2016. *The Montenegrin Warrior Tradition: Questions and Controversies over NATO Membership*. New York: Palgrave Macmillan.

---

23. On the Montenegrin warrior tradition, see Banović (2016).

Barjaktarović, M.R. 1948. Prilog proučavanju tobelija (zavetovanih devojaka). In D. Nedeljković (ed.), *Zbornik Filozofskog fakulteta Univerziteta u Beogradu*, Vol. 1. Beograd: Naučna knjiga, pp.343-51.

—— 1966. Problem tobelija (virdžina) na Balkanskom poluostrvu. *Glasnik Etnografskog muzeja u Beogradu* 28/29: 273-86.

Bennett, O.D. 1994. Foreword: Symbols of Contention. *Anthropological Quarterly* 67(2): 47-8.

Boellstorff, T. 2007. Queer Studies in the House of Anthropology. *Annual Review of Anthropology* 36: 17-35.

Brković, Č. 2013. The Quest for Legitimacy: Discussing Language and Sexuality in Montenegro. In T. Petrović (ed.), *Miroring Europe*. Leiden: Brill, pp.163-85.

Bromberger, C. 2008. Hair: From the West to the Middle East through the Mediterranean. *Journal of American Folklore* 121(482): 379-99.

Carrigan, T., R.W. Connell and J. Lee. 2004. Toward a New Sociology of Masculinity. In P.F. Murphy (ed.), *Feminism and Masculinities*. Oxford: Oxford University Press, pp.151-65.

Clatterbaugh, K. 1994. What is Problematic about Masculinities? In P.F. Murphy (ed.), *Feminism and Masculinities*. Oxford: Oxford University Press, pp.200-14.

Connell, R.W. 1995. Men at Bay: The 'Men's Movement' and Its Newest Best-Sellers. In M. Kimmel (ed.), *The Politics of Manhood*. Philadelphia: Temple University Press, pp.65-75.

—— 2000. *The Men and the Boys*. Berkeley: University of California Press.

Cvijić, J. 1991 [1922-1931]. *Balkansko poluostrvo*. Beograd: Zavod za udžbenike i nastavna sredstva.

Davis D.L., and R.G. Whitten. 1987. The Cross-Cultural Study of Human Sexuality. *Annual Review of Anthropology* 16: 66-98.

Douglas, Mary. 2002 [1966]. *Purity and Danger*. London: Routledge;

Drezgić, R. 2010. Religion, Politics and Gender in the Context of Nation-State Formation: The Case of Serbia. *Third World Quarterly* 31(6): 955-70.

Enguix, B. 2009. Identities, Sexualities and Commemorations: Pride Parades, Public Space and Sexual Dissidence. *Anthropological Notebooks* 15(2): 15-33.

Epprecht, M. 2006. 'Bisexuality' and the Politics of Normal in African Ethnography. *Anthropologica* 48(2): 187-201.

Eriksen, T.H. 1995. *Small Places, Large Issues*. London: Pluto Press.

—— 2003. Introduction. In T.H. Eriksen (ed.), *Globalization: Studies in Anthropology*. London: Pluto Press, pp.1-18.

—— 2007. *Globalization*. Oxford: Berg.

Fejes, F. 2008. *Gay Rights and Moral Panic*. New York: Palgrave Macmillan.

Gezeman, G. 1968. *Čojstvo i junaštvo starih Crnogoraca*. Cetinje: Obod.

Gutmann, C.M. 1997. Trafficking in Men: The Anthropology of Masculinity. *Annual Review of Anthropology* 26: 385-409.

Hannerz, U. 2003. Several Sites in One. In T.H. Eriksen (ed.), *Globalization: Studies in Anthropology*. London: Pluto Press, pp.18-39.

Johnston, L. 2005. *Queering Tourism*. New York: Routledge.

Jovanović, M. 2013. Silence or Condemnation: The Orthodox Church on Homosexuality in Serbia. *Družboslovne razprave* 29(73): 79-95.

Kahlina, K. 2013. Contested Terrain of Sexual Citizenship: EU Accession and the Changing Position of Sexual Minorities in the Post-Yugoslav Context. CITSEE Working Paper No. 2013/33. Edinburgh: Edinburgh Law School, University of Edinburgh.

Kelley, J. 2004. International Actors on the Domestic Scene: Membership Conditionality and Socialization by International Institutions. *International Organization* 58(3): 425-57.

Kimmel, S.M. 2004a. Masculinity as Homophobia: Fear, Shame, and Silence in the Construction of Gender Identity. In P.F. Murphy (ed.), *Feminism and Masculinities*. Oxford: Oxford University Press, pp.182–96.

—— 2004b. Masculinities. In S.M. Kimmel and A. Aronson (eds), *Men and Masculinities: A Social, Cultural and Historical Encyclopedia*. Santa Barbara: ABC CLIO, pp.503–7.

—— 2005. *The History of Men*. New York: State University of New York Press.

King, V.E. 2000. Men's Definitions of Masculinity and Male Power. PhD dissertation. Fort Collins, CO: Colorado State University.

Klein, U. 1999. Our Best Boys. *Men and Masculinities* 2(1): 47–65.

Lyons, P.A., and D.H. Lyons. 2004. *Irregular Connections: A History of Anthropology and Sexuality*. Lincoln: University of Nebraska Press.

Mead, M. 1963 [1935]. *Sex and Temperament in Three Primitive Societies*. New York: Morrow.

Milenković, M. 2008. Problemi konstitucionalizacije multikulturalizma – pogled iz antropologije, deo prvi – o 'očuvanju' identiteta. *Etnoantropološki problemi* 3(2): 45–57.

Miljanov, M. 1964 [1901]. *Primjeri čojstva i junaštva*. Beograd: Branko Djonović.

Mole, R. 2010. Sexuality and Nationality: Homophobic Discourse and the 'National Threat' in Contemporary Latvia. CEPSI Working Paper No. 2010/2. London: Centre for European Politics, Security and Integration, School of Slavonic and East European Studies, University College London.

O'Dwyer, C., and K.Z.S. Schwartz. 2010. Minority Rights after EU Enlargement: A Comparison of Antigay Politics in Poland and Latvia. *Comparative European Politics* 8(2): 220–43.

Pearce, C.S. 2014. 'Gej' (Gay) in Southeast Europe: LGBTI Rights in a European Global Corner. Policy brief, Global Europe Program, Woodrow Wilson Center. Available at: www.wilsoncenter.org/sites/default/files/SE%20Europe%20Policy%20Brief%20Pearce%20Jan%202014_Formatted_Rvsd_3.pdf (accessed 5 January 2015).

Pešić, V. 1996 [1986]. *Patrijarhalni moral Crnogoraca*. Podgorica: Unireks.

Rihtman-Auguštin, D. 1988. The Communal Family between Real and Imagined Order. *Narodna Umjetnost* 2: 209–19.

Šarčević, P. 2004. Sex and Gender Identity of 'Sworn Virgins' in the Balkans. In M. Jovanović and S. Naumović (eds), *Gender Relations in South Eastern Europe: Historical Perspectives on Womanhood and Manhood in Nineteenth and Twentieth Century*. Münster: Lit Verlag, pp.123–44.

Slenders, S., I. Sieben and E. Verbakel. 2014. Tolerance towards Homosexuality in Europe: Population Composition, Economic Affluence, Religiosity, Same-Sex Union Legislation and HIV Rates as Explanations for Country Differences. *International Sociology* 29(4): 348–67.

Solomon, L.S. 2007. War. In F. Malti-Douglas (ed.), *Encyclopedia of Sex and Gender*, Vol. 4. Detroit: Gale Group, pp.1518–22.

Sonenschein, D. 1966. Homosexuality as a Subject of Anthropological Inquiry. *Anthropological Quarterly* 39(2): 73–82.

Stychin, C.F. 2004. Same-Sex Sexualities and the Globalization of Human Rights Discourse. *McGill Law Journal* 49: 951–68.

Thompson, H.E., and J.H. Pleck. 1986. The Structure of Male Role Norms. *American Behavioral Scientist* 29(5): 531–43.

Tsing, A. 2002. The Global Situation. In J.X. Inda and R. Rosaldo (eds), *The Anthropology of Globalization*. Oxford: Blackwell, pp.453 Ed., 453–87.

Turner, V. 1975. Symbolic Studies. *Annual Review of Anthropology* 4: 145–61.

Zick, A., B. Küpper and A. Hövermann. 2011. *Intolerance, Prejudice and Discrimination*. Berlin: Nora Langenbacher, Friedrich-Ebert-Stiftung.

# 12. 'We're Far Too Far Down This Road Now to Worry about Morals'
## The Destabilising of Football Fans' Identities in an Overheated World

*Keir Martin*

Manchester United fans have had to negotiate some sharp changes in identity over the past twenty years. United had been the most supported club in the country since the 1950s, with a fan base that spread geographically across the country (and indeed overseas) to an extent that marked it out from most other clubs (Mellor 2004: 28–9; White 2009: 5–7). The establishment of the Premier League in 1992 restructured English professional football in a manner that consolidated a concentration of growing income into the hands of the top clubs (Conn 1997: 17; King 2002; Poulton 2013: 58). The gap in wealth between the richest and poorest professional clubs had been commented on in English football for decades. Hopcraft noted back in the 1960s that 'the gap in wealth between the small League clubs and the biggest ones widens week to week' (Hopcraft 2006: 162), but it was the establishment of the Premier League that probably marked the single most important entrenchment of that tendency.

The Premier League's establishment coincided with United regaining the league title for the first time in over a quarter of a century. The increased support and revenue that came with success at a time when English football grew in importance as a major branch of the TV entertainment industry, first domestically and then internationally, helped to contribute to United consolidating both sporting and financial success, as they went on to dominate the following twenty years of English football.[1] Likewise, United were at the forefront of changes in the ownership structure of English football during this period. Several clubs floated on the Stock Exchange in order to raise more funds, the first being Tottenham Hotspur in 1982, but the most important of which was undoubtedly United in 1990.

---

1. This was also the time when football cemented its dominance as the primary global sport at the expense of other sports (e.g. see Eriksen 2007: 48).

This transformation of English football from an institution mainly run by locally based family businesses to a financialised arm of the global entertainment industry (see e.g. Giulianotti & Robertson 2004: 554) has led to changed perceptions of the relationship between the club and its support base, not only for United but also for rival teams. United became for many emblematic of ambiguously received trends within the game, in particular a perceived shift towards rampant commercial exploitation on the one hand (White 2009: 310) and the emergence of a more passive and inauthentic set of supporters on the other (e.g. Conn 1997: 45–6; White 2009: 361–2). The fact that United had the largest set of supporters outside their home catchment area had been seen as a source of pride in the 1970s, for example, an indication of United's special status, even at a time when the team was often second-rate (e.g. Poulton 2013: 101–2). These fans were often held up as the best and most loyal of all, sacrificing more than local fans in terms of the dedication that they demonstrated in following the team (e.g. Poulton 2013: 101–2; see also White 2009: 161). By the 1990s, whilst welcomed by the club's owners as an indispensable foundation of their financial success, these supporters had become 'glory seekers' or 'plastic' or 'day trippers' in the eyes of many, both of opposition teams and indeed long-term United fans, to whom they had become a financially necessary embarrassment from whom it was necessary to distinguish themselves (e.g. White 2009: 333; Pearson 2012). As Cohen observes, 'One aspect of the charged nature of cultural identity is that in claiming one, you do not merely associate yourself with a set of characteristics: you also disassociate yourself from others' (Cohen 1998: 24).

The identity of United's support base (true fans or glory-seeking customers) and of United itself (club or business) became an increasingly fractious on-going debate. Even those fans who claim to be unconcerned about the club's identity or the nature of its fan base often seem forced to assert that debates about the club's changing identity are missing the point – a claim that is in and of itself of course an intervention in these debates. The club's identity is a problem for those who identify with an idea that the club should not be a business, or at least should be more than 'just a business', with ideas of 'identity' being seen as an irrelevance by those who also strongly push the idea that the club is at heart just a business, and that others should lose their sentimental attachment to the idea of it being somehow different (see also Critcher 1974). For those for whom the club's identity as more than just a business is an important source of concern, it is the idea that the club is at the heart of some kind of community that in part makes supporting it worthwhile.

Elsewhere, I have written about contested perspectives on the relationship between supporters and clubs, and in particular contested evaluations of the meaning of buying a ticket as a means of support (Martin 2012: 484–5; 2013: 235–7). This contested transaction and the ongoing relationship (or lack thereof) that it is seen to help to constitute is one relationship that goes to the heart of the issue of the identity of the purchaser as a fan and/or customer and the vendor as a club and/or business (see also Gregory 1982).

Although tensions between fans and owners, and as a consequence tensions between fans, as to how they should relate to owners have been present since the establishment of professional football in England, the main visible act of dissociation between fans throughout much of the twentieth century was between fans of different clubs. The fan base itself was largely viewed from a perspective in which it appeared a fairly homogeneous and undifferentiated mass of working-class white males (Taylor 1971; Hornby 1992). The predominant view prior to the overheating of the Premiership era was summed up in a 1985 *Sunday Times* article that described English football as 'a slum game played in slum stadiums watched by slum people' (cited in Goldblatt 2006: 542). What has emerged with the economic overheating of English football is the creation of schisms within new supporter communities, who although united by support of the same club now share such openly divergent life positions and perspectives that the desire to disassociate oneself from the characteristics of others who claim allegiance to the same team (being 'plastic' or a 'muppet')[2] can often be more keenly felt than the desire to dissociate from supporters of other clubs. Particularly for those for whom the club is important as a manifestation of a local working-class community, the tendency to unproblematically view it simply as a 'business' like any other is taken as a position representative of a new kind of fan from whom they wish to differentiate themselves.

## DEBATING GLOBALISED IDENTITIES
## IN AN ONLINE COMMUNITY

I have conducted initial fieldwork with United fans in Manchester, but for the purposes of this chapter, I draw on a conversation from the internet forum Redcafe. Redcafe has several thousand members, encompassing a wide range of United fans across the generations and across geographical

---

2.  'Plastic' tends to imply an inauthentic and glory-seeking fan, whilst a 'muppet' is one who is considered not to really understand the game and to get carried away with media-generated hype about potential big-money star signings, for example.

locations, and it is currently the most popular United web forum in terms of both members and 'guests' (the even larger number of people who view the discussions and debates amongst members without joining themselves). Redcafe also tends to cover a wide range of opinions regarding the controversial ownership situation of the club.

Manchester United plc was bought in an aggressive debt-leveraged takeover in 2005 by the family of the American businessman Malcolm Glazer. This takeover saddled the club with several hundred million pounds of debt that is still being serviced, and was hugely unpopular with large numbers of fans (e.g. White 2009: 10; Poulton 2013). Unlike other popular web fora, such as the forum associated with the fanzine *Red Issue* – whose home page at one point declared 'This is a *forum* for people who love United, but hate the fucking Glazers' – Redcafe is home to a range of fan opinions, from the kind of militant anti-Glazer perspective found on the *Red Issue* website to those who celebrate the Glazers as good owners who have seen and exploited United's unique potential to capitalise on a global fan base in the interests of increasing the club's revenue.

Redcafe has over the years been the site of a number of vitriolic debates amongst United fans as to the nature of the club, and the conversation that I discuss here is only one example that could have been taken to illustrate these tensions. I can only scratch the surface of these debates here, but I want to make a number of points about how United fans experience and attempt to shape the boundaries of supporter identity with different takes on these conceptual distinctions. As Cohen observes, 'cultural identity' is a matter of the careful 'symbolic marking' of the boundaries between those who view themselves as sharing this identity and those who they view as others (Cohen 1998: 24). Football of course provides many obvious examples of the clear symbolic marking of cultural identity between fans of different clubs, distinguished by such markers as coloured scarves or banners, whose meaning, whilst often provoking strong emotion, is almost universally shared and understood. But the overheating of a previously subdued tension between the idea of a football club as a business and as the receptacle of an identity that goes beyond business has led to a series of more confusing and complex battles over the cultural identity of being a fan amongst those who claim allegiance to the same club. In these battles, the disputed meanings of key words, such as 'business', 'club' and 'identity' itself, have become contested markers of the boundaries of cultural identity. The distinction between 'business' and 'club' appears to be a vital one to maintain, at least from the perspective of those for whom the maintenance of a boundary between a community of real fans and 'plastic' fans is a matter of personal importance.

Football clubs have of course always been businesses when viewed from one perspective.[3] As soon as they charge money for admittance – that is, a transaction that can be characterised as a business transaction – they can be characterised as a business entity, even if they are supporter-owned, take part in community-building exercises or prioritise on-field success over financial accumulation.[4] But it is also possible to characterise these commercial transactions as being in the service of and subordinate to a greater good, or as not fundamentally being commercial transactions at all despite their legal appearance as such (Martin 2013: 235–7). The question that frequently arises in such discussions is variant of: Is the club/should the club be a business or not? In such discussions, it is less the case that the term 'business' fully describes the entity, such as Manchester United, or not, but rather what kind of transactions, relationships and obligations does the term 'business' prioritise at the expense of what other kinds of obligations? We are used to thinking of businesses as things. Even when we accept their socially constructed nature as 'legal' or 'fictive' persons (e.g. Martin 2012), they are still described predominantly as social entities that act upon the world. But the construction of a business entity such as a company that runs a football club for profit is based upon the *idea* of business as the moral justification for the construction of and actions of such entities. When the character Stagg in Dickens's *Barnaby Rudge* announces, 'Listen to me. This is a matter of business, with which sympathies and sentiments have nothing to do' (Dickens 1841: 199), he does so, not in order to describe an organisation that he represents, but to justify his actions – in this case ignoring the pleas of poverty that are directed to him by the impoverished mother that he has been sent to extort money from. What Dickens's example powerfully illustrates is that the idea of business is an idea that is used to justify or delegitimise certain relations (those based upon sentiment, sympathy or class solidarity perhaps). In that case, appeals to business as an ethic for organising social relations presuppose the building of entities and companies of a certain kind that may often show a lack of concern for the maintenance of other kinds of community identity based upon different kinds of obligation or sentiment.

---

3. See Tischler (1981: 51–68) for an overview of the early history of this phenomenon.

4. Community-building exercises include coaching schemes run for local children and other community outreach programmes run by the breakaway club FC United of Manchester (see below).

## THE RISE OF THE PRAWN EATERS

In 2006, shortly after the Glazer takeover, a thread appeared on Redcafe entitled 'Glazer's Business Plan'.[5] In this thread, Wibble responds to complaints about threatened ticket price rises by observing: 'on a purely business basis it is probably correct … That further increases in price will possibly increase the proportion of "prawn eaters" is the price of allowing Glazer to take over and one he will be quite willing to pay'. Here we see an example that could be repeated hundreds of times of the term 'business' being used not purely or so much to describe an entity or situation, but rather as an idea about what kinds of values need to be prioritised. That this is not an uncritical celebration is shown by the coda to this statement that it will increase the number of 'prawn eaters' – a reference to the famous attack a few years earlier by United's then captain Roy Keane about the lack of support shown to the team by the new, more success-oriented fans who did not support the players when things were not going well. 'Away from home our fans are fantastic, I'd call them the hardcore fans. But at home they have a few drinks and probably the prawn sandwiches, and they don't realise what's going on out on the pitch'.[6] Wibble's formulation here is one in which he accepts that prioritising the business basis of the club is problematic and will eventually favour 'prawn eaters' over real fans. In characterising the plan as being correct from a '*purely* business' perspective, he introduces an implicit distinction between 'pure' business run for purely or predominantly financial reasons, and other forms of business in which the business element of operations is a means to an end.[7]

As is often the case with people who attempt to put forward a nuanced position in the middle of a highly emotional dispute, Wibble ends up

---

5.   Available at: www.redcafe.net/threads/glazers-business-plan.137552/ (accessed 30 June 2015). All subsequent quotations are taken from this thread unless otherwise specified. Original spelling and punctuation has been retained, and participants in the thread are identified by their web-forum usernames.

6.   Roy Keane, quoted in 'Angry Keane Slates United Fans', *BBC News*, 9 November 2000 (available at: http://news.bbc.co.uk/sport2/hi/football/champions_league/1014868.stm, accessed 30 June 2015).

7.   A similar distinction is implicitly made by Inglis when he argues that, 'Modern observers of the game complain that football is *too much of a business* nowadays' (Inglis 1988: 19, emphasis added). Inglis goes on to observe that, 'It was ever thus', which whilst true overlooks the extent to which this perception is now widespread and felt with a new intensity in some quarters. Inglis's book is an official history of the Football League, published on the occasion of its centenary, and his claims that football was always (too much of a) business chime with those of the Glazer supporters twenty years on who make similar arguments in order to support a position that remains indifferent to the problems that others claim to experience as a result of the industry's economic overheating.

being shot by both sides. Within minutes, Wibble's post is responded to by Fred the Red who declares, 'So the average working class man and his family get even further excluded from going to see their local team, whilst some twat in a suit who can afford it is welcome … Yeah … fecking great'. But even though Wibble is trying to advance a middle position, in which, even if change brings unwelcome consequences we may have to accept aspects of it, his position is still based upon some fairly stark implied conceptual oppositions, such as that between 'pure' business and other forms of business. Wibble's position that changes in the experience of being a United fan are the inevitable, if sometimes regrettable, outcome of the current owners moving towards a more 'pure' form of business are voiced by many others in this discussion as well. For example, Leadpig interjects: 'We're too far down this road now to worry about morals, if the Glazers business plan means the end of the hard working local man watching his team than so be it as sad as that is, if it's needed for our financial stability than [sic] it must be done rather that than watch our empire turn to dust … I rue the day the Glazers took over'. Despite the fact that he makes clear his dislike of these trends, what Leadpig shares with the Glazer enthusiasts in this discussion is the assumptions that, first, football is a business, and second, that means that certain other non-economic values have to be de-prioritised. In doing so he provokes the predictable response from Fred the Red: 'so you'd rather see the club stay rich than the people of Manchester not be able to afford to go see their local team?' Like Leadpig, Sincher, advances a position suggesting that resistance is futile:

due in no small part to the complete failure of communism, there are more and more people around now who can afford to pay more for football, if they choose to … It's still very tough on those who can't, though, and will remove some of the soul from the club – no doubt. But complaining against it is very much pissing in the wind.

Meanwhile, Leadpig responds to Fred the Red:

My point wasn't what I'd prefer but rather what's now essential for financial stability, regardless of opinion, of course I'd love to see the stadium packed with local support, but the Glazers have put an end to that, so we just gotta suck it up.

In all the above exchanges there is an acknowledgment that there is some 'soul' or 'identity' that commercialism (or at least rampant commercialism) threatens, whether we rail against it or whether we reluctantly accept that this is the spirit of the age. That this change in fan identity and demographics was far from an unwelcome surprise to those in charge of managing Manchester United's transition to an era of overheated commercialism is made clear in this extract from an interview with a club official in the early 1990s:

> We are already seeing a change at Old Trafford [Manchester United's home ground] to a crowd which is more 'family orientated' … It also means that the idea of segregation and confrontation, which has been with us for so long, will eventually go. Also there is a move to what we may term executive accommodation. It needs to be stressed that though this only comprises 4% of our attendance, such accommodation generates 25% of our admission revenue. So this is very good business from the club's point of view. (quoted in Murray 2001: 95)

Much of this discussion relies upon sharp conceptual distinctions, such as that between club and business, or between pure business and other kinds of business. These conceptions are best understood more as means of asserting what the writer believes should be the limits of reciprocal obligation between fan and club (or customer and business) and the purposes of the organisation than they are descriptions of an empirically existing and clearly visible separation. Or at least if there is a clearly visible separation it is one that is only perceptible if one chooses certain perspectives. The parties to this debate are all too aware of the existence of perspectives other than their own. Their argument is not so much that other perspectives are impossible, but rather that other perspectives (or sometimes even their own perspectives) are best dismissed as being the result of intellectually faulty or morally dubious standpoints. The perspective that is advanced by many as being the superior perspective is that a historic shift has occurred, in which United have gone from being a club to a business, or from being a business of a special type to being a 'pure' business.

A few minutes after his initial intervention, Fred the Red returns to the fray with the following comment: 'It's not going to be a football club anymore, it's going to be like a Theatre with an Asda [a UK supermarket chain] attached to the side'. Later on he admits, 'The PLC was bad. I don't dispute that, but between the two I know which one I would take every time … At least they did have some understanding of the club and did show even the slightest interest in the welfare of the supporters'. Here a distinction is drawn between two forms of ownership, in which the former form, although bad, at least showed some understanding of the club as a 'club', in contradistinction to the current state of affairs.

The idea that the club might be a business that is more than just a 'pure' business raises the question of what makes a business, or perhaps more accurately what work is done by characterising a set of social relations and obligations as a 'business', '(not) just a business', 'a pure business' or whatever. The distinction between different kinds of business is raised by those who wish to acknowledge that the club, of course, has a commercial aspect, but that, contra the opinion advanced by Dickens's Stagg to the widow Rudge, business does not necessarily have to mean the abandonment of all other values, whilst in other contexts the word 'business' is used in a Stagg-like manner precisely to advance acceptance (reluctant or unconcerned) of the primacy of non-sentimental claims and obligations. The use of the word 'business' acts not so much as the description of an organisation but as a means of asserting the desirability or inevitability of a studied ignorance of these non-economic claims. So Leadpig's response to Fred the Red's previously quoted statement about 'twats in suits' pricing out local fans is a simple restatement of Stagg's philosophy, 'there's no sentiments in business', a response so short and pithy as to imply that this is so well-known it is not even worth arguing about. Fred the Red responds with, 'You tell that to the dads who can't take their kids to games because the cnuts[8] have made it far too expensive to go' – an appeal to a different morality that makes clear that prioritising business morality involves other undesirable moral consequences.

As we have seen, the club/business distinction is rhetorically advanced by many who dislike the current state of affairs but – in a tendency that mirrors a related trend in anthropological theory over the past thirty years to dissolve such conceptual distinctions, such as that of Appadurai (1986: 11) and his influential critique of the related gift/commodity distinction – its very utility is called into question by others. Snooty Jim, for example, makes the observation that this is all a matter of perspective:

> It's all about whether you view it as a business or a club, etc.
> Fans – Customers/Market
> Club – Business/Brand
> Match – Entertainment
> Raising the prices until people can't afford to go and OT
> [Old Trafford] doesn't fill – Supply/Demand

### 'YOU CAN'T GET ANGRY AT A BUSINESS PLAN'

Snooty Jim's observation that the distinction is one of perspective, and that whether or not one chooses one side of the division or the other shapes your position on different issues, follows the business/club

---

8. 'Cnut' is here a deliberate misspelling common on Redcafe, and used to avoid being hauled up for breaching anti-swearing regulations.

distinction with a list of associated binaries in the typological style of Gregory's well-known discussion of gifts and commodities: reciprocity/non-reciprocity, non-alienation/alienation, human/object, interdependence/independence and so on (Gregory 1982). Snooty Jim makes explicit what is implicit in the previous contributions, namely that how and when one characterises United's identity as a club or a business is a matter of contested perspective. But for others, normally those who are more sanguine about the current state of affairs, it makes sense to question the utility of the distinction itself. So Cali Red responds to a claim by Fred the Red that the Glazers only care about money and not what happens on the pitch with the claim that: 'I don't think on and off the pitch can be separated anymore. At the highest level they go hand-in-hand'. That the attempt to collapse binaries can be seen in and of itself as a morally loaded rhetorical move that reflects a particular social perspective is eloquently summed up by Fred the Red in his retort: 'Only to greedy cnuts like the Glazers. To the fan on the terrace there's a hell of a difference'. Much as Gregory argues that many contemporary attempts to blur the distinction between human and non-human forms of agency reflect a particular elite position, namely that of the Wall Street trader (Gregory 2014: 61), so Fred the Red argues that attempts to blur the boundary between United's boardroom identity and its sporting identity also reflect the social perspective of a business elite, in this case the Glazers and their (enthusiastic or reluctant) supporters. In another response to Fred the Red, Checkone tells him:

> United is a business and the sooner you understand this the happier you will be. In the context of the business plan, who makes the most money is very important but you seem to have lost sight of this for another one of your trademark anti-Glazer rants. You can't get angry at a BUSINESS plan and claim that what happens on the pitch is all that counts, they go hand-in-hand and you can't be successful with one and not the other … Am I happy about the ticket prices increases? No I'm not. Will I continue to go? probably.

Later on Checkone observes, 'As a match-going Red I personally don't view United as a business, doesn't mean that it isn't though does it?'[9] On the one hand, Checkone denies the importance of or existence of a distinction between football and business activities, yet on the other he acknowledges the truth of Fred the Red's observation that from his

---

9.  'Red' is a colloquial term for a Manchester United fan, derived from the colour of the club's kit.

perspective he does in fact see such a distinction that means that he does not see the club as a business. He does this in part as a rhetorical piece of self-positioning to avoid being cast by the likes of Fred the Red as a 'prawn eater', but instead positions himself as an authentic fan, 'a match-going Red'. But he performs this piece of self-positioning only as a prerequisite to denying the perspective that his position affords: Yes, I would see it like that, but that is because my position predisposes me to see things from the wrong angle. It may not look like a business to me, but that does not mean that that is not its fundamental character. Much as Lukacs (1971: 48) seemed to think that the social position of the bourgeoisie made them incapable of seeing the true nature of class relations in capitalist society, Checkone seems to think that his own position as a match-going 'true' supporter makes him incapable of seeing the true nature of the social relations that constitute United as a business.

What much of the previous discussion shares is a sense that, whether we like it or not, or whether we accept it or not, these changes have been imposed by outside forces. Descriptions of these forces vary from the market, through the collapse of communism to the greed of the Glazers. Some advance market forces as an explanation that absolves the owners of moral responsibility. So Sincher argues: 'On a pure demand-and-supply basis, I doubt the proposed ticket prices will be a problem. They'll still sell. On the basis of some United fans and families not being able to afford to see the team any more, it's very sad, though not the fault of the Glazers directly'. However, this is not always how the situation is depicted. On occasion, some fans (normally those who reluctantly accept the inevitability of the current situation) present things in a significantly different manner. In this depiction, we are all partly responsible for these changes, however much we may legitimately deplore some of them. Later in the discussion, Leadpig responds to depictions of true United fans as victims of market forces and commercialisation, observing that:

> We can't have it both ways a club doesn't get as big as Man U on local support alone, we operate in a global market, the Glazers are business men and don't care about the 'true' fans they care about increasing profit revenues, we're all quick to draw up our transfer lists where do you think that money's coming from?[10]

Of course this position places opponents in a double bind. If they walk away they are derided for disloyalty, as happened to supporters of the semi-professional supporter-owned breakaway club, FC United of

---

10.  Transfer lists are wish lists of star players that, in the view of fans, the club should buy.

Manchester, formed in protest against the Glazer takeover. If they stay, however, they are derided as hypocrites for contributing to the very processes that they claim to disavow. But what is perhaps most interesting here is the way in which this presentation rhetorically constructs the commercial transaction as one that has enduring moral effects that cannot be disavowed (see Hornby 1992: 222). Contributors who are most willing to accept the inevitability of United as an overheated business are normally associated with asserting that buying tickets or other commercial transactions with the club involve pure commodity transactions on a stand-alone basis, but here suddenly the position is turned on its head and fans are held to be responsible for the intangible wider outcomes of the transactions that they enter into. Rather than the commodity transaction being a stand-alone transaction without enduring moral effects, it is one whose enduring effects cannot be denied, and neither can moral responsibility for those effects. Indeed, it would appear that the characterisation of the transaction as a commodity transaction itself appears not to be as natural as its proponents sometimes assert, but is itself the outcome of an implicit assumption that such transactions themselves are responsible for creating an abstracted economic field (the amoral market) within which these transactions are themselves embedded.

It is worth noting at this point that although communities often experience symptoms of overheating as external imposition, this is a perception that can be challenged or altered and that is itself as much an implicit moral evaluation of these trends as it is an automatic outcome of them. Moreover, arguing over how to characterise the extent to which these trends should be characterised as external forces or as the outcome of our own choices is a central part of trying to shape the course of future trends. This discussion comes from 2006, but interestingly, my reading of these threads over the past decade suggests that there has been an increase in descriptions of the situation that stress fans' partial moral responsibility for tendencies over recent years, perhaps in part due to the intensification of financial inflation with regard to phenomena such as transfer fees, players' wages, sponsorship deals and TV rights.

## THE GLOBALISATION OF FOOTBALL AND AN OVERHEATED TENSION

Such tensions are neither new nor unchanging. The most fundamental revolution in English football was not the establishment of the Premier League in 1992, but the end of the prohibition on the previously hidden practice of professionalism in 1885. This change led to the establishment of football as a mass spectator sport and set in train a number of changes that were fundamental to the creation of new clubs as private businesses or the transformation of existing amateur clubs – such as United, which was originally created as a Lancashire railway workers' team (White 2009: 17) – into professional business organisations. The new mass stadiums that had to be built for this transformation to occur involved the transformation of amateur clubs into limited liability companies (LLCs) that were able to raise the necessary money (Holt 1990; Taylor 2008). This transformation introduced many of the tensions over clubs' identities that we still see today, but in different forms. In the early days of professionalism, the main tension was between players and owners, with the latter imposing a strict maximum wage on their new employees and regulations that tied players to clubs until their new club paid an agreed transfer fee, even if the player's contract with their original club had expired (Tischler 1981: 61–5). These ties were only cut by a threatened player's strike in England in 1961 that broke the maximum wage (Inglis 1988: 218–27), and a European Court of Human Rights ruling in 1995 that confirmed players' rights to the free movement of labour within the EU (Blanpain & Inston 1996). Today there are ongoing struggles between top players and clubs over the astronomical levels of remuneration involved, but rather than this primarily being a collective struggle waged by organisations such as the Professional Footballers Association, it is now often an individual process in which players attempt to maximise the amount of money they can receive in exchange for their unique talents by pitting rival clubs against each other in a bidding war. This transformation has introduced a new tension to the heart of the English game, in which fans now often pour as much opprobrium on their own players, whose new freedom means that they are often suspected of mercenary disloyalty, as they traditionally gave out to players on rival teams. This leads in turn to new kinds of division within the community of fans as those who pride themselves on a more realistic and less romantic appraisal of the political economy of football patiently attempt to point out to those with a different construction of the club's identity, one based upon the idea that players and fans should share some special kind of spiritual communion, that football is in fact 'just a business' and that this is the nature of the world in which we live, particularly for clubs such as United who aspire to compete with Europe's elite.

More important, perhaps, is the intensification of a tension between some sections of fans and owners in this period of football financialisation, and the corresponding emergence of a tension between different sets of supporters of the same club, that is by contrast a largely new phenomenon. Such concerns are not limited to Manchester United, although their unique status in world football leaves them as perhaps the most extreme manifestation of these tensions. Hayton, Millward and Petersen-Wagner for example describe the fears of Hull City fans that their 'identity' would be threatened by a proposed name change to Hull City Tigers, suggested by an overseas owner keen to 're-orientate the club towards seemingly lucrative East Asian markets' (Hayton et al. 2015: 2), a prospect that would have been unimaginable in the less overheated and globally interconnected business environment prior to deregulation and satellite television technology.

The claim made by Giulianotti and Robertson, namely that seeing trends like this as simply the imposition of globalisation is too simplistic as they are actually instances of 'glocalisation' (Giulianotti & Robertson 2004: 545), would doubtless be met with hollow laughter by the fans cited above or those Manchester United fans who have had enough and have left to form FC United of Manchester. Whatever the academic merits of Giulianotti and Robertson's claims, the fact that these trends are experienced as an imposition of the 'global' by these sets of people is profoundly important in shaping their own creation of new movements and fan identities. Giulianotti and Robertson argue that there are limits to how far football clubs can remove themselves from local communities, on the basis of, 'symbolic ties to "home"', such as their 'name, headquarters, home stadium' (ibid.: 552). Manchester United's economic base and headquarters could now be said to be the Cayman Islands, where the Glazers incorporated the company recently for tax purposes. In other cases, both the name and the footballing home of the club has changed, most recently in the case of the MK Dons, the team formerly known as Wimbledon (an area of south-west London) who played in the Premier League during the 1990s, and whose owner was allowed by the English football authorities to move them to Milton Keynes in search of a bigger fan base in the face of much opposition. Although this move was seen at the time as being emblematic of the total rise of business values at the expense of all others, it is worth mentioning that it is not without precedent in English football, with the move of Woolwich Arsenal to their current home in north-east London for similar reasons in 1913 being equally controversial.

That the tension between fans and owners has always been present is clear, for example, in the work of George Poulton, who writes about the emergence of the supporters' owned breakaway club FC United of Manchester in 2006, formed in protest against the Glazers. Poulton details instances of similar tensions in the 1920s and 1930s (see also White 2009: 38, 49–52).[11] The formation of FC United has contributed

---

11.   It is also implied in Hopcraft's claim that, 'fans are wealth to a football club, yet until the most recent years they were largely ignored' (Hopcraft 2006: 194).

to massively intensified antagonism among United fans, with some of those remaining at Old Trafford expressing sympathy for those whose principles have led them to leave, whilst others threaten violence against them as 'Judases' or 'rebel scum'.

The claim that money distorts the sport date back to its earliest manifestations as a mass event (e.g. Inglis 1988: 11). But such tensions are far more visible today, and now constitute the basis for an ongoing crisis of identity amongst fans who bitterly argue amongst themselves about the extent to which either opposition to or support for the club's owners is compatible with true membership of a community of supporters. The rapid financialisation of the game that followed its Stock Market flotation (itself almost inevitably followed by an aggressive debt-leveraged private takeover) and the establishment of the Premier League has led to an overheating in which potential tensions between the club's nature as a commercial entity and the sense that the business operations were at least in part in the service of creating a community that stood, as Mauss puts it, for more than the 'tradesman's morality' (Mauss 1970: 65), have now reached a point of permanent controversy. As Andy Walsh, one of the leading figures in the establishment of FC United, describes the situation as he saw it develop in the 1990s:

> About that time there became two Uniteds. The people you went with were United, the relationship you had with the players on the pitch, that was United. But Martin Edwards [club chairman and chief executive] had a different vision of what United was. You had to block out all the embarrassment and the shit, the shirt changes, the corporate boxes, the money-making. If you didn't you'd have to defend it and it was indefensible. What you defended was your experience of going to United with your friends and family. It was the sense of belonging, of being part of the Man United movement that was what United was. (quoted in White 2009: 333)

In 1984, Manchester United was valued at £10m.[12] In 2014 it was valued at US$3.6 billion, or £2.1 billion at the exchange rate current at the time – an increase by a factor of 210 over thirty years.[13] Over the

12.   Michael Nighton's £20m Bid for Manchester United Was Doomed to Failure, *Daily Telegraph*, 17 August 2009 (available at: www.telegraph.co.uk/sport/football/teams/manchester-united/6043241/Michael-Knightons-20m-bid-for-Manchester-United-was-doomed-to-failure.html, accessed 1 July 2015).

13.   Wall Street Says Manchester United Most Valuable Team in World after Adidas Deal, *Forbes*, 15 July 2014 (available at: www.forbes.com/sites/mikeozanian/2014/07/15/wall-street-says-manchester-united-most-valuable-team-in-world-after-adidas-deal, accessed 1 July 2015).

same period, the average annual wage of a footballer playing in the English top division had risen from around £25,000 in 1984 (or roughly 2.5 times the average UK salary) to £1,163,000 in 2010 (roughly 34 times the average) and £1,600,000 in 2013 (roughly 60 times the average).[14] Top players at elite clubs such as United receive far more than this, with the club's top earner Wayne Rooney reportedly signing a contract in 2014 worth £300,000 per week, or £15.6 million per annum (or 585 times the average annual salary).[15] In 1989, fans could watch a United match for £3.50, roughly equivalent to £7 at today's prices. The cheapest tickets available at Old Trafford today, however, are approximately £35, a five-fold increase, and these seats are almost impossible to obtain, with most fans paying far more. It is no wonder that complaints that 'genuine' supporters are being priced out of the game are widespread, and no wonder either that increasingly bitter divisions have opened up between those who represent these interests on the one hand, and on the other, those who seek to defend these trends as inevitable and claim that the club's financial interests are more important than the sentimental relationship between the club and its more loyal supporters. There always was potential for tension over clubs' identities in the relationship between club owners and their supporters. But what the financial overheating of English football has done is exacerbate these tensions, entrenching them and making them more permanently visible.[16] This overheating has provided an example of the kind of 'cultural change and ... attendant value conflicts' that cause those undergoing them, 'to experience their existence as morally fraught' (Robbins 2007: 306) in new ways. The end result has been to fracture the cultural identity of a community of supporters in ways that would have been unimaginable a few decades ago.

---

14. Revealed: Official English Football Wage Figures for the Past 25 Years, *Sporting Intelligence*, 30 October 2011 (available at: www.sportingintelligence.com/2011/10/30/revealed-official-english-football-wage-figures-for-the-past-25-years-301002/, accessed 1 July 2015).

15. Wayne Rooney: Manchester United Forward's £70m Deal, *BBC News*, 21 February 2014 (available at: www.bbc.com/sport/0/football/26246939, accessed 1 July 2015).

16. Poulton provides a discussion of how the 'intensification' of pre-existing 'commercialism', and the subsequent 'transformation of English football to a hyper-commercialised form' in this period has impacted supporter identity (Poulton 2013: 48, 57). Even Sir Alex Ferguson, the legendary Manchester United manager, was moved to comment in the late 1990s that 'football is now big business' leading to 'a danger of over-commercialisation' and the possibility that 'fans will get priced out of grounds' (Ferguson 1999: 11). The following 15 years of his tenure saw the realisation of these fears, with little resistance from Sir Alex himself.

# REFERENCES

Appadurai, A. 1986. Introduction: Commodites and the Politics of Value. In A. Appadurai (ed.), *The Social Life of Things: Commodities in Cultural Perspective*. Cambridge: Cambridge University Press, pp.3–63.

Blanpain, R., and R. Inston. 1996. *The Bosman Case: The End of the Transfer System?* Leuven: Peters, Sweet and Maxwell.

Cohen, A. 1998. Boundaries and Boundary Consciousness: Politicizing Cultural Identity. In M. Anderson and E. Bort (eds), *The Frontiers of Europe*. London: Pinter, pp.22–35.

Conn, D. 1997. *The Football Business: Fair Game in the '90s?* Edinburgh: Mainstream Publishing.

Critcher, C. 1974. *Football since the War*. Birmingham: Centre for Contemporary Cultural Studies, University of Birmingham.

Dickens, C. 1841. *Barnaby Rudge: A Tale of the Riots of 'Eighty*. London: Chapman and Hall.

Eriksen, T.H. 2007. Steps towards an Ecology of Transnational Sports. In R. Giulianotti and R. Robertson (eds), *Globalization and Sport*. Malden, MA: Blackwell, pp.46–57.

Ferguson, A. 1999. Foreword. In S. Hamil, J. Michie and C. Oughton (eds), *The Business of Football: A Game of Two Halves?* Edinburgh: Mainstream Publishing, pp.11–12.

Giulianotti, R., and R. Robertson. 2004. The Globalization of Football: A Study in the Glocalization of the 'Serious Life'. *British Journal of Sociology* 55(4): 545–68.

Goldblatt, D. 2006. *The Ball is Round: A Global History of Football*. Harmondsworth: Penguin.

Gregory, C. 1982. *Gifts and Commodities*. London. Academic Press.

—— 2014. On Religiosity and Commercial Life: Toward a Critique of Cultural Economy and Posthumanist Value Theory. *Hau* 4(3): 45–68.

Hayton, J., P. Millward and R. Petersen-Wagner. 2015. Chasing a Tiger in a Network Society? Hull City's Proposed Name Change in the Pursuit of China and East Asia's New Middle Class Consumers. *International Review for the Sociology of Sport*. Available at: http://irs.sagepub.com/content/early/2015/06/02/1012690215588526.full (accessed 30 June 2016).

Holt, R. 1990. *Sport and the British: A Modern History*. Oxford: Oxford University Press.

Hopcraft, A. 2006 [1968]. *The Football Man*. London: Aurum Press.

Hornby, N. 1992. *Fever Pitch*. London: Gollancz.

Inglis, S. 1988. *League Football and the Men Who Made It*. London: Willow Books.

King, A. 2002. *The End of the Terraces: The Transformation of English Football*. London: Bloomsbury Academic.

Lukacs, G. 1971 [1921]. *History and Class Consciousness: Studies in Marxist Dialectics*. Cambridge, MA: MIT Press.

Martin, K. 2012. Big Men and Business: Morality, Debt and the Corporation. *Social Anthropology* 20(4): 482–5.

—— 2013. *The Death of the Big Men and the Rise of the Big Shots: Custom and Conflict in East New Britain*. New York: Berghahn Books.

Mauss, M. 1970 [1925]. *The Gift: Forms and Functions of Exchange in Primitive Societies*, trans. I. Cunnison. London: Cohen and West.

Mellor, G. 2004. 'We Hate the Manchester Club Like Poison': The Munich Disaster and the Socio-Historical Development of Manchester United as a Loathed Football Club. In D. Andrews (ed.). *Manchester United: A Thematic Study*. Abingdon. Routledge, pp.28–42.

Murray, C. 2001. *Manchester United at the Millennium: Development and Diversification*. Stockport: Chris Murray Publications.

Pearson, G. 2012. *An Ethnography of English Football Fans*. Manchester: Manchester University Press.

Poulton, G. 2013. FC United of Manchester: Community and Politics amongst English Football Fans. PhD dissertation. Manchester: University of Manchester.

Robbins, J. 2007. Between Reproduction and Freedom: Morality, Value and Radical Cultural Change. *Ethnos* 72(3): 293–314.

Taylor, I. 1971. Soccer Consciousness and Soccer Holiganism. In S. Cohen (ed.), *Images of Deviance*. Harmondsworth: Penguin, pp.134–64.

Taylor, M. 2008. *The Association Game: A History of British Football*. London: Pearson Education.

Tischler, S. 1981. *Footballers and Businessmen: The Origins of Professional Soccer in England*. New York. Holmes and Meier.

White, J. 2009. *Manchester United: The Biography*. London. Sphere.

# 13. Frozen Moments
## Visualising the Polity in Times of Overheating

### Iver B. Neumann

Barth and associates noted that identity is what has later been named a thing of boundary, in the sense that it turns on the differentiation between Self and Other, and this differentiation is strongest at the boundary (Barth 1969). In the 1970s and 1980s, poststructuralists theorised this insight under the rubric of the constitutive outside; given that the inside Self must be actively limned off from its outside Others, the Other is a constitutive part of the Self. The 1990s and early 2000s saw an explosion in identity studies, the main value of which was to apply these insights in empirical research.[1] With the saturation point for this kind of study reached and the basic insight dispersed throughout the human sciences, identity studies were no longer a key focus of creativity. After a decade or so of relative silence, the present volume returns to issues of Self and Other with fresh angles. This chapter increases the time scale used by other contributions significantly, to five thousand years, and looks at a specific class of boundary markers or diacritics of polity identity, namely monuments.

By monument I mean any vertical or horizontal structure – megalith, mound, building, fountain, obelisk, statue and so on – that is large enough to put a mark on the landscape and/or seascape that is noticeable by the culturally uninitiated. Monuments are one kind of that 'organisation of thought and social relations imprinted on the landscape' mentioned by Douglas (1972: 514–5). They are of key interest to identity studies because they not only tell, but are also *intended* to tell a visual story of Self, and by implication, of the Self's constitutive outside.[2] Here, the spatial focus is exclusively on the Fertile Crescent, Eurasia and Europe. The question that concerns me is how the Other is represented. I argue that three distinct Neolithic and Bronze Age responses to this issue – the Other as constitutive absence, the Other as death and the Other as a live and conquered force – are still with us. Indeed, it seems that these three ways of attempting a freezing of the Other in time were wholly dominant until after the Second World War, when sundry attempts at depicting the

---

1. For my own contributions to this movement, see Neumann (1996, 1999).

2. For similar reasons, Young (1994) theorises monuments as a sub-group of memorials.

Other *without* freezing it in time come into view. If we cannot speak of an overheating of the genre of monuments, we may at least speak of a thaw in ways of depicting the Other.

## THE NEOLITHIC: THE OTHER AS ABSENCE

If we define cities as the steady abode of a certain number of humans, cities are by definition a sedentary phenomenon, for they exist by dint of their steady human population. In this case, the first cities are to be found in Sumer. If, however, we also consider another defining factor, namely the dense existence of human-made structures, then city history antedates sedentarism and goes back to the Neolithic structures for worship found at Catal Hüyük in Anatolia. Centres of congregation, which invariably have spiritual significance, go back to mounds, megaliths and other phenomena that pop up in the Neolithic.

It has become conventional to see these phenomena as reflections of emergent society, in the sense that monuments mirror the groups that build them. While it is certainly true that monuments are being built in the image of the group, it is also true that the group is constituted by, among other things, their monuments. 'Image' suggests that the concept of community came before the material symbol of community, but how can we really say more than that the two are co-constitutive? Monumentalisation is a constitutive social act, and nowhere is this clearer than in the Neolithic, where, for the first time, we see the emergence of groups of a scale larger that the hunter-gatherer band.

Consider Stonehenge, the largest and justly most famous of the many megalithic centres of Britain, Brittany and Ireland, work on which was begun somewhere between 3000 and 2400 BCE. This well-known group of megaliths in Wiltshire is the centre of a huge, now subterranean, structure which it took some 30 million man-hours to build. Given its obvious religious significance, a first attempt at understanding Stonehenge is found in Durkheim's well-known theory of religion (Durkheim 1995). Stonehenge, like all religious and spiritual phenomena, is a materialisation of the community celebrating itself. For a more specific answer, however, we have to turn to archaeology. Colin Renfrew answers the question by drawing attention to the fact that, in a cold and wet climate, a community could not celebrate itself by building mud huts which, as the generations passed and new huts were built on the top of old ones, failed to make a mark in the landscape. That left so-called 'tells'. There is a sense in which the tell is a kind of plinth, with the village on top becoming the rest of the monument. Instead of such tells, which were the rule in the Fertile Crescent and the Balkans, but which would literally have melted away in Northern Europe, the local answer was stone, which was made to build free-standing monuments. Renfrew points out that in order to bring about the first part of the Stonehenge complex:

> The rather small group of occupants of the territory in question would need to invest a great deal of their time. They might need also to invoke the aid of neighbours in adjoining territories, who were encouraged no doubt by the prospect of feasting and local celebration. One can imagine that when the monument was completed it might itself have become the locus for further, annual celebrations and feast days. It served henceforth as a burying place and as a social focus for the territory. The suggestion here is that it was as a result of these ongoing social activities, along with other activities of a ritual or religious nature, that the cairn or barrow came to be the centre of a living community. It is reasonable to suggest that this community would not have come into being had it not been for the ongoing activities centred upon the cairn. (Renfrew 2007: 155–6)[3]

Stonehenge and megaliths seem to have been intended as magnets for firming a Self. The Other is not frozen, but is rather that which refuses to be drawn in.

### THE BRONZE AGE, I: THE OTHER AS DEATH

In order to receive their rewards, Indo-Europeans residing in the Eurasian steppe had to bring the severed heads of their enemies to their chiefs. The practice was perpetuated when people from groups speaking Turkic and Altaic languages rose to become the main kinship lines in the steppe. It is hard to say when building monuments out of the heads of the vanquished began, for the skulls would have been fairly rapidly swallowed by the shifting sands of the Eurasian steppe where this practice was conducted. We know of it from countless descriptions stretching from Greece in the fifth century BCE to Persian and European descriptions of Mongol ways in the thirteenth century, but the practice stretches back in all probability to Indo-European peoples who established a unified set of political practices in the steppe during the fifth and fourth millennia BCE.

Why did various Indo-European steppe peoples and their steppe successors do this? Historian of religion Bruce Lincoln has a convincing

---

3.   Renfrew (2007: 158) actually goes on to argue that this process is an example of the birth of ethnicities. Renfrew builds on his earlier work on Stonehenge as a focus of what he then termed 'group-oriented chiefdoms' (Renfrew 1974).

answer. Indo-European myths of creation have the universe created out of the body parts of a god – the Rig Veda has him as Purusha – so that 'The priest was his mouth, the warrior was made from his arms; his thighs were the commoner, and the servant was born from his feet' (Rig Veda 10.90.11–14, quoted in Lincoln 1991: 7). The king's body encapsulates all of society; he is its head. So, enemies of the king are, as it were, anti-kings, and so anti-heads. 'Just as Scythian warriors negated their enemies' arms in practices based on a cosmogonic myth that were designed to augment their own power, Scythian kings thus seem to have done the same with their enemies' heads', Lincoln (ibid.: 203) concludes.

Any ideal-typical undertaking, and my search for a typology of mon-umentalised Self–other relations is definitely such, must be grateful to the peoples of the Eurasian steppe, for the building of a monument that consists exclusively of the Other's severed heads to celebrate the Self's victory is, shall we say, as clear-cut an example of the opposite of Stonehenge as could possibly be. Where, at Stonehenge, the Other is only present as an absence, in the Eurasian steppe, the Self is only present as the absence that once wielded the blade. Death is definitely a frozen moment. The Self celebrates itself by putting the dead Other on display.[4]

### THE BRONZE AGE, II: THE OTHER SUBORNED

The Bronze Age also saw another innovation in monuments to stand beside megaliths and skulls. Beginning with the Babylonian ziggurats, pyramidal structures crop up in assorted adjacent polities. From around 2700 BCE, Egypt takes over as the major innovator. The pyramids are still megalithic in the sense that they are huge and built of stone, but we are no longer talking about huge slabs of stone but fashioned brick. Pyramids are also similar to megaliths in celebrating the community, but they are mausoleums for one person rather than mass-grave monuments.[5] For our purposes, it is of key interest that the ziggurats, although they sometimes had the names of kings engraved on them, did not have any other graffiti. Some younger Egyptian temples, on the other hand, sported representation of the Other, in the form of vanquished enemies. Consider the reliefs on the temple at Medinet Habu, Thebes. The drawings on the temple depict a triumphant Ramses lording it over captured 'sea peoples', that is, raiders and traders from elsewhere in and

---

4.  Skull-taking and display on a minor scale is of course well known from a number of other settings, such as Fiji (see Carneiro 1990: 195–7).

5.  Note that, given my definition of monuments, memorials would be a sub-category thereof.

around the Great Green, or what we know as the Mediterranean. Here, the Other is not present in the flesh (or, as it were, in the bones), but in represented and suborned form.

Why would the Other make such a dramatic entrance on historic monuments? First of all, it must be made clear that the motive of the slaying king was itself nothing new in Egyptian tradition. One of the very earliest pictures we have of an Egyptian king hails from the thirty-first century BCE (Baines 1989). The so-called Narmer Palette depicts Narmer, pharaoh of the First Dynasty, holding a captured enemy by the hair. The obverse side has the pharaoh and soldiers parading in front of the corpses of beheaded enemies, which are subsequently shown being eaten by wild animals. At the time of Ramses, then, the artistic tradition of depicting suborned Others was very well established, so the question must be reformulated: Why move the Other from the small format of painting to the large format of monuments at this particular juncture?

The answer seems to lie in a need to re-establish superiority. In 1550 BCE, Egyptians finally managed to remove the Hyksos from the throne. This was a major event, so much so that the re-established series of dynasties is known as the New Kingdom. The Hyksos seem mostly to have been Semitic speakers who migrated into Egyptian lands (Booth 2005). With the help of Indo-European war technology (composite bows, chariots, stratagems) from the Eurasian steppe, probably brought to them by Hurrians (which also made up parts of their number), and definitely new to the region, they were able to establish themselves as pharaohs. The intermezzo left a memory of what migrants could do that was not lost on later pharaohs, however, and when the so-called 'sea peoples' emerged, by sea and over land, to raid and migrate into the kingdom, memories of what in-migration could do were still fresh in the memory.

The 'sea peoples', a term that is in steady contemporary use where migrations are concerned, has actually been a catch-all for waves of migrants on the move from around 1600 BCE. These migrations seem to have been brought about by, among other things, the eruption of the volcano at Thera (today's Santorini) (Manning 2014). It is impossible to determine how much of the social overheating was volcanically generated, but this is not important for our undertaking here. What is important is, I think, a basic functional point. With increased strain on what we are definitely warranted in calling the body politic, inasmuch as the body of the pharaoh was the *pars pro toto* of the polity, the maintenance of political authority called for wider broadcast of depictions of how the cosmic order was being upheld. Since it was impossible to increase the qualitative power of the pharaoh by representational means – how do you further enhance a god? – this was done qualitatively, not only in the sense that depictions increased in size, but first and foremost by making these images widely available by having them engraved on public monuments. The campaigns against the 'sea peoples' took its toll, and it seems to have been in this context that the 'sea people' become the first Other in history to appear in represented form on monuments, more specifically on temple gates, where all that passed could see larger-than-life representations of Ramses II (1279–1213 BCE) defeating foreign soldiers and lording it over captured enemies.

There is a possibility that representatives of one 'sea people' are depicted as part of the pharaoh's guard, which would be important, for it would suggest that incorporation into the Self, a practice that we know was present, was also discursively acknowledged. At present, however, our knowledge about this is insufficient for any argument to be made.

The Egyptian innovation of depicting live enemies in battle and post-battle scenes stands beside the megalithic depiction of the Self and the skull-like representation of the Other as a relational alternative for how to depict the Other on monuments constituting and celebrating the Self. What is frozen here is a relational moment when the Self is on top. It is a small stretch to see this kind of monumentalisation as a cooling down of hostilities, a halting of a situation where the Other threatens to overheat the Self.

## TRANSFORMATIONS

The three themes established so far – the Other as absence, the Other as death and the Other as suborned – have stayed with us. I will look at their continued emergence in turn.

### The Other as Absence

There is a direct line to be drawn from Stonehenge via large houses and places of worship of specific groups to monuments with global pretensions. In what is today Europe, megaliths gave way to houses, more specifically, to chiefly halls that could be 50 to 60 metres long and 8 to 10 metres wide. These were the sites of feasting, a key practice for the chief to secure the allegiance of his bondsmen. In central Europe, these buildings were usually fortified. Sometimes they were perched on hilltops, and were then called *acropoleis* (Greek: 'the highest cities'; Kristiansen & Larson 2005: 226, 277; note also the similarity between the tell and the acropolis as markers of the landscape and instantiations of the Self). In terms of Self–Other relations, these *acropoleis* are straightforward; they instantiate the Self and serve as bulwarks against Others. They are part of a series, in the sense that those who build them are peer-group polities that are similar in building fortifications, sometimes in the shape of *acropoleis*, but who differ in having their very own acropolis.

Bronze Age monumentalisation in Europe also involved an import from the Eurasian steppe, namely barrows. In the steppe, these are known by their Russian moniker, kurgans, and used to contain chiefs in full gallop with their retinue. Herodotus describes how, amongst the Scythians, household servants as well as fifty horses and fifty young male Scythian slaves were strangled. Stakes were driven through their corpses and they were then hoisted onto their horses and rigged to a buried wagon wheel, escort fashion, before a kurgan was built above them. A number of such kurgans have been excavated, bringing to light the remnants of the ritual as described by Herodotus (Cunliffe 2008: 305; Ivantchik 2011). The barrows of Viking northern Europe were not so grandiose in style – only household servants were strangled and left there – but the point for us is that the Others are nowhere to be found in physical form. Their presence remains indirect, in the form of weapons designed specifically to kill them. Note that, where the steppe is concerned, there is a perfect symmetry in monuments that celebrate the Self: they either denote the Other as death (pyramids of skulls) or the Self as death (kurgans).

From their acropolis beginnings, monuments celebrating the Self spread amongst the Ancient Greeks. As archaeologist Barry Cunliffe puts the point in the context of change around the Mediterranean during the fifth century BCE:

Growing social complexity ... created greater divisions of labour and greater expectations. The number of people no longer engaged in genuine production increased dramatically while society now sought to monumentalise itself with massive temples, public buildings, elegant funerary monuments and the like – all trappings of status and communal self-esteem requiring massive inputs of labour. (Cunliffe 2008: 319)

The result is well known: *acropoleis* that were grander than ever, hippodromes, life-size statues, even standing columns and, first at Leuktra in 371 BCE, monuments (Garlan 1975: 60). The Other was not in sight, however. Once again, as in Egypt, this was not for lack of a pictorial tradition. Pictorial representation was probably not a practice of the Greek Dark Ages, and seems to have taken its time to appear in the first millennium BCE, but when Athens was at its apex, it was well established (Smith 1999). A famous example is the fifth-century BCE illustration on a wine jug, the so-called Eurymedon vase, which shows a Greek dressed only in a flowing robe, penis at the ready in one hand, approaching an awaiting Easterner from behind. The inscription reads: 'I am Eurymedon, I am bent over'.[6] Contrary to what happened in Egypt, however, representations of Others did not make it onto the monumental Greek erections of the day.

After the fall of Rome, official monuments in what we now call Europe took the shape of churches. Church depictions of Others turn on the salvation/damnation binary, and then there is the constitutive outside of the heathen, the not yet converted. I shall leave that to one side here. There is, however, an important point to be made about church architecture, and it has to do with how new empires in the broad civilisational tradition of Rome have always, without exception, in some direct or circuitous way tried to claim a rebirth and continuation of Roman imperial authority.

The rebirth of the Self takes on a new intensity with the advent of nationalism. Contrary to Renaissance rebirth, nationalism displays a conscious and willed historicity; it is a rebirth not of something copied, as was Charles the Great's church, but of something transformed. Enormous monuments that attempt to encapsulate the nation by means of larger-than-life people, pillars or symbols crop up everywhere.[7] One example of these monuments that allegedly represent what once was and was supposed to be again is Millet's statue of Vercingetorix, erected at Alésia in 1865 (Dietler 1998).

Vercingetorix was a noble of the Arverni tribe of the mainly Celtic-speaking people that the Romans called Gauls. He owes his fame to having won a battle at Gergovia against Julius Caesar in 52 BCE. Significantly, Gergovia was a fortified hilltop, what the Greeks had called an *acropolis* and the Romans called an *oppidum*. Caesar went on to capture Vercingetorix at the battle of Alésia, win the war in Gaul, parade Vercingetorix through Rome, and later execute him. Beginning with the revolutionaries of the late eighteenth century, French nationalists used what they insisted on calling 'our ancestors the Gauls' in general and Vercingetorix in particular as a temporal anchor for the French nation. It was Napoleon III who built him a seven meter tall statue

---

6. This is a much-discussed representation. For a non-theoretically informed overview, see Gruen (2011: 44).

7. There is a line to be drawn here to another kind of monument that celebrates origin myths, from another ethnographic area, namely the totem pole.

on a hilltop that was supposed to have been his headquarters during his last stand. Since the signifier monument and the signified person were almost two millennia apart, the relationship between them is particularly indeterminate. There is, for one thing, the matter of the nineteenth-century French understanding of themselves not only as a nation succeeding the Gauls, but also as a civilisation succeeding Rome. Napoleon III tried not to solve but to get round this contradiction by linking Vercingetorix and the French nation he represented to France's contemporary civilising mission as follows:

> In honoring the memory of Vercingetorix, we must not lament his defeat. Let us admire the ardent and sincere love of this Gallic chief for the independence of his country, but let us not forget that it is due to the triumph of the Roman armies that we owe our civilisation; our institutions, our customs, our language, all of this comes to us from the conquest. (quoted in ibid.: 76)

This is not the place to discuss how French intellectuals have had a field day with all this nineteenth-century celebration of freedom fighters during twentieth-century French imperial wars. I simply note that the Self that is celebrated on a hilltop in France – and all the countless monuments elsewhere that celebrate unsuspecting ancients as press-ganged forerunners of some nationalism – is of the kind that represents the Other simply as an absence.

Something new emerged in Hyde Park in 1851. For the Great Exhibition that year, a prefabricated iron-and-glass building, the Crystal Palace, was erected to house it. To posterity, the full title of the undertaking – the Great Exhibition of the Works of Industry of All Nations – gives us the absent Other on a platter: it was the non-industrialised peoples of the world, be they formally colonised or not. This was emphasised at the exhibition, but is not inscribed on the building itself. The fact that the explicit goal of the undertaking was to stress Great Britain's status as the leader of the industrialised world further underlines that the monument was chosen as a specimen of a particular kind of building – hi-tech engineering – where Great Britain could excel over other industrialised nations. There is a double constitutive outside here: the close Other of other industrialised nations, and a further removed one of the non-industrialised.

I think there is a line to be drawn from Stonehenge to the Crystal Palace. Both are intended as magnets to steady a Self. Both target specific groups (tribes, industrialised nations) of the same kind and invite them to join in, and both do so in a new and abstract building idiom. We know that

Stonehenge was refused by certain groups. So was the Great Exhibition and its housing monument (Dostoevsky, who was there, famously saw it as the very epitome of the proud and dismal spirit of materiality). Nonetheless, they both usher in a new sub-genre: the monument that aims to celebrate a seemingly global vision of humankind. London is still at it: the eighty-seven-floor Shard of 2013 is a recent example.

You may ask why I have not used the American skyscraper – for example, the Empire State Building – as an example of global pretensions. The reason is that the American tradition in monuments does not celebrate the universal; it is stuck in the particular. Perhaps the most famous of American monuments, the Statue of Liberty, was a gift from the French and is a very good example of the serial logic of nationalism – the world consists of nations, each with its symbols. These symbols usually come in series of similar monuments (parliamentary buildings, opera houses, squares). In the case of the Statue of Liberty, however, the series is not one of similar monuments but of identical ones – the French gift was, insidiously, a replica. Reinhart Koselleck writes about American commemorative monuments that they:

> distinguish themselves foremost by their shimmering finish and use of expensive materials. In this respect, they contrast with those of other nations, and are most similar to post-1918 British memorials. In terms of their content, the memorials depict on marble plaques in crypts and memorial halls how the bygone conflict was strictly Manichaean, a struggle only between good and evil. There are victory monuments without a visible enemy; the enemy is bathed in the nothingness of the color black, displaced and outshone by the gold of the victor. (Koselleck 2002: 308–9)

The best example of this genre is probably the Vietnam Memorial in Washington, which, as Auchter nicely puts it, 'heralded a new kind of monument that completely separated individual death from ideological cause' (Auchter 2012: 11). A long wall lists names of American dead. There is a drop as one walks past the ever taller wall, so the effect is not dissimilar to a Neolithic passage grave. I look at the wall and I see my own reflection. Three dazed soldiers stand looking. The Other is absent, but this is a historically new kind of absence. It is not the absence of a Stonehenge or a Crystal Palace, inviting incorporation. It is not the absence of an Other still out there, ready to fight another day. It is as if the Other has been eradicated twice, first killed on the battlefield, then removed as a worthy enemy. The only trace of the Other is as the implied cause of the Self's grief about its own losses. Metaphorical murder is added to battlefield murder, insult is added to injury. What was overheated has returned to its normal temperature.

To sum up, the Other as absence is still very much with us, be that as an unknown absence of humanity understood as the entire species in the form of a future polity of unknown status, or as an absence of something quarrelsome that is best forgotten.

## The Other as Death

As already noted, the Eurasian steppe tradition of celebrating the Self by heaping the skulls of killed enemies on top of one another was also a Mongol practice in the thirteenth century, and it was perpetuated by the Ottomans. A good example is still standing in today's Serbia. In the third largest Serbian town, Nis, stands the more than 3 metre tall Ćele-kula, or 'skull tower', built in 1809 by Turks out of at least 192 Serbian skulls to demonstrate what would happen to those who oppose Ottoman power (Quigley 2001: 172). In line with ancient traditions of bringing the heads of defeated enemies to the leader, the skulls were sent to the sublime porte in Istanbul before serving as building material.[8]

This tradition is still with us. In order to celebrate Iraq's victory over Iran in the 1980s, Saddam Hussein had a war memorial built in the centre of Baghdad.[9] Below two swords hang nets. In the nets dangle the helmets of Iranian soldiers. In the tarmac around the monument, over which cars and lorries are forever on the move, there are more helmets. The enemy and, if not their heads then at least their helmets, have been run into the ground, where they are clearly in sight and can be desecrated on a continuous basis. The helmets may be metaphorical of heads of enemies frozen in time, but the ongoing desecration sees to it that the conflictual relationship remains heated.

---

8. In 1892, Serbs built a cathedral around the tower, and so transformed the monument by indexing Serbian Orthodox religion, a key diacritic of the Self pitted against the Muslim Ottoman Other. I should like to thank Novak Galić for discussions about this monument.

9. I should like to thank Johan Spanner for having brought this monument to my attention. Note that, from a world-historical perspective, the use of helmets rather than actual heads is probably best read as a hybridisation of the steppe tradition of the Other as death on the one hand, and a metaphorical tradition of the same that seems to have begun when Ancient Greeks began hanging pieces of enemy armour from tree branches. The use of armour and weapons carried over to our times, in practices of decorating victory columns with captured canons (such as Siegsseule in Berlin), the use of melted and so quite literally overheated captured canons for statues (for example, the Vendome column in Paris) and medals (for example, the British Victoria Cross) and so on. At this point, the classification scheme used here breaks down.

After the Second World War, an inverted Other as Death motive emerged in the many monuments that were and still are built to commemorate the Self's perpetuation of the genocide of the Jews and, in a much more limited degree, Roma Others.

## The Other as Suborned

Egyptians reacted to social overheating by placing the suborned Other on public display on monuments. Greeks stopped somewhat short of building monuments depicting the Other as suborned or as death, although they did perfect a tradition of hanging pieces of captured armour from tree branches, and, as we know from its depiction on a surviving coin, this motive was monumentalised at Leuktra in 371 BCE. In this monument, all three traditions of how to depict the Other seem to meet. It was left to the Romans to echo the Egyptian depicting of the suborned Other. Roman triumphal arches emerge during the early second century BCE (Claridge 2010: 55) and are full of reliefs of conquered enemies. One example would be the arch of Titus, built around AD 82 by the Roman emperor Domitian to commemorate his brother Titus and his victories, which included the sack of Jerusalem. Captured Jews being led away in chains, and booty, including a menorah (a Jewish seven-pronged candelabra), feature prominently. The arch was built where this very procession had passed into Rome, so the reliefs were presented as a representation of an *in situ* event. When this particular arch went up, arches had been around for a century, so it had no claim to novelty as a monument. Neither have I chosen the arch of Titus for its continued relevance as a hated piece of architecture by the Jewish community in Rome. Rather, I have chosen the arch of Titus as an example because of the history of its reception further north in Europe. One practice of the Renaissance, that is, the European mnemonic ethno-politics which commemorated past greatness, was (from the sixteenth century onwards) to build arches of triumph, and the arch of Titus was a favoured exemplar.

Now, why would the Greeks refrain from depicting the Other directly on monuments, while the Romans featured them prominently? The standard work on the arch of Titus tells us no more than that arches grounded the building of colonies and the arch was a Roman power symbol (Pfanner 1983: 95). Once again, it seems to me that the question is overheating. Greeks were famously fighting a number of comers, but Greek *poleis* (city states) were not that cosmopolitan. With the exception of Corinth, which owed its stature to trade, and which owed its trade to its strategic position and the man-made canal that made it possible to cross the isthmus on which it was placed, and which due to its trade harboured a number of foreign traders at any one time, Greek *poleis* were fairly homogeneous affairs. In imperial Rome, on the other hand, the known world rubbed shoulders. Order, the famous Pax Romana, was predicated on showing these people, and also people in the colonies, their respective places, with Roman citizens on top, other free men in the middle and everybody else at the bottom. This was made perfectly clear on monuments, as everywhere else. There were attempts at cooling down social overheating by displays of what should be the 'natural' situation, namely one where the Self was on top and the Other was at the bottom.

Note, however, that as time wore on, monuments specified how the Other could become less radically different. For example, on the arch of Severus of AD 203, captured Parthians are not only depicted in chains, but also out of them, handled solely by Roman civilians as opposed to soldiers. This monument begins to depict incorporation into the Self, which, depending on whether or not the Egyptian representations of the pharaoh's guard includes 'sea people', may be a historical first.

With the Renaissance, the arch reappeared, with the suborned Other still in place, but usually as a fighting force, not as a captured one. The most famous them all, the Arc de Triomphe de l'Étoile, was built by Napoleon following his triumph at Austerlitz in 1806, and stands in the heart of Paris. Echoing the arch of Titus, it has battle scenes prominently displayed, so the Other is back in view, but this is not the vanquished and integrated Other highlighted by the Romans. There is no social contact and hybridisation on display here, only the Other depicted as a fighting force. The Other is reduced to some other detachment of humanity, distinct from the Self. Nationalism thinks of humanity in terms of a series of distinct, backward-looking, rebirthing detachments of sameness, be that when the Self is celebrated with the Other absent or, as in arches, when the Other is present as a force about to be suborned.

We also have a parallel genre that depicts the suborned. Perhaps we may think of the Roman triumphal arch having split in two, with the arches themselves keeping the topic of fighting the Other and some equestrian statues taking up the shared topic of the resulting suborned Other. One example can be found in St Petersburg, in Catherine the Great's statue to her predecessor and founder of the city, Peter the Great, who is depicted on horseback while putting down a snake. Such depictions of the Other as an animal (fantastic or otherwise; there are dragons galore) abound in the period. Later on, there are also examples of the Other being depicted in human form, as with the equestrian statue of Eugene of Savoy. It hails from the year 1900, stands in Buda Castle and depicts how Eugene liberated Budapest from the Ottoman Empire at the Battle of Zenta (1697). Reliefs with fighting scenes and statues of defeated Turks crowd the plinth, so this particular monument actually takes up both aspects of the Roman arch: the fighting of the Other as well as the resulting suborned Other. The relational presentation of the Other in monuments that began in Egypt and thrived in Rome is still with us, it still crops up where overheating is in evidence and it still represents the Other as suborned or about to be suborned.

A caveat and a footnote are in order. The caveat: An overarching discussion like this one cannot go into depth about different ways of representing the suborned. I simply note that the overwhelming majority concerns the Other suborned in battle or taken prisoner after battle. There are variants, however, such as the 1888 Columbus Monument in Barcelona, where grateful child-like natives may be seen kneeling down to sundry Christian cultic specialists.[10] The footnote: I mentioned that, in Egypt as well as in Greece, the pictorial tradition of the suborned enemy antedates the presence of such images on and in monuments. Mention should be made of the fact that we have, in today's Europe, rare and small-scale examples of the Other being presented amongst the Self in memorial monuments. One example is the black tablet of stone on one of the walls of Magdalen College, Oxford, which celebrates the members of college that fell during the First World War. It lists the names, and the only way of knowing which side they fought for is to try to infer their nationality and citizenship from those names. An elite community nested within a state was able to put state othering to one side and celebrate its fallen members, regardless of citizenship. Here we have a non-suborning way of including the Other in memorialisation that, at least to my knowledge, has not made it onto monuments.

## CONCLUSION

One of the innovations of the Neolithic was the megalithic monument, which celebrates the Self and excludes the Other by absence only. This form survived into the Bronze Age, when it was joined by two other ways of representing the Other in monuments: the practice in the Eurasian steppe of piling skulls in pyramids to show the Other as death, and the Egyptian practice of depicting the Other as suborned. The Romans honed the latter practice.

The European Middle Ages knew the celebration of Self through mounds in the Eurasian steppe and in northern Europe, and also attempts at replicating Roman practices. It also knew the Other as death in the continued Turko-Mongol practice of piling up the severed heads

---

10.   I should like to thank Simone Friis for alerting me to this monument.

of enemies. It also knew the Other as suborned through the still-standing earlier Roman monuments, but the Middle Ages did not construct new specimens in this genre.

With the coming of modernity, we see a postulation of previous instantiations of the Self, in the form of nationalist monuments of symbols, including historical persons. There is historical innovation in the shape of monumental buildings that purport to celebrate universal humanity. Skulls remain, but seem to be going out of fashion. We also see the return of representations of the Other, first as animal, then as humans.

At present, seemingly universal monumental buildings seem to be all the rage. The representation of the Other as death has fallen on hard times; the only recent example I have found is a monument that makes do with metaphorical skulls, in the shape of helmets. Recent depictions of the Other as suborned have also been hard to find in the area covered here. I should also note a major innovation from the last century or so, namely the monument of the Other as liberator. These may be built by the Other on the territory of the Self, as was, for example, the Stalinist high-rise in downtown Warsaw which was a replica of similar structures in Moscow. In these cases, we are simply talking about a foreign polity marking new territory as its own fiefdom. They may also be built by the Self itself, though – as in the case of Norwegian monuments that honoured the British, American and Soviet allies that liberated Norway from the Nazi occupation of 1940 to 1945. Such monuments tend to be personalised (busts of Churchill and Roosevelt on plinths), but may also be in the form of graves to unknown soldiers.

Inventory and classification are the easy parts. What does this tell us? One thing is that, while war and genocide remain as practices, monuments no longer celebrate the importance of slaughtering enemies. The Vietnam Memorial is built as a site of downcast reflection. Controversy has sprung up regarding minor monuments, for example the one in London commemorating Bomber Harris. Another is that monuments, that eminent genre for freezing moments in time, may serve as an indicator of a perceived risk of overheating. Dynamic representations of how the Other is being suborned invite a reading of how the Self tries to cool down social dynamism by freezing moments where it is on top, and the Other is on the bottom. We saw this in increasingly multi-ethnic settings in Egypt, and then in Rome. Perhaps the most interesting finding is that we do *not* find something similar today. There are certainly worries about the overheating of the social, and of the Other's part in this, but Western societies no longer try to ward all that off by building monuments where the Other is depicted either as death, or as suborned.

## ACKNOWLEDGEMENTS

Many thanks to Thorgeir Kolshus and the audience at the Overheating seminar in Oslo, 26 October 2014, and to Ina Blom, Thomas Hylland Eriksen, Simone Friis, Lene Hansen, Johan Spanner and Bjørnar Sver-drup-Thygeson for comments. The article is part of a project titled Images and International Security based at Copenhagen University and funded by the Danish Research Council for Independent Research (grant no. DFF–132–00056B).

## REFERENCES

Auchter, J. 2012. Ghostly Politics: Statecraft, Monumentalization, and a Logic of Haunting. PhD dissertation. Phoenix: Arizona State University.

Baines, J. 1989. Communication and Display: The Integration of Early Egyptian Art and Writing. *Antiquity* 63(240): 471–82.

Barth, F. (ed.). 1969. *Ethnic Groups and Boundaries*. Oslo: Universitetsforlaget.

Booth, C. 2005. *The Hyksos Period in Egypt*. Princes Risborough: Shire.

Carneiro, R.L. 1990. Chiefdom-Level Warfare as Exemplified in Fiji and the Cauca Valley. In J. Haas (ed.), *The Anthropology of War*. New York: Cambridge University Press, pp.190–211.

Claridge, A. 2010. *Rome: An Oxford Archaeological Guide*. Oxford: Oxford University Press.

Cunliffe, B. 2008. *Europe Between the Oceans: 9000 BC–AD 1000*. New Haven: Yale University Press.

Dietler, M. 1998. A Tale of Three Sites: The Monumentalization of Celtic Oppida and the Politics of Collective Memory and Identity. *World Archaeology* (special issue) 30(1): 72–89.

Douglas, M. 1972. Symbolic Orders in the Use of Domestic Space. In P.J. Ucko, G.W. Dimbleby and R. Tringham (eds), *Man, Settlement and Urbanism*. London: Duckworth, pp.513–22.

Durkheim, E. 1995 [1912]. *The Elementary Forms of Religious Life*, trans. K.E. Fields. New York: Free Press.

Garlan, Y. 1975. *War in the Ancient World: A Social History*. London: Chatto and Windus.

Gruen, E.S. 2011. *Rethinking the Other in Antiquity*. Princeton: Princeton University Press.

Ivantchik, A.I. 2011. The Funeral of Scythian Kings: The Historical Reality and The Description of Herodotus (4.71–72). In L. Bonfante (ed.), *The Barbarians of Ancient Europe: Realities and Interactions*. Cambridge: Cambridge University Press, pp.71–106.

Koselleck, R. 2002. War Memorials: Identity Formation of the Survivors' In *The Practice of History: Timing History, Spacing Concepts*. Stanford: Stanford University Press, pp.285–326.

Kristiansen, K., and T.B. Larson. 2005. *The Rise of Bronze Age Society: Travels, Transmissions, Transformation*. Cambridge: Cambridge University Press.

Lincoln, B. 1991. *Death, War, and Sacrifice: Studies in Ideology and Practice*. Chicago: University of Chicago Press.

Manning, S.W. 2014. *A Test of Time and A Test of Time Revisited: The Volcano of Thera [Santorini] and the Chronology and History of the Aegean and East Mediterranean in the Mid-Second Millennium BC*. Oxford: Oxbow.

Neumann, I.B. 1996. *Russia and the Idea of Europe: A Study in Identity and International Relations*. London: Routledge.

—— 1999. *Uses of the Other: The 'East' in European Identity Formation*. Minneapolis: University of Minnesota Press.

Pfanner, M. 1983. *Der Titusbogen*. Mainz am Rhein: Philipp von Zabern.

Quigley, C. 2001. *Skulls and Skeletons: Human Bone Collections and Accumulations*. Jefferson, NC: McFarland.

Renfrew, C. 1974. Beyond Subsistence and Economy: The Evolution of Social Organisation in Prehistoric Europe. In C.B. Moore (ed.), *Reconstructing Complex Societies*. Cambridge, MA: Sawyer, pp.69–96.

—— 2007. *Prehistory: The Making of the Human Mind*. London: Weidenfeld and Nicolson.

Smith, A.C. 1999. Eurymedon and the Evolution of Political Personifications in the Early Classical Period. *Journal of Hellenic Studies* 119(1): 128–41.

Young, J. 1994. *The Texture of Memory: Holocaust Memorials and Meaning*. New Haven: Yale University Press.

# 14. Eurovision Identities
## Or, How Many Collective Identities Can One Anthropologist Possess?

*Chris Hann*

Social anthropologists generally emphasise the collective aspects of human identity. As this volume reminds us, the nature of the groups we form varies enormously. Despite the disclaimers of the editors in the Introduction, ethno-national identity still seems to have a special status. It is often taken to be the prime form of collective identity, by citizens around the globe if not by anthropologists such as Jeremy MacClancy (this volume).

It was not always thus. In the first half of the twentieth century in Eastern Europe, millions did not yet have a clear ethno-national consciousness. I met old people in south-east Poland in the 1970s who had grown up as Eastern Christians and as 'locals'.[1] They lacked a clear group identity between the level of their village and that of 'eastern Slav Christian'. Modern secular ethno-national identities were eventually imposed on the populations of this region through the brutal ethnic cleansing and deportations of the 1940s. Most of my interlocutors had learned to think of themselves as members of Poland's Ukrainian minority. But even now in the twenty-first century, in the heart of old Europe in the Carpathian Mountains, there exists a significant indigenous population that confounds scholarly classification. People disagree among themselves as to who they really are according to what Eriksen and Schober (this volume) call the 'global grammar for talking about identity'. Paul Robert Magocsi, the most distinguished historian of this population, which he calls the Carpatho-Rusyns, titled a two-volume collection of his essays about them *Of the Making of Nationalities There Is No End*. He explains that his unusual title was inspired by a passage in Ecclesiastes. His paraphrase goes as follows:

---

1. In other parts of prewar Poland, the term *tutejszy* (literally 'the people of this place') was an official category in the national census, applied not only to describe people but also their language.

Of the Making of Nationalities There is No End, And Much Diversity is a Richness of the Human Spirit. Put another way, the various peoples, or nationalities inhabiting our planet all deserve to have their cultures preserved and fostered, because it is their manifold diversity that makes life worth living. (Magocsi 1999: xi; see also Magocsi 2016)

Magocsi thus adds 'people', 'nationality' and 'culture' as further synonyms for the ethno-national unit. But can these all be perfectly congruent?

One anthropologist who has written extensively about identity is Günther Schlee. For Schlee, collective identities change dynamically to reflect competition for resources according to optimisation principles of group size outlined long ago by Niccolò Machiavelli (Schlee 2008: 35–6). It makes no sense, from this perspective, to distinguish between 'resource-based' and 'identity-based' conflicts, since all conflicts involve both (Schlee 2016). Where states are weak or barely exist, as in the Horn of Africa, approaches grounded in rational-choice theory are seductively plausible. But how malleable is the sense of belonging to an evolved collective identity in responding to material incentives? Schlee supports his argument with reference to relatively wealthy Slovenia's prompt secession from the former Yugoslavia in 1991 (Schlee 2008: 37). But strong Slovak support for breaking up the federation of Czechoslovakia in the same postsocialist period seems to contradict the assumptions of rational-choice theory. Even if certain Slovak elites stood to gain from controlling their own state, for most of the population the 'velvet divorce' from Bohemia and Moravia looked like a bad deal in resource maximisation terms. The theory can only be saved if we assert that Slovaks were maximising not material resources but some mysterious symbolic resources pertaining to identity when they voted to create their own nation-state. This carries a danger of tautology. Without detailed knowledge of competing interests within the population, and of the various cut-off points at which symbolic benefits are deemed to outweigh material costs by all the diverse actors involved, the approach has no predictive power.

Let me provide a more personal illustration. One identity available to me through birth, descent and early socialisation is Welsh. My nation of origin is relatively small (around three million) and relatively new, at least in its current form. Although its origins can be traced back over millennia, it is easy to demonstrate that the symbols of contemporary Welsh identity were an invention of the early nineteenth century (see Morgan 1984; Williams 1985). Wales lost the last traces of its political independence in the sixteenth century. It lost its economic clout with the decline of the South Wales coalfields in the twentieth. Yet despite its economic dependence on England, as in Scotland a significant proportion of the population would vote for independence if given the opportunity. Wales has almost entirely lost its teaching programmes in social anthropology as a result of recent university reforms. But this early victim of English imperialism (as it seems to some of us today), even if by some measures less productive than Greater London or metropolitan Paris, still has an old language and a vigorous contemporary identity, in which the game of rugby plays a major part. A Welsh politician of the twentieth century committed to the principles of electoral socialism, Aneurin (Nye) Bevan, is widely recognised as the father of Britain's National Health Service. In addition to the landscape (rugged mountains and a spectacular coastline), rugby and the health service are among the factors which shape my lingering sense of belonging to Wales, though in my family the language died out with my grandfather. But since childhood I have lived most of my life in England and Germany. I have to admit that a British or even an English identity remains more subjectively meaningful in many contexts than a nebulous European identity.

Classical work by Polish sociologist Stanisław Ossowski is helpful in theorising these complexities. Drawing primarily on the Polish case, Ossowski (1946: 10–13) distinguished between the 'private fatherland' (*ojczyzna prywatna*) and the 'ideological fatherland' (*ojczyzna ideologiczna*). The former refers to the immediate community or region in which one is raised, to the population of which one feels strong ties of loyalty and solidarity. For most of the population of Polish states in the course of history, this has meant a village community. For some subjects or citizens, especially in peripheral or borderland regions, the private fatherland might coincide with a distinctive ethnic, religious or linguistic identity.[2] In any case, this level of identification is undermined by the rise of national consciousness. With the re-emergence of a Polish state following the First World War, people such as the Carpatho-Rusyn minority were exposed to strong nationalising pressures. Most of them were deported following the Second World War, on the grounds (in most cases false) that they identified themselves as Ukrainians and supported terrorist attacks against the Polish state. But even in regions that were Polish-speaking and Roman Catholic, consciousness of the 'ideological

---

2. Ossowski's conception of the 'private fatherland' is reminiscent of Fredrik Barth's formulation of ethnicity as a categorical ascription that 'classifies a person in terms of his basic, most general identity, presumptively determined by his origin and background' (Barth 1998: 13–14). But Ossowski's conception is more general, since (as critics of Barth have pointed out) an ethnic consciousness in the sense considered by Barth and his collaborators in 1969 is far from universal.

fatherland' was a relatively recent phenomenon, linked to new forms of polity and economy.

Can Ossowski's binary be updated and applied in contemporary conditions? Has accelerating social change so altered the scale of our subjective identifications that even a rather large nation-state such as Poland (population circa 40 million) might play the role of 'private fatherland'? Perhaps not for the majority of the country's permanent residents, since in my experience of Poland, loyalties to one's town and/ or region still run rather deep, despite the convulsions of twentieth-century history. But what about millions of labour migrants working and bringing up their families in cities such as London and Glasgow? Is it possible that, at least for some of these people, Britain comes to function as the 'ideological fatherland'? For their children and grandchildren, Poland may be a 'private fatherland' they experience only vicariously.

Thus Stanisław Ossowski's ideal types of *ojczyzna prywatna* and *ojczyzna ideologiczna* may still be useful in contemporary social conditions, in which identifications are complicated by increased mobility and new technologies of communication. One new element is the emergence of supra-national identities. The European Union is primarily an interest-based alliance based on economic and political integration, but it has for decades been financing top-down pedagogical programmes to promote a European 'cultural' consciousness. It seems to me unlikely, given the diversity of this macro-region, that 'Europe' will ever function as a 'private homeland'. Rather, it remains somewhere in the background, analogous to being 'eastern Christian' in the pre-industrial village community. In spite of the rhetoric they might use, I doubt that even the most cosmopolitan 'Eurostars' of Brussels or Berlin can actually raise families in this spirit, without more localised sources of attachment. But it does seem conceivable that 'Europe' might increasingly come to occupy that ideological space that was formerly colonised by the nation state.

If Ossowski's paradigmatic case was that of the *tutejszy* ('the people of this place') at home in a village community and lacking any national con-sciousness, he also drew attention to cases in which private and ideological communities might coincide, and to the 'national nominalism' that could ensue in border regions among the members of a population claimed by rivals at the ideological (nation-state) level (see Wierzbicki 1977: 182–4). In such cases, 'indifference' develops to remote centres of power and the localised ties of the 'private fatherland' are the only ones that matter. This seems to be an accurate description of the situation in many parts of the mountainous zone inhabited by the Carpatho-Rusyns.

In my own case, the town of Cwmbran and the historic county of Monmouthshire would come closest to the status of a 'private fatherland'. For me there is already something ideological about claiming a Welsh identity, since I never learned the language and my ancestry includes English and Irish immigrants as well as native speakers of Welsh. My passport identity has always been British. Curiously, however, the document does not actually state 'Britain'. Instead it proclaims 'European Union – United Kingdom of Great Britain and Northern Ireland'. I find it hard to feel any emotional identification at either of these levels.

## POLITICAL ECONOMY AND THE FUTURE
## OF THE NATION-STATE

The nation-state model that lies behind Ossowski's ideal types derives primarily from European experience. It can be theorised, following Louis Dumont (1994), as a synthesis of the universalist and the particularist, the former exemplified by the luminaries of the French Enlightenment and the latter by the Herderian relativist response to *les Lumières*. Its spread was shaped on the one hand by romantic ideals of the *Volksgeist* and self-determination, and on the other by the need to educate citizens in a single 'high culture' to meet the functional requirements of industrial society (Gellner 1983). This model seemed to approximate closely to reality after the First World War, at least in Europe, with the almost simultaneous collapse of the multicultural empires of the Habsburgs, Ottomans and Romanovs. Whereas nation-states took shape on the territories previously governed by the first two of these polities, the Russian Empire was replaced by a socialist federation. Socialism was the dominant ideology of twentieth-century Eurasia. It provides an instructive example of the inadequacy of rationalist universalism in accounting for the collective identities that matter to human beings. Socialist ideology proclaimed class interest as the basis of group solidarity, but in practice nationality continued to count for more. Anthropologists contributed to theorising the *ethnos* or *minzu*, sometimes participating actively in the construction of these collectivities.

The legacies of Stalinist theory and practice are still evident everywhere in the former Soviet Union (including contemporary Ukraine and its Transcarpathian *oblast*, where the largest sub-group of Carpatho-Rusyns is to be found). Mao's China emulated Soviet patterns, the major difference being that communist power holders in China upheld the unitary nature of their multi-ethnic state. Whereas the Russian Empire has fragmented into over a dozen nation-states, that of the Qing (with a major Mongolian exception) remains unified a century after its demise.

One of the 55 recognised national minorities is the Uighur, a people numbering some ten million, concentrated in Xinjiang, in north-west China. Closely related Turkic speakers in Central Asia formed new nation-states in the wake of the Soviet Union's collapse, but the Uighurs must content themselves with an 'autonomous region' in which effective power is wielded by Han Chinese. Recent years have witnessed intensifying conflict, with Han accusations of terrorism (secessionist and fundamentalist) drawing counter-accusations of repression and assimilation from Uighurs.

But when one looks more closely, the ideal type of the nation-state ('one polity, one culture') is increasingly remote from twenty-first-century realities everywhere in Eurasia. In Europe, it is contradicted above all by the 'super-diversity' to be found in all larger cities. How can these European developments be connected with the permutations of collective identity in Eastern and Central Asia? How can the authorities in Beijing resolve explosive tensions in Tibet and Xinjiang? Ethnographic research in these regions is difficult, but in collaboration with Chinese partners it has proved possible to undertake fieldwork in eastern Xinjiang to study Han–Uighur interaction at the local level (see Bellér-Hann 2015). Anthropologists at the Max Planck Institute seek to continue dialogues with partners in large multi-ethnic states such as China, Russia and Vietnam in order to investigate comparatively the evolution of forms of collective identity throughout Eurasia, and not all of us are constrained by rational-choice theory.

There is no consensus as to how to theorise the flux of identities, either positively or normatively. In recent years, as the editors of this collection note in the Introduction, there have been numerous calls to abolish the concept, to puncture illusions of groupness, and instead return to our 'common humanity' (MacClancy, this volume). One way to escape the nationalist trap is to insist on multiple scales of collective identity. For example, in my own case I am at liberty to move up and down situationally between being Welsh, British, European and Eurasian (since I consider Europe to be a macro-region of Eurasia; see Hann 2016). But this seems inadequate since, as noted above, my authentic 'private fatherland' is smaller and thus 'below' Welsh national identity, while at the other end of the scale there are many contexts in which a universal humanity trumps everything else. My 'ideological fatherland' is dispersed, and the level of Europe is especially problematic. In the wake of the Second World War, governing elites in the land of Herder and Fichte shifted away from a German identity to embrace the continent. Angela Merkel frequently invoked the mantle of Europe in 2015, both in dealing with economic rebellion against the constraints of the single currency in Greece, and when opening German borders due to a 'humanitarian imperative' to assist refugees stranded in Hungary. During the tense political standoff between Berlin and Budapest, Hungary's prime minister, Viktor Orbán, also claimed to be acting on behalf of Christian European values and identities (he also uses the term 'civilisation'). For many citizens of the European Union, Orbán's concept of Europe appears to be more convincing than that of Merkel. The upshot is confusing and highly problematic for the future of our representative democracies. Berlin elites see themselves as the better (Christian) Europeans, yet their policies are not very popular with their own electorate, let alone outside Germany. So the rest of Europe will continue to classify Angela Merkel and her allies as German, just as people will continue to label Orbán a Hungarian populist.

On the eastern borders of the EU, the violence that broke out in Ukraine in 2014 also raises fundamental issues of ethno-national identity in an instructive way. Kiev elites seeking closer ties to the EU are simultaneously dedicated to imposing a homogenised national identity of a sort that this vast territory, with its richly diverse population and frequently changing borders, has never known in the past. Richard Sakwa calls the new elite project 'monist nationalism' (Sakwa 2015: 20–3) and argues instead for a plurality of identities within Ukraine, as in the larger European polity. The tragedy is that, having won freedom from the domination of Moscow following the break-up of the Soviet Union, the prospect of admission to the EU seems to go hand in hand with the repression of valued collective identities, among them that of Carpatho-Rusyn, by the power holders in Kiev.

In the anthropological literature, the case of the former Yugoslavia is better documented. It is represented in this volume through Banović's study of Montenegro, where the identity of the LGBT minority has to confront a strong patriarchal nationalism. Robert Hayden has argued that anthropologists should acknowledge the strength of these ethno-national identities, notably in Bosnia-Herzegovina, rather than invoke an imaginary past harmony and emphasise the contingencies of the original constructions (Hayden 2007). Like Ukraine and its neighbours in the east, these Balkan countries are excluded from the EU. They are thoroughly peripheral to European capitalism and condemned to high rates of labour migration. Under these circumstances, it is hardly surprising that national identities remain strong. What other sources of cohesion do these populations have on which to fall back? As a result of poor management of the 'refugee problem', there is currently a resurgence of populist nationalism almost everywhere in Europe. But this is clearly a symptom. The present *Völkerwanderungen* (migrations) cannot be understood independently of neoliberal political economy on a global scale. Political economy approaches, in combination with ethnographic and historical analysis, offer more insight into contemporary 'identity politics' than economistic theories of rational choice.

## EUROVISION IDENTITIES

The examples discussed above should suffice to demonstrate that symbolic or 'residual' sentiments of belonging and identity can be powerful drivers of action. Identity is always more than a cost–benefit calculus (though such calculations may play a significant role for many actors). As Eriksen and Schober explain in the Introduction, it is basically a question of connecting the past with the present to make meaningful identities. Belonging can prove elusive in an 'overheated' world in which persons, technologies and ideas are all more mobile than ever before. The uneven acceleration of globalisation often leads to an accentuation of national identity, which proceeds hand in hand with the negative stereotyping of others, especially among those who perceive themselves to be 'losers' as a result of these processes (Hann forthcoming). But I want to close on a more optimistic note with a brief analysis of a contemporary ritual that is quintessentially national, yet at the same time European and cosmopolitan.

The Eurovision Song Contest is a media extravaganza which can be relied upon every year to provide much food for thought concerning identity. The 2015 competition was held in Vienna, glamorously hosted by the previous year's winner, drag queen Conchita Wurst. The European Broadcasting Union has long been in the forefront of disseminating more generous conceptions both of Europe and of the gendered person. Israel has been a stalwart in both respects. The end of the Soviet Union opened the competition not only to the Baltic republics (soon to become full members of the EU and NATO) but also to others located somewhere in the antechambers. Azerbaijan won the event in 2012. Thanks to its oil, it had the wherewithal to host the spectacle impressively in Baku a year later. It is hard to exaggerate the significance of such events in modifying, even transforming, the social imaginaries of Europe. Small northern countries such as Norway have long been conspicuously successful, as has Ireland. Patterns of regional-bloc voting encourage viewers to question the evolved mosaic of nation-states which at first sight Eurovision appears to entrench. If Scots, Catalans and Kurds notice the success of artists from Ireland, Estonia or Latvia, they inevitably ask why their own people should go unrepresented at this annual Olympics of popular culture.

The 2015 contest was a close race between Sweden, the eventual winner, and Russia. This was in itself remarkable. Just one year earlier in Copenhagen, Russia's representative had been loudly booed by the audience, which had been fed a diet of anti-Russian propaganda since the 'invasion' of Crimea two months earlier. In Vienna, the dulcet tones of Conchita Wurst silenced such protests. Austro–Russian relations were highly conflictual in the not so distant past, and Vienna is a city that, in its Habsburg days, played a very significant role in the genesis of the Ukrainian national movement. But the Viennese public knew better than to allow its moment in the limelight to be instrumentalised by those whose demonisation of Russia is eerily reminiscent of the era of Carol Reed's classic film *The Third Man* (1949). Thanks to Polina Gagarina's honourable second place, Russia remained a part of Europe in the Eurovision Song Contest of 2015.[3]

The contest is a mammoth media event managed by the European Broadcasting Union, a bureaucracy dominated by its largest members, obliged to work within commercial dictates (and smart enough to call upon the services of PricewaterhouseCoopers as the ultimate auditor of the voting mechanism). Like the equivalent bodies in the world of football when they allow Kazakhstan to compete in the European Championships, these bureaucratic-commercial actors provide a valuable corrective to the tunnel vision of the politicians and officials who shape the policies of the EU and NATO. The spectacle in Vienna in May 2015 completely overshadowed the EU summit in Riga, taking place at the same time, with the main aim of settling vital issues of foreign policy in Europe's eastern borderlands. Both types of mega-event are predicated upon nation-states, but only the Eurovision Song Contest provides sensory evidence every spring of the diversity of these units, and at the same time a reminder of the arbitrariness of national classifications. It also drives home the contingency of *continental* classifications, by helping viewers to imagine an alternative, more inclusive Europe. To my mind this is a welcome step in the direction of recognising the long-term unity of Eurasia. It seems especially important at a time of crisis in global political economy, when the policies of the West are strengthening anti-democratic, illiberal forces everywhere, inside as well as outside the EU.

---

3.  Though strongly tipped to win at the May 2016 competition in Stockholm, the Russian contestant, Sergey Lazarev, again missed out narrowly amid charges of illicit propaganda by a rival and an unfair new voting system. Lazarev finished third, behind Jamala, a Crimean Tartar who represented Ukraine with a tragic song about the deportations of her people by Stalin in 1944, and, in second place, Dami Im representing Australia(!). But third place could still be deemed honourable.

# REFERENCES

Barth, F. 1998 [1969] Introduction In F. Barth (ed), *Ethnic Groups and Boundaries: The Social Organization of Culture Difference*. Prospect Heights, IL: Waveland Press, pp.9–38.

Bellér-Hann, I. 2015. *Negotiating Identities: Work, Religion, Gender, and the Mobilisation of Tradition among the Uyghur in the 1990s*. Berlin: LIT.

Dumont, L. 1994. *German Ideology: From France to Germany and Back*. Chicago: University of Chicago Press.

Gellner, E. 1983. *Nations and Nationalism*. Oxford: Blackwell.

Hann, C. 2016. A Concept of Eurasia. *Current Anthropology* 57 (1): 1–27.

—— In press. Overheated Underdogs: Civilizational Analysis and Migration on the Danube–Tisza Interfluve. *History and Anthropology*.

Hayden, R.M. 2007. Moral Vision and Impaired Insight: The Imagining of Other Peoples' Communities in Bosnia. *Current Anthropology* 48(1): 105–31.

Magocsi, P.R. 1999. *Of the Making of Nationalities There Is No End*, 2 vols. New York: East European Monographs.

—— 2016. *With Their Backs to the Mountains: A History of Carpathian Rus' and Carpatho-Rusyns*. Budapest: Central European University Press.

Morgan, P. 1984. From a Death to a View: The Hunt for the Welsh Past in the Romantic Period. In E. Hobsbawm and T. Ranger (eds), *The Invention of Tradition*. Cambridge: Cambridge University Press, pp.43–100.

Ossowski, St. 1946. *Analiza socjologiczna pojęcia ojczyzna*. Łódź: Biblioteczka Myśli Współczesnej.

Sakwa, R. 2015. *Frontline Ukraine: Crisis in the Borderlands*. London: I.B. Tauris.

Schlee, G. 2008. *How Enemies Are Made: Towards a Theory of Ethnic and Religious Conflicts*. New York: Berghahn Books.

—— 2016. How Terrorists Are Made. *Max Planck Research* 1: 10–15. Available at: https://bc-v2.pressmatrix.com/de/profiles/99f9c77d7a2c/editions/6ac2b059b113e787305d/pages/page/6 (accessed 27 June 2016).

Wierzbicki, Z.T. 1977. The Development of National Consciousness in the Polish Peasant. In J. Turowski and L.M. Szwengrub (eds), *Rural Socio-Cultural Change in Poland*. Wrocław: Ossolineum, pp.181–200.

Williams, G.A. 1985. *When Was Wales? A History of the Welsh*. Harmondsworth: Penguin.

# Notes on Contributors

**Branko Banović** is a social anthropologist and director of the regional museum in Pljevlja, Montenegro. His research covers many aspects of Montenegrin history and national identity, and he is the author of *The Montenegrin Warrior Tradition* (Palgrave, 2016).

**Heike Drotbohm** is Professor in the Department of Anthropology and African Studies at University of Mainz. Her research focuses on Afro-Atlantic societies, concentrating on transnational livelihoods with a special focus on cross-border families, the social and emotional meaning of migrant law as well as on migrants' access to human, cultural and social rights.

**Thomas Hylland Eriksen** is Professor in the Department of Social Anthropology, University of Oslo and principal investigator of the European Research Council project 'Overheating'. His latest books are *Fredrik Barth: An Intellectual Biography* (Pluto, 2015) and *Overheating: An Anthropology of Accelerated Change* (Pluto, 2016).

**Chris Hann** is a Director at the Max Planck Institute for Social Anthropology, Halle and principal investigator of the European Research Council advanced grant project REALEURASIA. He has published extensively on postsocialist societies, Eurasia and anthropological theory, and is co-author (with Keith Hart) of *Economic Anthropology* (Polity, 2011).

**Amanda Kearney** is Associate Professor of Social Anthropology at the School of Social Sciences, University of New South Wales. Her latest book is *Violence in Place, Cultural and Environmental Wounding* (Routledge, 2016).

**Jeremy MacClancy** is Professor of Anthropology and Director of the Anthropological Centre for Conservation, the Environment and Development at Oxford Brookes University. He is the editor of *Anthropology and Public Service: The UK Experience* (Berghahn, in press).

**Keir Martin** is Associate Professor in the Department of Social Anthropology, University of Oslo. He is the author of *The Death of the Big Men and the Rise of the Big Shots* (Berghahn, 2013).

**Iver B. Neumann** is Montague Burton Professor of International Relations at the London School of Economics and a lifelong associate of the Norwegian Institute of International Affairs, Oslo. He is the author of several books, including *At Home with the Diplomats* (Cornell University Press, 2012).

**Robert J. Pijpers** is a PhD fellow with the 'Overheating' project in the Department of Social Anthropology, University of Oslo. His research focuses on the micro-politics of large-scale foreign investment and processes of social and economic change in Sierra Leone.

**Elisabeth Schober** is a postdoctoral fellow with the 'Overheating' project in the Department of Social Anthropology, University of Oslo. She has carried out fieldwork in South Korea and the Philippines, and is the author of *Base Encounters: The US Armed Forces in South Korea* (Pluto, 2016).

**Astrid B. Stensrud** is a postdoctoral fellow with the 'Overheating' project in the Department of Social Anthropology, University of Oslo. Her research in the Peruvian Andes focuses on economic practices, informality, water management, climate change, globalization, state practices, everyday politics and power.

**Cathrine Moe Thorleifsson** is a postdoctoral fellow with the 'Overheating' project in the Department of Social Anthropology, University of Oslo. She is the author of *Nationalism and the Politics of Fear: Race and Identity on the Border with Lebanon* (I. B. Tauris, 2015).

**Torunn Wimpelmann** is Senior Researcher at the Christan Michelsen Institute, Bergen. She has published on conflict management, gender and women's rights, as well as post-conflict development issues, mainly with a regional focus on Afghanistan.

# Index